NUMBE

Yale French Studies

FRANCE/USA: The Cultural Wars

Yale French Studies

Ralph Sarkonak, *Special editor for this issue*
Alyson Waters, *Managing editor*
Editorial board: Edwin Duval (Chair), James F.
    Austin, Ora Avni, R. Howard Bloch, Peter Brooks,
    Mark Burde, Shoshana Felman, Catherine Labio,
    Christopher Miller, Leon Sachs, Naomi Schor,
    Susan Weiner
Editorial assistant: James F. Austin
Editorial office: 82-90 Wall Street, Room 308
Mailing address: P.O. Box 208251, New Haven,
    Connecticut 06520-8251
Sales and subscription office:
Yale University Press, P.O. Box 209040
New Haven, Connecticut 06520-9040
Published twice annually by Yale University Press

Designed by James J. Johnson and set in Trump
    Medieval Roman by The Composing Room of
    Michigan, Inc. Printed in the United States of
    America by the Vail Ballou Press, Binghamton, N.Y.

ISSN 044-0078
ISBN for this issue 0-300-09074-9

RALPH SARKONAK

Editor's Preface: Just How Wide Is the Atlantic Anyway?

> And here, I cannot leave this great and good country, without expressing my sense of its pre-eminence of character among the nations of the earth. A more benevolent people I have never known, nor greater warmth and devotedness in their select friendships. Their kindness and accommodation to strangers is unparalleled, and the hospitality of Paris is beyond anything I had conceived to be practicable in a large city.
>
> —Thomas Jefferson[1]

> One should not consider America as the center of the world. It is the largest world power? Granted. But be careful. It is far from being its center. As a European, one has a duty not to consider it as the center, one needs to carry one's gaze, to manifest one's interest, to prove one's solidarity with all the Vietnamese, Cubans and Africans, all our friends in the Third World who are gaining their independence and freedom.
>
> —Jean-Paul Sartre[2]

Twenty years before Sartre's statement, Willy Ronis took the photograph that appears on this issue's cover. The photo, entitled "8 mai 1945-Paris," was taken on VE (Victory in Europe) Day. As in the photos of the liberation of Paris in August 1944, we see an American flag, American soldiers, and French men and women. But unlike the 1944 photos that we remember—photos of soldiers being kissed by French women, of soldiers drinking bottles of wine offered to them by their grateful hosts, of soldiers beaming in their battle-stained fatigues—the Ronis photograph is an altogether more serious affair. Almost all the people know they are posing for a history-making shot: Many of the

---

1. *The Life and Selected Writings of Thomas Jefferson*, edited and with an introduction by Adrienne Koch and William Peden (New York: Modern Library, 1993), 101.
2. Jean-Paul Sartre, "Pourquoi je refuse d'aller aux États-Unis," *Le nouvel observateur* (1 April 1965), quoted by Jean-Philippe Mathy, *Extrême-Occident: French Intellectuals and America* (Chicago: University of Chicago Press, 1993), 154.

YFS 100, *FRANCE/USA: The Cultural Wars*, ed. Ralph Sarkonak, © 2001 by Yale University.

American men and the French men and women face the camera in a polite but tired manner. Despite the festive air of one woman, here there is a *gravitas* that is absent from Liberation photographs of the previous year. It is as if these *spectra* recognize that, while the past may be past, the future that awaits them is uncertain. (For example, rationing would continue in France, and conditions in the winter of 1944–45 had been worse than during the Occupation.) To be sure, one couple seems to be pretty serious about their future together. Perhaps the war bride is now living in New York, or the Great Plains . . .

Whatever each individual's stance, posture, and gaze, there is a dignity to each and every one, as well as a sense of relief. At the same time the people photographed by Ronis seem to acknowledge that this is not really the end, but rather the beginning of something else, a new era and perhaps a new episteme. Because of the pageant-like setting, the cover photograph speaks to us of a time simpler than ours—this despite the tremendous sacrifices of the war—and of an optimism about the future that would soon be smashed to smithereens with the bombing of Hiroshima and Nagasaki, and the advent of the not-so-Cold War, including the Communist Blockade of West Berlin in 1948–49. The new episteme would not arrive until the 1960s as far as thinking differently about war and peace, about a different type of Franco-American relations, or—to put it in the context of the writings of one of the most popular of theorists in French departments across the U.S.A. for many years, Michel Foucault—"just" about thinking differently:

> There are times in life when the question of knowing if one can think differently than one thinks, and perceive differently than one sees, is absolutely necessary if one is to go on looking and reflecting at all.[3]

From Jefferson's eighteenth-century euphoric francophilia to Sartre's 1960s bitter rejection of an America engaged in a war against Vietnam, a war the French had already lost, it is indeed a long way, a long time in the ever changing relations between France and the U.S.A., relations that have been and continue to be full at once of love and hate, of rivalry and envy, of silly mimicry and stubborn nationalism. The former American ambassador to France from 1936 to 1940, William Bullitt, wrote these prophetic words about American self-interest just days before the liberation of Paris:

---

3. Michel Foucault, *The Use of Pleasure*, trans. Robert Hurley (New York: Vintage Books, 1990 [1984]), 8.

France was our first friend. But gratitude is the rarest of human qualities and gratitude between nations is even rarer than between individuals. The memory of battles long ago grows dim; and it was not gratitude but a cool estimate of our own vital interests that led us to side
with the French against the Germans in the World War of 1914 and in
the present war—which is its second phase.[4]

As for the French, they would deplore, in turn, modernization (Fordism,
Taylorism), Americanization, globalization, and American fast food
(*malbouffe*), although they consume the latter in great quantities apparently.[5] Americans would both ape and mock French style and chic—
whether in the areas of food, clothing, and what used to intimidate us
so, "French theory," a pleonasm since it really came down to theory
pure and simple, other theories being less popular or entirely ignored.
But within not so long a time, Adorno, Benjamin, and Habermas would
be the references to which the American academy would turn, especially after the death of Paul de Man. For French intellectuals, mean-
time, the euphoria of liberation led to the anti-Americanism of Sartre
and company, as Jean-Philippe Mathy has described so succinctly:

> Between World War II and Vietnam the perception of American culture
> and society in French intellectual circles changed considerably. During
> the moment of euphoria following the liberation of France, a period
> marked by the political alliance of the various ideological streams (com-
> munists, socialists, Christian democrats, Gaullists, and liberals) that
> had resisted fascism, the United States appeared as a nation of libera-
> tors who had made the key contribution to the victory over Nazi bar-
> barity. The onset of the Cold War . . . rekindled the anti-Americanism
> of many in the French intelligentsia, regardless of political persuasion.
> The United States had become, with no serious rival, the largest indus-
> trial nation . . . , the self-appointed "leader of the free world," and the
> police officer of the planet. [*Extrême-Occident*, 137][6]

4. William C. Bullitt, "The Future of France," *Life* (14 August 1944): 75.

5. McDonald's sales in Europe in 1999 were reported to be $9.6 billion. It appears that
"[t]he French continue to smoke and drink with reckless abandon while spending heav-
ily on public health. . . . But, with all that, their average life expectancy of 73 places them
third in the world, well ahead of 24th-place America at 70. Little wonder that in a just-
released World Health Organization survey, France ranked first in 'overall health system
performance' compared with anti-socialist America at 37th." (John R. MacArthur,
"French Toast: Here's to our Gallic Cousins for Putting America in its Place," *The
(Toronto) Globe and Mail* [27 July 2000]).

6. ". . . postwar America appeared as both a model and a menace. The issue for the
French was to find the way to possess American prosperity and economic power and yet
to avoid what appeared to be the accompanying social and cultural costs. The challenge

Since the 1990s there has been a rash of French-baiting in American media. The French are slow to take advantage of email and the Internet, the French are hopelessly old-fashioned in their attempts to preserve a social-security net, the French don't think as well as they think they do, the French don't have any good writers these days, and so on *ad nauseum*.[7] The French, of course, also have their beefs, as mentioned above. Just as serious—or more so—are French concerns and deep doubts about political correctness, multiculturalism, and the expansion of the canon of French studies in the U.S.A. (see Francesca Canadé Sautman's article *infra*).

> The news coming from the other side of the Atlantic did nothing to alleviate the fears of the self-appointed guardians of republican civic virtues. The American people, it seemed, had simply gone mad. They were quarreling over sexual harassment, ethnic diversity, and gay rights, and their puritanical obsession with sex spread into the remotest corners of an individual's privacy. Every day the French media reported new horrors from the politically correct front that only confirmed what was in store for France as the deleterious influence of American society became more and more prevalent. Two elements of the new transatlantic developments went to the heart of the French malaise: the canon wars and multiculturalism. [Mathy, *French Resistance*, 14–15][8]

There have been numerous areas or arenas where these and other concerns—or better, fears—have been played out in France, whether it be

---

was to become economically and socially 'modern' without such American sins as social conformity, economic savagery, and cultural sterility. Cast in its grandest terms, the issue was, how could France follow the American lead and yet preserve a French way of life?" (Richard F. Kuisel, *Seducing the French: The Dilemma of Americanization* [Berkeley: University of California Press, 1993], 3). We should not forget the links between modernization and decolonization in post-World War II France, as Kristin Ross points out in *Fast Cars, Clean Bodies: Decolonization and the Reordering of French Culture* (Cambridge, Mass.: The MIT Press, 1995).

7. "France-bashing is not limited to the halls of academia, however. Not a week goes by, it seems, without some article in the mainstream press in America taking on the French for being incapable of worthwhile aesthetic creation, for foolishly refusing to get on the Internet, or for persisting in defending outdated conceptions of the welfare state in the age of capitalistic global competition." (Jean-Philippe Mathy, *French Resistance: The French-American Culture Wars* [Minneapolis: University of Minnesota Press, 2000], 9). For a short description of Alan Riding's famous article, "Where is the Glory That Was France?", *New York Times* (14 January 1996), see *French Resistance*, 10.

8. Two French perceptions of political correctness can be found in Françoise Gaillard, "Politiques ou corrects, l'Amérique nous oblige à choisir," *Crises* 1 (1994): 117–24, and Claudine Haroche and Ana Montoia, "La codification des comportements et des sentiments dans la *political correctness*, ou comment prétendre imposer le respect et garantir la dignité de chacun," *Revue française de science politique* 45/3 (June 1995): 379–95.

the flying of the Rainbow flag in the Marais district of Paris, the scarf affair, or the *parité* and "pacs" debates.[9]

This brings us to the issue at hand, this volume of *Yale French Studies, FRANCE/USA: The Cultural Wars*, that I have been fortunate enough to edit. A suitable subtitle might be "What is it the French don't get about what is going on in America?", as one of the contributors suggested I could name this project. This volume examines and illustrates various ways in which the developing field of cultural studies contributes to French studies. Divided into three sections ("Crossing the Atlantic," "Studying Cultures," and "Crossing over Cultures/Knowledge"), this collection targets the gap—the "schism" or the *dialogue de sourds*—that in recent years has increasingly characterized the manner in which cultural phenomena in France and the United States are perceived by the intellectuals of both countries. Using comparative approaches, seven scholars tackle the cultural differences that have divided France and the U.S.A. not only recently but as far back as de Tocqueville. At the same time, this intellectual and ideological conflict reflects the "culture wars" that have occurred and continue to occur within each country. For to speak of the cross-Atlantic divide—whether it be a question of universalism, democracy, pornography, rap music, or the politics of gender—is already to focus on the internal divisions that characterize both France and the U.S.A. Revolutionary independence and critical interdependence necessarily inform and critique each other in this Franco-American battle of ideas and of the diverse ways in which are constructed two imperfect cultures caught up in the no man's land of changing epistemes.

The first part, "Crossing the Atlantic," describes several transatlantic journeys. Susan Weiner quotes Pierre Nora on the "strange impermeability" between the two cultures.[10] Her examples, taken from

---

9. On the flag issue, see David Caron, *"Liberté, Égalité, Séropositivité:* AIDS, the French Republic, and the Question of Community," *French Cultural Studies* 36/3 (1998): 281–93. On the scarf affair, see Naomi Schor's article in this volume; on the *parité* debate, see Schor's and Anne Garréta's articles; on the *pacs* debate, see Garréta.

10. Two examples of what might be perceived to be aggressive French attitudes to culture are the following quotations: "Gentlemen, with respect to *esprit*, civilization, and culture, France doesn't take advice from anyone; it gives it!" (Serge Lifar, *Combat* [30 April 1950] quoted by Kuisel, 28); "It's not sinning by chauvinism or traditionalism to think . . . that European culture still has a word to say, that it, more than ever, has its values to express, in a civilization that risks becoming, for the first time perhaps in the history of the world, a *civilization without culture*." (André Piettre, *Le monde* [23 December 1967], quoted by Kuisel, 209).

Tocqueville, Aron, and Baudrillard, demonstrate how each of these social theorists arrived at the same paradigm: ". . . the French were theoretical and intellectual, the Americans were pragmatic and concrete."
But then even nonideology can be recast as ideology in this "our current postnationalist world."

David Bell's article tackles the Sokal affair.[11] He interprets it in light
of two of the less well-known literary genres, the *canard* (as in Balzac's
Illusions perdues) and the *sottisier* (as in Flaubert's *Dictionnaire des
idées reçues*). The debate about relativism, the relationship between
scientific research and literary theory, and the wider implications constitute for Bell "a truly remarkable misreading of the wider context of
French intellectual developments since World War II." Just how serious some took this debate can be seen from the following quotation:

> To compare Starr's report with Sokal's relentlessness at first seems in-
> congruous or shocking. Although the parallel doesn't hold for very long,
> it may have something to teach us. We would see two faces of rigorous
> puritanism, two ways of fostering a particular type of hate, two ways of
> attempting to disqualify people on the grounds of proximity. The Sokal
> affair may well be exemplary of the links that the scientific order may
> have with the moral order.[12]

We shall return to the Starr report about President Clinton in Christie
McDonald's article, "Changing Stakes: Pornography, Privacy, and the
Perils of Democracy."

The second part of this issue, "Studying Cultures," is an illustration and a defense of comparative cultural studies in the Franco-American context.[13] Naomi Schor's article demonstrates how modern
French universalism is a result of the convergence of three separate

---

11. A physicist teaching at New York University, Alan Sokal performed a hoax on
more than one research community by publishing an article in *Social Text* about the convergence of scientific and cultural knowledge, which he subsequently revealed in an article that appeared in *Lingua Franca*. He and a Belgian colleague, Jean Bricmont, later
wrote a book entitled *Fashionable Nonsense: Postmodern Intellectuals' Abuse of Science* (New York: Picador USA, 1998), whose original French title was *Impostures intellectuelles* (Paris: Odile Jacob, 1997).

12. Roger-Pol Droit, "Nous sommes tous des imposteurs!", *Le monde*, 2 October
1998.

13. "A skeptical and sociological, as opposed to appreciative and aesthetic, image of
France is becoming more common. The tendency of French departments in the U.S. to
move away from the intensive reading of classic texts and toward interdisciplinary and
francophone studies has inevitably brought French institutions under more critical
scrutiny." (Daniel Gordon, "Democracy and the Deferral of Justice in France and America," in this volume).

streams: the religious, the linguistic, and the ethical. As she states, the French culture wars "oppose the upholders of the Republic and the advocates of a French multiculturalism and democracy." The Franco-French debates brought into the light of day the "central paradox of French universalism": "the very universalism that is enlisted to press forward claims to human rights is reviled as legitimating oppression and masking inequity" toward, for example, slaves, women, and Jews. Her final question ("To what extent does universalism rely on exclusion to function?") will be taken up by Anne Garréta in her article on the Symbolic.

Daniel Gordon's article treats the wars over multiculturalism in the U.S.A. and the cultural wars between French and American professors "over whether this kind of dispute is meaningful at all." Whereas "the French tend to see America as heading toward multicultural anarchy, ... Americans tend to see the French as stuck in franco-solipism." Gordon's main point is that "[e]ach country sustains a magnificent tradition, but each one has also reached an impasse in its pursuit of justice: a point where the official concept of peoplehood blocks it from pursuing reforms that are necessary to complete its egalitarian mission. As a result, each nation perennially defers the pursuit of justice for certain of its members." He raises the specter of hostility to Jews in France, an issue that took on new relevance in 2000.[14] Taking a fairsided approach to transatlantic debates about multiculturalism, Gordon finds that "[t]he flaw in American multiculturalism is not its enthusiasm for diversity *per se* but its complacency with regard to the problem of commonality." This reminds us that one of the advantages of the field of cultural studies is that it allows authors to take strong critical and ethical stances vis-a-vis both sides in any comparative debate.

The last piece in "Studying Cultures" is Christie McDonald's article on "pornography, privacy, and the perils of democracy." As Schor did, McDonald goes back to the eighteenth century by referring to the *Declaration of the Rights of Man and the Citizen* and its feminist

---

14. A Reuters news report noted the following: "Racist attacks in France hit the highest level in a decade last year, said a survey released yesterday by a human-rights group that found most French people believed there were too many foreigners in the country. The report, commissioned by the government, was issued by France's National Consultative Commission on Human Rights, which tied the surge in racist violence in 2000 to a wave of new anti-Jewish feeling. It said the increase in racist attacks, threats, graffiti and propaganda developed after the renewal of a Palestinian uprising against Israel last September." ("France: Racist Attacks Highest in Decade," *The (Toronto) Globe and Mail* [22 March 2001]).

equivalent by Olympe de Gouges, *Declaration of the Rights of Woman and the Citizen*. Her hypothesis is that "the focus on sexual scandal . . . both translates and fosters the uncertainty surrounding ethics in the socio-political sphere." McDonald deals not only with pornography and the split among feminists concerning it, but leads us through the scandalous investigation of Clinton by Special Prosecutor Starr and the way it was perceived in France. In the end, it seems that

> American public opinion was thus consonant with what opponents came to call the "French solution." Coded positively, this solution indicated a way of being discreet about private sexual matters; coded negatively, private character was excluded from the judgment of leadership.

Part III, "Crossing over Cultures/Knowledge," studies two fields of research that have taken on great importance in the American academy in recent years: francophone and gay/lesbian studies. But both articles in this section go far beyond the rather restrained field of comparative discipline-building in France and the U.S.A. Despite the "continental drift," to use Mathy's expression (*French Resistance*, 170), cross-cultural practices and societal changes take on new meaning *and* a new vividness in these articles.

"Hip-Hop/scotch: 'Sounding Francophone' in French and United States Cultures" by Francesca Canadé Sautman addresses "the relationship between 'being/speaking Francophone' and forms of ethnic-cultural dissent in France and the U.S.A." The author provides us with information concerning the term *francophone*, the first francophone texts in Africa, and even a French-language book published in New Orleans in 1845. And to bring us up to date, Sautman raises an all-important point about the position of black francophone immigrants to the U.S.A. Discussing the work of French rappers, she describes the use of intercultural textuality in songs where "multilingualism, polyglossia, interweavings of different linguistic traditions and practices were distinctive features." The canon has expanded, indeed, and this article is a vibrant demonstration about just how necessary and exciting that expansion is for French studies.

Anne Garréta's "Re-enchanting the Republic: "Pacs," *Parité*, and *Le Symbolique*" begins with the fact that "there is no such thing as gay and lesbian or queer studies in France." To be sure, individual research is not impossible, but there is not even a fledgling movement in the direction of a new academic discipline, as has happened here in North America. Garréta reads "French institutional erasures of gender and sexuality behind the mask of the Universal or of Objectivity." Like Schor, she discusses the *parité* debates, which do not seem to have an equivalent on this side of the Atlantic, as well as the "pacs" issue, which does have a *homologue*, albeit a chiasmatic one, in Vermont. In France, it seems, the "prepolitical conditions of the subject's construction trump, precede, the determination of the citizen," which leads me to wonder if essentialization is still alive and well in post-Sartrean France.

Several of my favorite pages in Sartre are the ones in *La nausée* that describe the artistic partnership between a Jewish American song-writer and an African American singer.[15] The archetypical enemies of the Nazis—and later, Vichy—worked to produce "Some of These Days" in a steamy Manhattan. The result is the one and only way Roquentin can cure his existential nausea brought on by his newfound knowledge about contingency and the absurd. Indeed, hearing the song for the last time, he wonders if he too could become a creator of something as hard and pure as the song on the old, fragile record, thereby assuming his stature as a free man, one who up until then was attempting to sit between two chairs, as the French say, namely, between essentialist copouts, coverups, and falsehoods, on the one hand, and an existence fraught with spells of ontological *angoisse* accompanied by debilitating episodes of nausea, on the other. The link between American jazz and French Existentialism is, of course, a rich one: witness the existential nightclubs (*caves*) of the Saint-Germain-des-Prés quarter in the 1940s.[16]

---

15. Jean-Paul Sartre, *La nausée* in *Oeuvres romanesques*, Bibliothèque de la Pléiade, ed. Michel Contat and Michel Rybalka (Paris: Gallimard, 1981), 207–09.

16. In an article about early devotees of Existentialism, one finds the following passage: "The setting for these reunions was the Cave des Lorientais in the Rue des Carmes, and later the Club Saint Germain and the Rose Rouge. Cognac teamed up with jazz. This period saw the beginnings of Claude Luter, perfervid devotee of the New Orleans style. 'The catacombs of the early Christians,' murmured Raymond Queneau as he entered the Cave des Lorientais, fascinated by externals first of all but then by the 'community of tastes' that appeared to reign. All that once was forbidden in the name of a so-called 'moral order' could now spring up again: Judeo-Negro-American music, dancing in public, the drinking of spirits, the right to speak one's mind and to go to bed at four in the morning. . . . Perhaps one disagreed with American policy, which had already begun to exercise a perceptible pressure, but how could one fail to be won over by the charm of a young American soldier initiating one of the girls into the mysteries of jitterbugging, who passed on to us the latest news of Hollywood and Broadway, testified to the effects of penicillin and related deeds of violence that seemed to come straight from the pages of Hemingway and Faulkner?" (Jacques Guicharnaud, "Those Years: Existentialism 1943–1945," trans. Kevin Neilson, *Yale French Studies* 96 [1999]: 57. The article was first published in *Yale French Studies* 16 [1955–56].)

As the world's oldest modern republics, France and the U.S.A. need, complement, and—to a certain extent—emulate each other. They also have great cultural and political differences regarding multicultural-ism, globalization, as well as the notion and practice of democracy it-self in a republican context. As one contributor said to me, "The At-lantic is getting wider these days." The authors who have contributed to this volume come to grips with that divide from their own perspec-tive, and it is a rich one, indeed. But let us not forget that wars—whether cultural or not—do not exclude truces, peace treaties, and al-liances, whether old or new.[17]

It only remains for me to thank the authors of this volume for their unflinching loyalty and their patience in what has been a long and sometimes difficult enterprise. And, of course, none of this would have been possible without the generous aid and counsel of Alyson Waters, the general editor, whom I wish to thank here. In this the tercentennial year of the founding of Yale College and in this the one hundredth vol-ume of *Yale French Studies*—there could be no more appropriate fo-rum—it seemed timely to come back, once again, to the relations be-tween the United States of America and her oldest ally. That the task fell to me, a Canadian, is perhaps ironic, but I can and do identify with both of my adopted cultures.

17. "In short, and in long, what we have here is a profound mutual misunderstand-ing [between France and the U.S.A.]; it's a rock-solid foundation that ensures a great fu-ture together." It is with these words that Louis-Bernard Robitaille concludes his chap-ter "The La Fayette Syndrome" in his humorous book, *And God Created the French*, trans. Donald Winkler (Montreal: Robert Davies, 1997 [1995]), 255.

I. Crossing the Atlantic

SUSAN WEINER

Terre à Terre: Tocqueville, Aron, Baudrillard, and the American Way of Life[1]

In a 1978 article entitled "America and the French Intellectuals," Pierre Nora wrote of the "strange impermeability" between the two cultures, which neither psychoanalysis nor politics could explain: a "deeper structural reality . . . the idea of Revolution itself."[2] The American Revolution was the discrete and definitive event that founded the nation, its consensus and the status quo. In France, revolution remained an idea, a dream, and a discourse of transcendence that instead established the Left as the counterpower paradoxically central to the nation (Nora, 334). The event as opposed to the idea: this deep structural difference between France and the United States, as Nora noted, was first remarked and analyzed by Alexis de Tocqueville in *Democracy in America*,[3] then most notably by Raymond Aron in *The Opium of the Intellectuals*.[4] In the decade following Nora's article, the sense that different experiences of revolution were the underlay of French and American cultural differences continued to stand in the *America*[5] of Jean Baudrillard. Nora did not engage with the specificities of Tocqueville's and Aron's observations, focusing instead on how the conceptual and material results of revolution in France and the United States had defined each nation's particular claim to universalism.

1. This essay benefited greatly from Debarati Sanyal's careful and critical reading, bibliographic suggestions from Romy Golan and Michael Mosher, and Jeremy Sabol's seminar presentation on Descartes.

2. Pierre Nora, "America and the French Intellectuals," *Daedalus* (Winter 1978): 325, 334.

3. Alexis de Tocqueville, *Democracy in America*, vol. 2, trans. Henry Reeve (New York: Alfred A. Knopf, 1956).

4. Raymond Aron, *The Opium of the Intellectuals*, trans. Terence Kilmartin (London: Secker & Warburg, 1957).

5. Jean Baudrillard, *America*, trans. Chris Turner (London and New York: Verso, 1988).

YFS 100, *FRANCE/USA: The Cultural Wars,* ed. Ralph Sarkonak, © 2001 by Yale University.

From the "structural reality" that Nora posited in 1978, a return to the writings of Tocqueville and Aron and a step forward to Baudrillard brings together cultural phenomena from three distinct moments that led each of these social theorists to articulate the same observable paradigm. In mentalities as they created everyday life, the French were theoretical and intellectual, the Americans were pragmatic and concrete. The contrast is by now so familiar to appear banal. But even banalities have their history, and that of the long-standing view that there exist distinctly French and American ways of thinking is particularly relevant for our present moment. Tocqueville and Aron no longer go unread in their own country, as was the case in the 1970s[6] (Nora, 327). In our current postnationalist world, we can fully appreciate how their exploration of the "strange impermeability" between France and America carried with it a dream of transcendence different from that of revolution. By idealizing neither mode and imagining the infusion of French abstraction with American pragmatism, both of these thinkers call into question the French intellectual identification with revolution and its discourse. Tocqueville and Aron rehearse the dichotomy of national identity as expressed in modes of thought in order to enact, in their own writings, its effective end.

Despite these important discursive gestures, the contrast between French abstraction and American pragmatism remained in place throughout the early 1980s as an automatic reference for popular and intellectual culture, as did the paradoxically dominant position of the oppositional Left in France. In 1983, Baudrillard could describe America as an "achieved utopia,"[7] in contrast to a France stranded in the sea of its nineteenth-century ideas and ideals—and have his stark vision

---

6. On Tocqueville, see for example Tzvetan Todorov, *On Human Diversity: Nationalism, Racism, and Exoticism in French Thought*, trans. Catherine Porter (Cambridge: Harvard University Press, 1993); François Furet and Françoise Mélonio, Introduction to *The Old Regime and the Revolution*, trans. Alan S. Kahan (Chicago: University of Chicago Press, 1998); Françoise Mélonio, *Tocqueville and the French*, trans. Beth G. Raps (Charlottesville: University of Virginia Press, 1998); Pierre Manent, *An Intellectual History of Liberalism*, trans. Rebecca Balinski (Princeton: Princeton University Press, 1994). For Aron see Jean-François Sirinelli, *Deux intellectuels dans le siècle: Sartre et Aron* (Paris: Fayard, 1995) and Nicolas Baverez, *Raymond Aron: un moraliste au temps des idéologies* (Paris: Flammarion, 1993).

7. "Everything that has been heroically played out and destroyed in Europe in the name of Revolution and the Terror has been realized in its simplest, most empirical form on the other side of the Atlantic . . . All we do is dream and, occasionally, try to act out our dreams. America, by contrast, draws the logical, pragmatic consequences from everything that can possibly be thought" (Baudrillard, 97).

treated with the utmost of seriousness. Baudrillard positioned his comparative appraisal of America (for him, Los Angeles and New York City) as the final chapter of more than a century of French intellectual exploration of American pragmatism, as an end of history in its own right since American pragmatism and French abstraction had hardened into what he saw as timeless national identities and experiences. But Baudrillard's intellectual filiation with Tocqueville and Aron and his would-be final analysis must necessarily be reframed by the contemporary reality of the European Union and its goals of economic growth and cooperation. Pragmatism now necessarily filters into the "French way of thinking." And yet, the French self-identification with theory, abstraction, and ideas largely—and for some, reassuringly—remains.

In *Democracy in America*, the implicit point of comparison for Tocqueville's observations was the regime in France at the time: the July Monarchy (1830–1848), which was a testimony to the difficult course of shedding the mental structures of aristocracy as well as its institutions. Revolution alone could not undo a history that was centuries-old; the United States, on the other hand, had no such yoke of time to bear. The first half of the nineteenth century was a time of political and sociocultural self-invention for the new nation, and Tocqueville saw in America a laboratory for democracy whose experiments would prove useful for France. American government, the family, femininity, race relations, the multitude of civil associations—American particularities manifested themselves at every level of daily life, and for Tocqueville, all were worth comparing to the French context. As presented in *Democracy in America*, Tocqueville's findings are framed by what he identified in the first chapter as a specifically American mode of thought. The intellectual climate and style of inquiry, the philosophical references and debates familiar to Europeans, were nowhere in evidence; indeed, *Democracy in America*'s opening sentence is an affirmation as provocative today as it surely was then: "I think that in no country in the civilized world is less attention paid to philosophy than in the United States" (Tocqueville, 3). Not paying attention to philosophy, however, is immediately recast: neither reactionary nor hostile, inattention expresses blithe disinterest, a simple unawareness of Europe's established schools of thought and of the history and institutions of philosophy.

It took a French-trained mind to recognize that even without references to Plato and Aristotle at their fingertips, Americans had a common approach to problem-solving. Quite ingeniously, Tocqueville characterized the American way of thinking as Cartesian, though few Americans, he hypothesized, had ever read Descartes:

> To evade the bondage of system and habit, of family maxims, class opinions, and, in some degree, of national prejudices; to accept tradition only as a means of information, and existing facts only as a lesson to be used in doing otherwise and doing better; to seek the reason of things for oneself, and in oneself alone; to tend to results without being bound to means, and to strike through the form to the substance—such are the principal characteristics of what I shall call the philosophical method of the Americans. [Tocqueville, 3]

As Tocqueville delineated the typical American reasoning process, he presented French readers with their own idealized reflection. For while Cartesianism may have laid its claim as a form of universalism, the reference is also culturally French. Unlike their French counterparts, however, Americans were "naturally" Cartesian, according to Tocqueville, "because their social condition deters them from speculative studies . . . [and] this same social condition naturally disposes their minds to adopt [Descartes' maxims]" (Tocqueville, 4). In contrast, Descartes had arrived at his method by deliberately seeking isolation from his world, thus creating the conditions in which to cast off a body of socially circumscribed, acquired knowledge.

Descartes articulated plainly his intention that the *cogito* and the universalism to which it gestured be a revolution in thought, and that he himself be recognized as its incarnation: as the individual at the origin of universalism.[8] His was a philosophy predicated on the radical beginning. Tocqueville put aside the intentional radicalism of the Cartesian method and instead pointed to its suitability for both French and American contexts. Ultimately, Tocqueville's sense of Cartesianism was less a matter of revolution than it was of the ideal workings of democracy (Tocqueville, 6).

Cartesianism may have been the democratic ideal for both France and America, but it was too little applied in the American society Tocqueville observed in the early nineteenth century. Despite constitutional provisions for freedom of thought, it was only in the political realm that Americans sought to question, change, and search for truth outside of tradition. America's "natural" Cartesians were culturally contained, a

---

8. See Paul S. McDonald, *Descartes and Husserl: The Philosophical Project of Radical Beginnings* (Albany: SUNY Press, 2000); André Glucksmannn, *Descartes c'est la France* (Paris: Flammarion, 1987).

stasis he hypothesized to be the result of the society's religious under-pinnings. Christianity, a cornerstone of America's foundation along with the oft-trumpeted liberty and justice, remained unshakeable, unques-tionable, and ubiquitous, "an established and irresistible fact, which no one undertakes either to attack or to defend" (Tocqueville, 6). Tocqueville called Christianity "a religion which is believed without discussion" (Tocqueville, 6), subtle in its sovereignty, an ideological force ultimately more difficult to cast off than France's ostentatious monarchical past.

With this meditation on the cultural limits of Cartesianism in America, Tocqueville went back to aver his initial premise with re-newed conviction. While Americans and the French were equally ca-pable of independent thought, as a function of the moral imperative in the American context it remained the case that the truly pure and un-fettered thinkers, the masterminds of democracy in its theoretical conception and ideal, were French. Surprisingly hospitable to their free reflection, remarked Tocqueville, was the Old Regime. Only an aris-tocracy could provide the leisure and calm necessary to the pursuit of ideas, even if those ideas would come to be used against the very world that allowed for their formulation. The Enlightenment philosopher, unlike the American citizen, had to limit himself to abstraction as far as democracy was concerned and "could only speculate on the best manner of conducting [public affairs]" (Tocqueville, 18), but he had plenty of time in which to do so. In the "universal tumult" that was American democracy, theoretical notions were appreciated for their applicability and practicality, for their immediate potential to increase power, wealth, or efficiency, to improve material conditions. Queried Tocqueville, "where is that calm to be found which is necessary for the deeper combinations of the intellect?" (Tocqueville, 42).

Tocqueville was less interested in reifying the French and Ameri-can national characters than in analyzing their historical, political, and cultural specificities. Theorizing was an aristocratic pleasure, the ma-terial realization of ideas a democratic one. Would the French no longer take pleasure in abstract thought once the would-be transition to democracy had been made? Would such a profound social and political transformation transform in turn the nature and expression of French intellectual life? *Democracy in America* implicitly presents itself as a potential forerunner of the kind of work that a truly new breed of French thinker might produce: one that sought to understand through historical, philosophical, and economic analysis how to make democ-racy work outside of the limits of classic liberalism.

Tocqueville was alone in the France of his time; as the Revolution of 1848 would soon prove, the moment for thinkers like him had not yet arrived. In *Democracy in America* he recognized with prescience that just as aristocratic and democratic societies fostered certain modes of thought, so did the social conditions brought about by revolution— particularly in France, where the most impressive works of scientific thought had been produced in periods of upheaval. Revolutionary movements had not undone the nation's deep-seated social divisions, but had instead enduringly altered the world of ideas. Indeed, the greatest effect of revolution in France was to provide the conditions for the mode of thought that Descartes had theorized a century earlier:

> There are no revolutions that do not shake existing belief, enervate authority, and throw doubts over commonly received ideas. Every revolution has more or less the effect of releasing men to their own conduct and of opening before the mind of each one of them an almost limitless perspective. [Tocqueville, 7]

In Tocqueville's formulation, the figure of the solitary abstract thinker attached to the aristocratic sphere did not disappear with the king; moreover, the *penseur* acquired political urgency as the ways and means of equality began to take hold in the absence of monarchic institutions and authorities. "Excessively" independent and even distrustful of others, the thinker of revolutionary times as presented by Tocqueville "looks for the light" in himself alone. "That sort of intellectual freedom which equality may give ought, therefore, to be very carefully distinguished from the anarchy which revolution brings" (Tocqueville, 7), cautioned Tocqueville, who saw the fusion of Cartesianism and revolution as a transitional moment in France's progress toward equality, and the combative thinker as a transitional figure whose time would soon come to an end.

For Tocqueville, revolution belonged to the French past, and had little place in his formulation of the path to democracy. From this would-be consignment to memory, by the mid-twentieth century, 1789 and the idea of revolution had become a linchpin of French intellectual identity. Albert Camus was one of the few on the Left to connect the post-World War II climate to the Terror, where the tragic vocation of the authentic artist was that of the "éternel Girondin";[9] the dominant mood and discourse of the late 1940s and early 1950s were decidedly

---

9. Albert Camus, "Le témoin de la liberté," *Actuelles* (Paris: Gallimard, 1950), 266.

Jacobin. In Raymond Aron's concurring analysis, to be an intellectual in postwar France was to identify and to write as a revolutionary. *The Opium of the Intellectuals* compared French intellectuals' social position to that of their American and Soviet counterparts in order to criticize these French intellectuals' execration of their own country. Though unappreciated, France was "The Intellectuals' Paradise" (Aron, 218): a land of free expression where not only did the life of the mind represent the highest value, but the mind could be used to make a decent living.

At least this was the case in Paris, where novelists had greater social status than statesmen, even when addressing political matters. Aron described a world where the social structures and the mentalities of the aristocracy had remained in place, and where the thinkers were all of the clever yet useless variety:

> The tradition of the salon, presided over by women or dilettantes, has been allowed to survive in a century of technology. A general culture may still allow one to dissertate agreeably on politics, but it is no protection against silliness and it does not equip one for recommending precise reforms. In a sense, the intelligentsia is less geared to political action in France than anywhere else. [Aron, 220–21]

Effete, feminized, and ineffectual, the intellectuals who dominated postwar Parisian society were ready to hold forth on any or all subjects, but able to go no further than words. While Aron expressed contempt for the vague politics of the left-wing intellectual, he also hypothesized that their unrealized call to action was not simply a sign of bad faith. Excluded as rebels, as "prophets of subversion" (220), from the Fourth Republic's own incoherent spheres of economic and political decision-making, intellectuals found the euphoric yet unspecific calls they made for sociopolitical transformation during the Liberation relegated to back issues of weeklies.

In Aron's atypical view, Fourth Republic distrust and disinterest was what led intellectuals on the Left to a pro-Soviet stance. Support of the Soviet Union, even when tempered by the acknowledgment of the human cost of Stalinism, was one way to carry on the spirit of *engagement* and the project, announced in the first issue of *Les temps modernes*, to transform social conditions as well as consciousness.[10]

10. Although Sartre in 1945 envisioned carrying out this project without the underpinnings of dialectical materialism. Jean-Paul Sartre, "Présentation," *Les temps modernes* 1 (October 1945), 7.

Reproach of the rabid anti-Communism of the United States was another. But the anti-Americanism of French intellectuals went well beyond reproach. How to understand the virulence? Why was America a scapegoat for the French Left in the 1950s? "The United States is represented as the embodiment of everything most detested, and then all the resentment and hatred and gall which accumulate in people's hearts in a time of troubles are heaped on this symbolic figure" (224–25), observed Aron.[11]

Could this be, he wondered, the only possible reaction to the fact that through capitalism America had come closer than any other nation to goals communism had only ever theorized—the overall rise in the standard of living, the attenuation of class differences, and the increased powers for individuals and for unions? (Aron, 227). Would America reach the end of history without revolution and its theories ever even entering the national psyche? The counterexample of French intellectuals who claimed to be interested in the fate of the masses yet railed against the vulgarity of mass culture's offerings reinforced Aron's presentation of a French type of thinker who preached revolution yet ultimately remained aristocratic. *The Opium of the Intellectuals* shows that the solitary, abstract, and combative thinker was not the transitional figure Tocqueville had imagined him to be. Cartesianism simply had acquired a new urgency, that of situation: "Je pense en 1945, donc je suis"—one could even paraphrase a Sartrian use of the *cogito* for the phenomenology of the intellectual specific to the immediate postwar period and to the dream in those years of imminent revolution.[12]

The "natural Cartesianism" Tocqueville had seen in Americans also came to function in Aron's view as an expression of the times. He identified a distinct cultural type specific to the 1950s, distinct yet integrated into the workings of the nation: "the expert" (Aron, 229). In contrast to the self-identification of French intellectuals with revolution, the typical representative of the intelligentsia in America was a quantitatively-oriented economist or sociologist involved in practical

11. Aron cites Sartre's reading of the Rosenberg trial as a "new Fascism" and the sign of what could become a "war of extermination," ending in a call to all Europeans to break ties with an America he described as rabid: "or else we'll be bitten and infected ourselves." For Aron (who believed the Rosenbergs were guilty), American "rabidity" paled in comparison to this sort of French intellectual rage in the face of America. See *The Opium of the Intellectuals*, 224–25.

12. "Ce qui est relatif, c'est le cartésianisme, cette philosophie baladeuse qu'on promène de siècle en siècle [What is relative is Cartesianism, that roving philosophy that is taken for a stroll from century to century]." Sartre, 7 [my translation].

matters of state: national administration, business, the banking industry, and the press, spheres where "ideas and personnel never cease to circulate"[13] (Aron, 221). One can be sure that "experts" did not hold forth in salons.

Tocqueville had described how "not paying attention" to philosophy was a mode of thought in itself in nineteenth-century America; in the Cold War years, Aron was fascinated by the way in which ordinary Americans, just like the "expert," lived the negation of what Europeans understood as ideology. Unattached to any predefined conceptual system, set neither on a savior nor on the end of history, the "American way of life" as an expression of American pragmatic thinking combined respect for the Constitution with the Protestant work ethic, and a strong if vague humanitarianism. Such nonideology, wrote Aron, could also be recast as a specifically American ideology:

> [T]he cult of success; individual initiative and adaptation to the group; moral inspiration and humanitarian action; the violence of competition together with a sense of the rules of the game; optimism about the future and rejection of existential anguish; the reducing of every situation to technically soluble problems. [Aron, 297]

While Aron was dismayed by the rampant anti-Americanism on the French Left, he did not counter it with unequivocal admiration for the United States. Each of his observations sounded a simultaneously positive and critical note. The "American way" is efficient and practical; things work on every level, but at a cost: the loss of the complexity of human experience that comes with philosophical reflection on the causes and effects of acts in the world. Action without thought was the American ideology. Aron was a sociologist but always a philosopher. In his ambivalence toward the single-minded practicality and productivity of the United States, one can detect his personal preference for questions without quantifiable answers, for debate and discussion of ideas. To "reject" existential self-searching and to "reduce" systems and situations to problems was in essence to remain on the surface of things. Whereas French intellectuals could not get beyond words, Aron considered the American tendency to privilege the surface as the dimension of movement and problem-solving to be limited in its own way.

The same divide between surface and depth as qualities associated with American and French ways of thinking came to be reframed by

---

13. This was also true for Great Britain and even Germany, wrote Aron. But French intellectuals reserved their greatest contempt for the United States.

the rise of postmodern thought in Jean Baudrillard's *America*. No longer did superficiality signify limitation; instead it was both an authentic expression of the vastness of the West as well as the everyday experience of Americans who lived in what Baudrillard called an "achieved utopia," where, supposedly, everything wished for promptly materialized. A brasher observer than Tocqueville, Baudrillard suggested that only a European could recognize the conceptual interest of American pragmatism, "since he alone will discover here the perfect simulacrum" (Baudrillard, 28), whether in the form of the highway system, "the lyrical nature of pure circulation . . . the collapse of metaphor," or the language of advertising—"I did it! . . . a pure and empty form" (Baudrillard, 27, 20). America for Baudrillard was the sublime object of theory.

Like Aron and Tocqueville, Baudrillard advocated the value of a certain measure of abstraction. Unlike them, he also intimated that there was nothing more to say about French and American modes of thought as expressed in their individual cultures, his being the final analysis of their final forms. Whereas America was a "fait accompli," melancholic Europe was the land of the "déjà vu" (Baudrillard, 84), of "nostalgic utopians," agonizing over their ideals of revolution, progress, and freedom "but baulking, ultimately, at their realization" (Baudrillard, 77). In his contrast between American pragmatism and French abstraction, Baudrillard expressed what could be called post-anti-Americanism:

> We criticize Americans for not being able either to analyze or conceptualize. But this is a wrong-headed critique. It is we who imagine that everything culminates in transcendence, and that nothing exists which has not been conceptualized. Not only do they care little for such a view, but their perspective is the very opposite: it is not conceptualizing reality, but realizing concepts and materializing ideas, that interests them. The ideas of the religion and enlightened morality of the eighteenth century, certainly, but also dreams, scientific values, and sexual perversion. . . . Everything that has been dreamt about on this side of the Atlantic has a chance of being realized on the other. They build the real out of ideas. We transform the real into ideas, or ideology. [Baudrillard, 84]

Tocqueville and Aron had both begun their analyses by noting that philosophical reflection without a distinct material purpose had little place in the American context. They went on to admire American pragmatism—and concluded by regretting the loss of complexity that accompanied a way of thinking focused on results. When oversimplified, the substance of their analyses devolves into stereotype and anti-Americanism: the judgment that a culture without intellectuals (at least the kind one finds in France) is no culture at all. For Baudrillard, the comparison is flawed, a contingency of value weighted in favor of France. In his view, the two cultures were each closed systems that happened to be uncanny inversions of each other: in America, ideas took concrete form; in France, realities evaporated into the world of ideas. In this formulation, the opposition between national identities is more firmly in place than ever, and doubles as Baudrillard's own version of the end of history. When America was founded, he wrote, "Europe began to disappear" (Baudrillard, 81), a disappearance completed by the 1980s: "in Los Angeles, Europe has disappeared." Perhaps in the Los Angeles of the 1980s it had, but then again, Baudrillard could not have foreseen at the time the collapse of Communism and the rise of the new Europe, whose importance on the current global economic and political scene belies the finality of his dire declarations of just one decade past.

Yet the age-old figure of the idealistic abstract thinker has not disappeared either, in today's debates surrounding "la pensée unique" (neoliberalism), unemployment, and "exclusion" (race and class tensions). In a recent article in *Le monde* that lists some of the most important books to take on such questions, Sophie Gherardi notes the authors' tendency to analyze without offering solutions. "A very French debate ensues," she writes. "These writers oppose concepts and not case studies; examples and statistics are put into service to ideas."[14] Along with this resolutely unpragmatic approach to real social and economic problems, the image of France conveyed in these works is that of a nation poised—still—between its Old Regime past and a present it is not fully prepared to assume:

> A leitmotif returns in many of these works: that of a France halfway, between Anglo-Saxon capitalism and German corporatism; between archaism and modernity; between particularism and alignment; between egalitarian aspiration and the elitist reality. It is as if this country, so long a bearer of a message and a model, that of Jacobinism, literally no longer knew where to situate itself. [Gherardi, 2]

As the leaders of the European Union pledge to respect national and regional identities and sovereignty while fostering a shared economic and ethical project for the continent as a whole, the question of a specifi-

14. Sophie Gherardi, "Le débat est en librairie," *Le monde: économie* (24 February 1998), i (my translation).

cally French way of thinking gains renewed relevance. Only now, the counterexample of American-style pragmatism no longer serves as the automatic reference. State-level negotiations between European nations and the intellectual scrutiny to which they are subjected in the French press call attention to the way in which problem-solving can double as an expression of cultural specificity—without necessarily defining it as such. And while the revolutionary ideal has run its course, there remains a recognizably French mode of thought: abstract, theoretical, and often combative, a mode much akin to that of the "excessively" independent thinkers and "prophets of subversion" that Tocqueville and Aron had observed in their own times.

How then are we to understand the French tendency toward abstraction as distinct from the idealization of revolution? What sort of alternative genealogy might we trace, and what place would Cartesianism take? The idealization of revolution must enter into any historical understanding of the French way of thinking, but so must other ideas and ideals that have been consistently integrated into the cultural fabric and interrogated over the centuries—humanism, for example, and universalism. Perhaps such a reassessment might be of practical use as France continues to define its position within the European Union. In any case, reflecting on French abstraction beyond the "strange impermeability" between French and American ways of thinking stands as a liberation in its own right, a transcendence that Tocqueville, Aron, and Baudrillard could only ever imagine.

DAVID F. BELL

Text, Context: Transatlantic Sokal

Only with great trepidation would anyone undertake to write something more about the Sokal affair after over three years of relentless articles, letters to the editor, electronic mail messages, web forums, and cyber flaming of all sorts. The whole episode may, in fact, have been the first public intellectual polemic whose importance was defined by the sheer quantity of cyber words devoted to it. In the first phases, several of the principals seem to have believed that the volume of commentary generated by the debate could be taken as a plebiscite justifying their continued interventions and their attempts to explain themselves and to defend their positions.[1] Numerous websites devoted space to the electronic publication of texts related to the affair. To approach the affair in any comprehensive way would therefore seem to be a herculean task, one that could absorb a substantial amount of any researcher's lifetime. To my knowledge, the best recent attempt at such a comprehensive approach is Yves Jeanneret's *L'affaire Sokal*, but even Jeanneret freely admits that the texts he uses for his essay are but a sampling chosen for the purposes of exploring a very specific perspective and culled from a vast source whose true dimensions are ultimately difficult to measure.[2] The problems associated with intervening in the discussions swirling around the affair are more than quantitative, however; they are also directly related to the ideological passions excited by Sokal's publications. To write anything about the affair means to find oneself almost inevitably taking a position for or against the contemporary version of the hard sciences, for or against philosophy, for or

1. See, for example, Andrew Ross, "Reflections on the Sokal Affair," *Social Text* 50 (Spring 1997): 149–52.
2. Yves Jeanneret, *L'affaire Sokal ou la querelle des impostures* (Paris: PUF, 1998), 255–57.

YFS 100, *FRANCE/USA: The Cultural Wars,* ed. Ralph Sarkonak, © 2001 by Yale University.

against French "theory," for or against cultural studies and science studies. One of the main characteristics of the numerous discussions provoked by Sokal's publications is that they have not been particularly hermeneutical. Those who have written about the issues raised by the affair often have not been principally concerned with understanding and evaluating their adversaries' positions. The fundamental principle of a hermeneutical approach is to adopt an attitude of generosity toward the ideas proposed by one's adversary. This perspective compels a potential critic to assume the validity of opposing arguments in order to engage them fully and to decide whether or not they are compelling—but only after working through all of their nuances. Jean-Michel Salanskis puts it nicely: "I find meaning only to the extent that I construct it by assuming the coherence, sense, and pertinence of the text I am reading. To give credit to an argument is not a favor granted to its author for affective, extra-intellectual reasons. It is instead the primary and necessary operation of any attempt to comprehend."[3] I doubt that one could characterize much of the extended Sokal polemic in such terms—with numerous exceptions, of course. Since a substantial part of the debate has been conducted in the media—particularly in the new media of the Internet—the temptation has been to go for the kill, to construct a thirty-second sound bite in order to best adversaries without having to spend the time necessary to analyze what they have actually said or written.[4]

---

3. Jean-Michel Salanskis, "Pour une épistémologie de la lecture," in *Impostures scientifiques. Les malentendus de l'affaire Sokal*, ed. Baudouin Jurdant (Paris: Éditions de la Découverte/*Alliage*, 1998), 181. The translation is my own, as will be the case in the rest of this essay unless another translation is indicated.

4. For readers who might not have the broad outlines of the Sokal affair at their fingertips, a thumbnail sketch would be helpful. New York University physicist Alan Sokal published an article in the Spring-Summer 1996 issue of the review *Social Text* ("Transgressing the Boundaries: Towards a Transformative Hermeneutics of Quantum Gravity," *Social Text* 46–47 [Spring-Summer 1996]: 217–252). Shortly after the publication of that article, he published a second article in *Lingua Franca* ("A Physicist Experiments with Cultural Studies," *Lingua Franca* 6/4 [May–June 1996]: 62–64), in which he revealed that the first article had been a hoax. "Transgressing the Boundaries," he explained, had been an experiment to see whether an article that was patently scientifically false (for any scientist reading it) could make it through the stages of editorial review and be accepted in a journal that was one of the leading forums for articles in the cultural studies field of science studies. *Social Text* editors Andrew Ross and Stanley Aronowitz, as well as Stanley Fish, the director of the Duke University Press, the publisher of *Social Text*, immediately responded, and a debate ensued not only about academic publishing practices, but about the place and importance of science studies. The wider debate pitted believers in scientific truth against proponents of the notion that science is not culturally neutral. In the

It is by no means certain that I can avoid the pitfalls that have resulted from the passions of the early moments of the Sokal polemic. Just because one writes after the furor does not automatically ensure that one will get things right or even that one can attain the dispassionate stance that sometimes escapes the principal discussants in the heat of the moment. With a bit of distance, one can hope nonetheless to broaden the discussion by introducing a slightly wider perspective and to contextualize it in ways that show other dimensions. In the argument that follows, I would like to approach certain aspects of the affair from a more literary point of view in order to make some comments about the style of Sokal's arguments and about the way he deals with the contexts in which he constructs those arguments. In fact, as everyone who has followed the debate already knows, there were actually two Sokal affairs (see note 4). The first began with the publication of "Transgressing the Boundaries: Towards a Transformative Hermeneutics of Quantum Gravity," followed shortly by "A Physicist Experiments with Cultural Studies," in which Sokal revealed the hoax of the first article and commented on its purpose. The second act began with the publication in Paris of *Impostures intellectuelles,* co-authored with Jean Bricmont, in which Sokal and Bricmont leveled a broadside against French philosophers and theorists. The two affairs were a year and an ocean apart, and the differences in the contexts of the two publication moments will engage me principally here. Those differences dictated contrasting publishing strategies and literary forms. My reflections will be concentrated mainly on the literary forms used in the course of the debate and on the contextual constraints that both allowed and limited them.[5]

---

fall of the following year, 1997, Sokal took the debate to France, when he published an essay, cowritten with Belgian chemist Jean Bricmont, in which he accused major French intellectuals and thinkers of the past two decades of playing fast and loose with scientific concepts (Alan Sokal and Jean Bricmont, *Impostures intellectuelles* [Paris: Editions Odile Jacob, 1997]). English translation: *Fashionable Nonsense: Postmodern Intellectuals' Abuse of Science* [New York: Picador USA, 1998]). Sokal clearly believed that French thought was at the origin of American science studies and that the approach toward science it had instilled in American intellectuals was relativistic and threatened to undercut any belief in the notion of scientific truth.

5. Every literary critic and historian knows that the evolution and renewal of literary forms always takes place between the constraints created by conventions and the space of play they provide. See, for example, Mette Hjort, *The Strategy of Letters* (Cambridge: Harvard University Press, 1993), or Mette Hjort, ed., *Rules and Conventions: Literature, Philosophy, Social Theory* (Baltimore: The Johns Hopkins University Press, 1992).

The original *Social Text* article has been called at various times a hoax, a trick, a joke, a trap, a mystification, a parody, an experiment—the list could continue. Let us characterize it here by using the French term *canular*, a word that appeared often in French responses to the Sokal affair and that is defined by the *Robert* as a "mystification, blague, farce, fausse nouvelle [fictitious news item]." In journalistic and publishing circles, the *canular* has a long history, and no one, I think, has constructed its theory in a subtler manner than Balzac. It would be instructive to look at his *Illusions perdues* for insight into the meaning and the functioning of the *canular*. In reality, Balzac uses the term *canard* rather than *canular*. The appearance of the term *canard* to mean a journalistic hoax or fiction dates roughly from the mid-eighteenth century. By the mid-nineteenth, the word's meaning had been extended, and it referred as well to entire newspapers that dealt in sensationalistic, invented fictions.[6] *Canular* is a much more recent word that began to be used to designate journalistic hoaxes only after the beginning of the twentieth century. What, then, is a *canard* in Balzac's understanding of the term? We get an explanation in a scene following Lucien de Rubempré's first journalistic success in *Illusions perdues*, the article he writes in Coralie's boudoir describing the play in which she has a role, *L'alcade dans l'embarras*. The new and fresh style of the review article gives Lucien the entry he desires into the journalistic circles organized around Finot and Lousteau. Shortly after its publication, he is allowed to participate in a meeting of the journalists who will be working for Finot's new newspaper. During this discussion, the main contributors to the newspaper give Lucien one of his first extended lessons in journalism. It is not surprising that the term *canard* comes up immediately, because it is at the heart of journalistic praxis during the Restoration, as Balzac sees it.[7] Since he is a newcomer and does not understand the term, Lucien requests an explanation as soon as it is used:

> That is our word for a scrap of fiction told for true, put in to enliven the column of morning news when it is flat. We owe the discovery to Benjamin Franklin, the inventor of the lightning conductor and the republic. That journalist completely deceived the Encyclopædists by his

6. Hence the title of the modern-day French satirical newspaper, *Le canard enchaîné*, with its humorous mixture of speculation, innuendo, fact, and fiction.

7. See, for example, Honoré de Balzac, *Monographie de la presse parisienne* (Paris: J. J. Pauvert, 1965), 64–65.

transatlantic *canards.* Raynal gives two of them for facts in *Histoire philosophique des Indes.*[8]

The power of the *canard* is to be able to pass itself off as authentic by maintaining a high degree of probability. What is probably the case easily becomes what is actually the case for a naive reader—and given the conventions of journalism, almost any reader is at least occasionally naive.

It is important to note that Balzac's treatment of the *canard* quickly broadens to encompass much more than simple *faits divers* or *Faits-Paris,* as they were called during his period, and thereby has an impact on substantive ideological issues. Arguably one of the best-known passages in *Illusions perdues* describes the moment when Lousteau asks Lucien to write a negative review of Nathan's most recent book. Lucien is initially stymied by the assignment, because he likes and appreciates the book in question. This is the occasion for Lousteau to launch into a veritable theory of the polemic based on the idea of the *canard,* on the notion that what one writes is not necessarily—if ever—what one actually believes to be true: "'Oh, I say! you must learn your trade,' said Lousteau laughingly. 'Given that the book were a masterpiece, under the stroke of your pen it must turn to dull trash, dangerous and unwholesome stuff'" (9:208). Lousteau's point is that any position can be transformed into its opposite, any quality into its corresponding defect. The lesson continues over the next few days and the next few pages in Balzac's text, when Lucien is called upon to write a second article in favor of the very book he has just pilloried. Ultimately, he will also write a third, synthesizing article, the only one he signs with his real name, in which he summarizes the preceding articles and assumes the stance of an impartial observer—above and beyond the fray of the polemic unleashed by the first two articles.[9] As Émile Blondet puts it: "In literature, my boy, every idea is reversible, and no man can take it upon himself to decide which is the right or wrong side. Everything is bilateral in the domain of thought. Ideas are binary. Janus is a fable signifying Criticism and the symbol of Genius. The Almighty alone is triform" (9:225). I want to insist on the fact that the third position adopted by Lucien—supposedly beyond those expressed in the first two articles—is no more sincere than the viewpoints

---

8. Honoré de Balzac, *Lost Illusions,* in *The Works of Honoré de Balzac,* vol. 9 (New York and London: Harper & Brothers, n.d.), 201–2.

9. One cannot, however, speak unproblematically about signing with one's "real" name. See below.

taken in the first two: "You . . . end by averring that Nathan's work is the great book of the epoch; which is all as if you said nothing at all; they say the same of everything that comes out" (9:228–29). The perspective taken in the third article may be disguised as God's, but it is very far from transcendental, as much caught up in the fray as any of the ideas expressed in either of the other two articles.

What lessons does this summary of Balzac's analysis of the *canard* and its extensions contain? In the first place, the notion of the polemic is possible to imagine in the form Balzac gives it only if there is a free circulation among possible positions, none of which corresponds to a "true" position. When Lucien enters this journalistic universe, he must abandon all pretense that something like a principled position can be defended, and he must accept the idea that what drives any media-based polemic is precisely the absence of a standpoint above the fray that can be invoked to end the exchange. The novel eventually gives him ample proof of this principle when Lucien himself falls victim to this mechanism. Second, in order to assume any and all positions in a polemic of this sort, one must be extremely well-versed in the crucial issues of the ambient cultural debates at any given time. When Lousteau and later Blondet outline the form that the "for and against" arguments must take in order to be effective, they do so by situating in detail this particular instance of critique within the context of the literary debates that define Romanticism in their period. If the newspaper publishes principally not what is, but, rather, what is probable, then it behooves the journalist to make an article believable, probable enough to pass muster once released into the public domain.

Balzac's description of the *canard* and its extension into journalistic polemics can provide some perspective on Sokal's original "Transgressing the Boundaries" article. As Balzac points out, to defend a position is not to espouse it, to sign an article is not to authenticate it. It quickly becomes evident that Sokal has two signatures in the beginning of the American phase of the controversy: the one crowning the *Lingua Franca* article is meant to be different from the one attached to the *Social Text* article. The *Lingua Franca* signature is supposedly authentic. It authenticates the positions taken in the second article, and it identifies them as the opinions of the "real" Sokal.[10] I will come back

10. Yves Jeanneret analyzes the double signature in a very convincing way at the beginning of his *L'affaire Sokal*, 13–15. Jacques Derrida's "Signature Event Context," *Glyph* 1 (1977): 172–97, is, of course, the classic deconstruction of the notion of a "real" signature.

to this later, but I also want to point out that the success of the hoax or parody, the fact that it was accepted as a viable article by the editors of *Social Text* and ultimately published in their journal, had everything to do with Sokal's understanding and use of the context in which the article appeared. From the style of the writing to the set of references used in the notes, from the attack on objective science to the apparent agreement with the proponents of the social nature of the scientific endeavor, everything is geared to create resonances corresponding to the expectations of the editors and the public of *Social Text*.[11] One may debate the degree of subtlety displayed by Sokal. The editors of *Social Text* have claimed that what brought the article through the evaluation stage and eventually into the journal was not as much its style and content as the fact that it was signed by a physicist (and there is good reason to believe them). One can also surmise that Sokal likely had some assistance in the ultimate redaction of the article, since the rhetorical style of the argument is quite foreign to that practiced by professional physicists. Nonetheless, one cannot deny that a certain savvy understanding by Sokal of the generic and stylistic circumstances contributed greatly to what might be termed the success of the initial part of the Sokal operation, the very same kind of understanding that drives Lousteau's and Blondet's successes in *Illusions perdues*. In fact, the understanding and leveraging of context demonstrated in the *Social Text* article really go much deeper than would be the case in a simple stylistic exercise. The article puts to effective use the development of a certain antiscientific spirit within American culture in general over the past several decades. From Christian cultural conservatism to New Age Scientology on the left, culture in the United States has been marked by a *mise-en-question* of the validity of the faith in science and technology that characterized earlier moments in the twentieth century.[12] This wider context lends Sokal's *canard* a good portion of its probability and therefore its credibility. If science studies in the United States have had a certain success in putting the claimed objectivity and the presumed neutrality of science and technology into question, this is at least in part because a broad

11. And one might add that the particular difficulties of defining and constructing the objects of social science research make the rhetoric of presentation of results all the more crucial to the success of any publication in this domain.

12. See Michel Pierssens, "Science-en-culture Outre-Atlantique," in *Impostures scientifiques*, 106–17, for a very useful thumbnail sketch of this and other issues of context involving the American side of the controversy.

spectrum of doubts about the bases and validity of scientific knowledge pre-existed such critical exercises.

In many ways, the publication of "Transgressing the Boundaries" was a rather textbook example of a polemic in the manner imagined by Balzac in *Illusions perdues*. The *Lingua Franca* article, however, was an almost immediate and peremptory attempt to change the game in a substantial manner. In particular, it was stylistically considerably different from "Transgressing the Boundaries." It did not take the form of an objective presentation of supposed fact accompanied by reasoned interpretation of that fact (as is the case for a typical academic article—with all the difficulties implied by the notion of fact, of course), but instead was cast as an autobiographical statement, making liberal use of the first person pronoun and calculated to give the impression that its author was expressing his fundamental position—one that was beyond interpretive quarrels. Far from assuming the consequences of launching a polemic by means of a strategy of shifting positions, Sokal attempted to cut off the discussion by presenting what he wanted to be understood as his authentic position on the hoax he had just perpetrated when he had offered for publication in *Social Text* an article he knew to be nonsense. This subsequent and ultimate position taken in *Lingua Franca* was intended simultaneously to draw the conclusions of the demonstration and to silence those he was criticizing by invoking the weighty embarrassment of their error in believing that "Transgressing the Boundaries" had actually contained a viable argument.[13] The problem is that one cannot have one's cake and eat it too. One cannot so easily exit a polemical field with a pirouette of this sort, by invalidating in one fell swoop the very same textual strategy one has adopted as the primary means to open the debate. The double signature is the indication of a "schizophrenia" (I'm using the term metaphori-

---

13. The significance of the choice of *Lingua Franca* as the forum in which to carry out this autobiographical exercise should be lost on no one. The review willingly describes itself as the gadfly of the academic community and takes pleasure in exposing whatever university and intellectual scandals it can. Sokal's operation created a perfect occasion to draw attention to *Lingua Franca*, and the presentation of his article by the editors of the review explicitly invited an exchange that would put *Lingua Franca* at the center of the discussion: "In the essay printed below, Professor Alan Sokal of NYU discusses his unusual attempt to play with—some might say transgress—the conventions of academic discourse. *Lingua Franca* invites readers to respond to Sokal's article" ("A Physicist Experiments with Cultural Studies," 62). The provocation of the verb "transgress" is evidently calculated to provoke vigorous response—"playing with" suggests a lack of seriousness that cannot elicit strong, principled opinions. The terms of the invitation raise all the problems of the *canard* that I have analyzed.

cally, hence the quotation marks) that cannot be repaired by reference to the authentic nature of the critic's consciousness ever present unto itself.

I do not want to belabor the question of the double signature, however, since Yves Jeanneret has done a masterful job of analyzing its meaning. Rather, I want to raise the problem of the style of critique that Sokal chose in the first place. It is difficult, if not impossible, to imagine how a *canard* could actually function effectively as a mechanism of critique. Its very definition implies that its success must render it invisible. The best *canard* would appear to be so like what it is imitating that it becomes undetectable—it must be convincing enough to allow it to pass unnoticed for what it is not. In the end, the *canard* is a version of the simulacrum, one of those representations of the ideal that so haunted Plato as a potential source of philosophical, if not to say social, disorder. The danger of the simulacrum, as Plato understood it, is its potential for creating confusion by undoing the hierarchy of being. If left to its own devices, the simulacrum could provoke a general crisis and paralysis (reasoning in Platonic terms), hence Sokal's haste to put an end to what could quickly become a very vicious circle. He therefore intentionally belittles "Transgressing the Boundaries" in his *Lingua Franca* article, calling it and the arguments it purveys alternately "modest," "silly," and "egregious," in order to undo it qua *canard*.

Paradoxically, however, the *Lingua Franca* article did anything but put an end to the discussion. Fortunately or unfortunately, as the case may be, the debate that ensued was necessarily infected by the disordering effects of the *canard* genre, by the *canard*'s tendency to confuse rather than to clarify, to reproduce itself once a certain responsibility toward an allusive truth is abandoned in favor of probable arguments. I think one could put things this way: a successful simulacrum cannot really be an instrument of critique, because only one condition would make this possible—a commentary ex post facto on the strategy of creation of the simulacrum must accompany it in short order. But clearly such a commentary immediately undercuts the effectiveness of the device. I would compare this situation to the one created by renegade magicians, who coldheartedly reveal their sleight of hand techniques and thereby destroy in an instant the very magic they have so arduously created by dint of an ascetic initiation during which they must actually have given themselves over to the rules of sleight of hand in order to master the techniques. The change of registers that occurs through Sokal's revelatory gesture in *Lingua Franca* makes the debate bifurcate and go off in a different direction. It empties the simulacrum of its lightness, its playfulness, and attempts to turn it into something it could never be—an "experiment," a proof of something. The simulacrum cannot prove anything—it can only act, it can fool people, it can circulate in the domain of the *on dit* so enjoyed by Franklin, according to Balzac. Left over from Sokal's revelatory gesture ending his *canard*'s reign is a mixture containing a certain bitterness, a touch of irony and acid humor, and a corresponding solemnity that infects the rest of the debate, in short, a tone that invites a belittling of the adversary. These are the after effects of a *canard* gone bad.

In some ways, the context and style of the second part of the Sokal debate, the one that took place in France after the publication of *Impostures intellectuelles*, owe much to the abrupt bifurcation that occurred in the early part of the first Sokal affair on the American side of the Atlantic. Sokal's intervention in the French context simply could not take the form of a *canard*, in part because the inappropriateness of this form for its projected ends had already become manifest in the American phase of the debate. Sokal seems to have made a strategic choice to avoid the impression of *légèreté* that the *canard* had imparted to his first gesture and thus to justify the seriousness of his arguments by the solemnity of their tone. The abandonment of the *canard* form was due in large part also, however, to the fact that Sokal simply did not have the means at his disposal to position himself at the heart of an intellectual project and debate in France as he had done in the United States. To publish an article in *Social Text* was possible only because Sokal had been immersed in the American discussion about relativism in science studies—at least on an informal level—for some time, and he understood the American academic journal milieu well enough to know that *Social Text* represented precisely this science studies tendency. With only a bit of help, then, he could reproduce a rhetorical style mimicking the discourse of science studies, undermining in familiar ways the faith of an already skeptical American public in the objectivity of science and technology. These conditions were simply not present on the French side of the Atlantic. Sokal's attempts to understand and to position himself within the circumstances encountered in France were more difficult, more challenging in many ways. Furthermore, his ally and co-author, Jean Bricmont, a Belgian chemist, can himself arguably be located only on the distant periphery of Parisian intellectual debates. The ex-centric linguistic and cultural ally chosen by Sokal was clearly a reflection of the differences in the way in which Sokal had to situate himself on the other side of the Atlantic.[14]

The problem was fundamentally one of deciding how to invade the center of a territory from an ex-centric position.[15] In a situation where Sokal lacked the same feel for context that he had possessed when writing his *Social Text* hoax article, he was forced to adopt a simpler strategy, the essence of which was to confront the offending French intellectuals directly—from the position of the outsider. As one who was not directly involved in French intellectual and philosophical debates, he had an automatic claim to objectivity and could easily wear the mask of naïveté as well.[16] The aim was to put Parisian intellectuals and thinkers face to face with their own erroneous statements by assembling lists of direct quotations from their published works, passages in which they manipulated scientific theories incorrectly. The advantage of such an approach was to force French thinkers to go on the defensive, since their lack of expertise, not to say their stupidity—but Sokal generously conceded that he could not make such judgments—had thereby become a matter of public record. At stake here is no longer a *canard*, but, rather, a *sottisier*, a "collection of stupid remarks and platitudes especially those made by well-known authors," as the *Robert* defines it. Yves Jeanneret makes a telling and rather ironic connection to the famous manual of French literary history, known as "Lagarde et Michard" (184–85). But whereas Largarde and Michard compiled a primer containing what they considered to be the loftiest moments of French literary history, *Impostures intellectuelles* represents "Lagarde et Michard" turned on its head and containing what are, on the con-

14. It is possible, of course, to argue for the strength of such a peripheral position: to attack from without allows one to avoid the pitfalls of critics who are only too implicated in the very scene they wish to analyze. What interests me principally here, however, is the contrast between the two contexts and the different strategies they elicit as the result of those differences.

15. I am not going to treat directly here the question of why Sokal felt that the origin of the American malaise he was addressing could be found in "French theory" (whatever that might mean) and that he thus felt compelled to intervene within France itself. This issue was discussed exhaustively at various points during the French phase of the affair. Clearly, in the *Social Text* article, there was already an implicit anti-French agenda, since Derrida, Lacan, Irigaray, Deleuze, and Serres made prominent appearances in "Transgressing the Boundaries." That agenda became explicit as the second, French phase of the affair unfolded. At its origin is a complex history of American university intellectual politics since the early 1970s.

16. Voltaire's *Lettres philosophiques* are a classic example of how such a position can be used.

trary, the most unworthy and embarrassing passages in the works of a whole series of contemporary French critics and philosophers. This approach to the question of context clearly is radically different from the one that was adopted in the American phase of the discussion. When Sokal was transported to the French side of the Atlantic and confined to a peripheral, ex-centric position as a result of his unfamiliarity both with French publishing mores and with a different set of intellectual questions, he and Bricmont chose a radically dissimilar literary style— a compilation of quotations, as opposed to an academic article like the one that had been created for *Social Text.* Cut off from his new context, Sokal produced, with the help of Bricmont, a work that was itself marked by a technique of radical decontextualization: the compilation contained passages severed from the various circumstances of presentation and logical development that made them integral parts of broader arguments. The two scientists freely admitted, in fact, that they had read very little of the works from which they quoted in their essay and that they had relied instead on informants, many of whom are identified by name in a laboriously long list at the end of the introduction to the second edition of *Impostures intellectuelles.* Although Sokal and Bricmont also expressly claimed that their critique applied only to those parts of the works in question that contain major blunders in understanding basic scientific and mathematical theory, no amount of prior justification can hide the fact that decontextualized quotation necessarily disfigures the thought it is intended to represent. The choice of how to contextualize a given quotation implies, as any literary critic knows, an interpretation of the whole work from which the remark is taken. I can only refer back to the observation made by Jean-Michel Salanskis: absent the hermeneutical effort, then what one always has is a polemical confrontation, the motivation of which is not to understand.[17]

The literary manual composed by Largarde and Michard has rightly been criticized for nearly three decades now, not only because it enshrines a canon that excludes a great deal of French literary and cultural production, but also because it reduces French literature and culture to

17. I might add that Salanskis makes his observation in the course of an analysis of the place and importance of mathematical concepts in both Lacan and Deleuze. That analysis considerably enlightens the reader concerning the reasons why they used certain concepts and the relative weight such concepts bring to their arguments. Needless to say, both Lacan and Deleuze were roundly pilloried in *Impostures intellectuelles,* in part for their alleged misuse of mathematical concepts.

a series of decontextualized *morceaux choisis*. Likewise, *Impostures intellectuelles* reduces French critical and philosophical production in the past quarter of a century to a trash heap of excerpts, calculated not to be exemplary of the work of the thinkers at stake, but, rather, of their aberrations. The problem is a good deal more complex than this observation suggests, however, because the *sottisier* itself is a ticklish and subtle genre. If I turned earlier to Balzac for help with the *canard*, it will now be useful to invoke Flaubert, one of the great masters of the *sottisier*. I am thinking primarily of the *Dictionnaire des idées reçues*, of course, but also of *Bouvard et Pécuchet*. It is not particularly easy to decide exactly what the *Dictionnaire* really is. Conceived by Flaubert around 1850, and a regular object of his reflection as he was composing *Madame Bovary, L'éducation sentimentale*, and *Bouvard et Pécuchet*, the manuscript was never published during Flaubert's life. I think part of the reason for this is the intractable difficulty that arises in the writing of any *sottisier*. Is such a work destined for a public not aware of the critique it implies and therefore accepting it at face value as a sort of manual of behavior and etiquette, or, on the contrary, does it address an elite part of the public, a subgroup comprehending all the irony such a work wields as a fundamental cultural critique? Flaubert wants it both ways in his early conception of the work, as the following remark about the *Dictionnaire* in a letter to Bouilhet in 1850 shows:

> This book, when completed and preceded by a good preface in which one might indicate that the work was written with the intention of connecting the public to a tradition, to the established order, to general conventions, and arranged in such a way that the reader doesn't know if one is mocking him or not, would perhaps be a strange work, one capable of succeeding.[18]

The impossibility of reconciling those two perspectives—the fundamental dilemma they pose—eventually paralyzes the publication project and prevents its completion. It is possible for Flaubert to have his cake and eat it too in a novel like *Madame Bovary*, that is, to give a certain free reign to his irony while maintaining a reading level that makes the narrative palatable even for those who do not grasp all of its irony. Without the narrative dimension, however, there is little left but the brutal nakedness of an affront to bourgeois culture. *Bouvard et Pécuchet* is an interesting variation on the notion of the *sottisier* that

18. Quoted in Gustave Flaubert, *Oeuvres complètes*, ed. Bernard Masson, vol. 2 (Paris: Seuil, 1964), 303.

retains, if only in a pale version, a narrative structure, and it addresses the problem of ironic distance in an ambiguous way. The two copyists with whom the text begins return to their copying ways at the end (un-realized, but projected by Flaubert), so that the notion of copying be-comes a central trope. What does it mean to copy and thus to bring into the text of such a narrative a compendium of scientific and cultural knowledge, confused and decontextualized in various ways by the prin-cipals? Are we to take it at face value, or tragically, or are we to see the author laughing acidly in the wings? Such are the complexities of read-ing Flaubert's unfinished novel.

What I am suggesting here is that the *sottisier* is no less complex in its own right than the *canard*, perhaps even more so. To pull off the writing of such a text, there has to be a dimension of humor and irony that can be shared by an eventual reading public, at least in part. This would imply that in order to write a proper *sottisier*, one would have to be very familiar with the detail and depth of the culture of the reading public that is the target both of such a text's critique and of its com-plicity. This is clearly not the case in *Impostures intellectuelles* in its French version.[19] The repetitive nature of the running commentary that joins the excerpts together is remarkable for its heavy-handedness and its lack of wit—and for the absence of any detailed attempt to un-derstand fully the intellectual field where Sokal and Bricmont wanted to intervene. It is not just a question of having chosen a difficult liter-ary genre for such an exercise, but of having misunderstood the terms of the intellectual debate about science in France. Recall that Sokal in-tervened in the United States because he felt that relativism was rampant enough to put into question the public trust in the scientific endeavor. The situation in France differs substantially. Until very re-cently, the belief in the power and efficacy of science has been a funda-mental part of the profession of faith of French bourgeois culture, and that faith is changing its form only slowly. In a country that embarked on a nuclear program originally expected to culminate in a super reac-tor and that has only recently begun to back off this goal and to scale down its nuclear program because of environmental and political con-cerns, in a country whose boom in the 1950s and 1960s contributed to

---

19. If any readers have forgotten the fact that the French version of the book appeared well before the English version, I want to underline it here. It is also important to insist on the idea that a *sottisier* of French thinkers' mistakes obviously does not play the same way to an English-languge audience, and thus *Fashionable Nonsense*, the English trans-lation of the *sottisier*, has had negligible impact on the American side of the Atlantic.

a national fervor for technology and development strategies, in a country where major religious groups have steered clear of a critique of science, the sort of relativism that is Sokal's American *bête noire* can only
be an imaginary creation. The thinkers whom Sokal takes to task have
filled their essays with scientific parallels, terminology, and metaphors
not because they are attempting to undercut and relativize science, but
for precisely the opposite reason—because they have modeled their reflections on what they have seen as major scientific discoveries and theories in this century. The history of structuralism in the 1960s is very
clear: the ambition was to transform the *sciences humaines* and to
make them truly scientific in the modern sense of the word, to wrench
them free from positivisms of all sorts, in short, to give them the tools
with which to become modern disciplines capable of drawing on the
lessons of twentieth-century scientific advances.

The aftermath of that failed attempt may not be pretty. It has clearly
resulted in cases of metaphorical and lax uses of scientific concepts that
became potential and realized targets for Sokal and Bricmont. But the
absence of any indication of the fundamental differences between the
social and political attitudes toward science in the United States and
in France makes of *Impostures intellectuelles* a truly remarkable misreading of the wider context of French intellectual developments since
the Second World War. Only because it took to task an entire generation of French thinkers did it stir up so many passions on the Parisian
scene, but certainly not because it struck the same intellectual chord
as the *Social Text* debate in the United States. Without the frontal assault on the value of French philosophical and critical cultures embodied in *Impostures intellectuelles,* undoubtedly the argument made
by Sokal and Bricmont would have been hopelessly beside the point.
Vilified for their errors, the French thinkers attacked by Sokal and Bricmont soon had to answer for another sin: the so-called obscurity of postmodern French philosophical thought in general. The bourgeois yearn-
ing for clarity of expression, which has a long history in France, became
the fundamental rallying point for all those French citizens who wished
to take sides against French philosophy and criticism. But that is another discussion, one that differs substantially from a discussion about
the relativism of science studies. What I wanted to demonstrate here
was how two different contexts elicited two different forms of argument. Moreover, it should now be clear that the exportation across the
Atlantic of the Sokal line of argument concerning relativism, illustrated in the course of the *Social Text* hoax and its aftermath, could only

miss the point in a different context defined by another set of beliefs. Science studies are destined to have a different impact on the French from the one they have had on Americans. The Sokal affair in its transatlantic dimensions has perhaps been more of a distraction than an incentive to face the real problems of diminishing resources for scientific research and the subsequent need to set new priorities, as well as a fundamental need to reflect carefully on the impact of science on individual subjects and on the environment (both the material environment and the social environment created by a stunning series of key scientific discoveries in the twentieth century). Ultimately, neither the *canard* nor the *sottisier* would appear to be well chosen to promote a policy debate that might have effective political and intellectual consequences.

II. Studying Cultures

NAOMI SCHOR

The Crisis of French Universalism

To speak of French universalism is and is not an oxymoron: it is to the extent that universalism is defined as the opposite of particularism, ethnic, religious, national, or otherwise. It is not to the extent that French national discourse has for centuries claimed that France is the capital of universalism and, though often challenged, that claim has remained largely secure.[1] What has been contested is the essentialist move of identifying a nation with a particular quality or "character" on the one hand, and the implication that the image is descriptive of a true state of affairs on the other. To speak then of French universalism is both to risk essentialism and to engage in a literal reading practice: stereotypes are not to be confused with reality, or truth.

A SHORT HISTORY OF FRENCH UNIVERSALISM

Though French universalism has by definition no official, standard history it is possible to reconstruct a history that considerably enlarges the scope of French universalism, or rather the notion of the Frenchness of universalism. In most accounts French universalism is seen as intimately bound up with the universal revolution of 1789. It is the French appropriation of the universalism that lies at the heart of Enlightenment philosophies such as Rousseau's and Voltaire's. This widely accepted view completely obliterates a far more complex and ancient history and by the same token diminishes the significance of the French Revolution. While the origins of French universalism are elusive, this much is certain: at the beginning French universalism derives from its relationship to the Church; it is, as it were, borrowed from Catholicism

1. Slavoj Žižek, "A Leftist Plea for Eurocentrism," *Critical Inquiry* 24/2 (Summer 1998), "French republican ideology is the epitome of modernist universalism," 1007.

YFS 100, *FRANCE/USA: The Cultural Wars,* ed. Ralph Sarkonak, © 2001 by Yale University.

(from the Greek *Katholikos*, "universal"). Referred to since the Middle Ages as "the elder daughter of the Church," France drew from its privileged relationship to the Church its founding reputation and mission as a disseminator of a universalist creed. Indeed, in a paradoxical fashion, the very event of the French Revolution, which did so much to destroy the power of the Gallican Church, by the same gesture enabled French universalism to perpetuate and propagate itself. The French Revolution, in this view, did not mark a rupture between a pre-universalist and a post-universalist France but rather drew on and gave new impetus to France's time honored civilizing mission. "It's especially after the revolutionary upheaval that France became the missionary nation par excellence," writes René Rémond.[2] The history of universalism in France is then a history of the transvaluation of a fundamental religious belief into the prime means of desacralizing society.

The religious origins of universalism are buttressed throughout the early modern period by yet another form of universalism, which is bound up with the rise of the absolutist monarchy: I am referring to France's *linguistic* universalism. In the seventeenth century, French—the language of the king as well as of polite conversation and civility—was ever more widely viewed as the language of humanity. By virtue of the doctrine of *translatio imperii et studii*, France was seen as the heir to the Roman empire, and French was viewed as the legitimate successor to the ancient universal language, Latin. The eighteenth century marked the triumph of this claim to universality of the French language, following from Descartes's promotion of French as the language of reason and transparency and hence his adoption of the vernacular instead of Latin as the language of the cogito. The *philosophes*, and notably Voltaire in his influential *Encylopédie* entry on the French language, vigorously promoted the classical clarity of the French language. The foundation of the claim to France's linguistic supremacy is the linearity of the French sentence: linguistic universalism is essentially syntactical. What gave the claim its legitimacy was the fact that it was shared by other Europeans and notably by the Germans, or rather one very powerful German, the King of Prussia. Thus Frederick II in his 1780 essay on German literature contrasts German's linguistic disorder with the vaunted clarity of French. The official language of the Prussian

2. René Rémond, "La fille aînée de l'Église," *Les lieux de mémoire*, vol. 3. *Les France 3. De l'archive à l'emblème* (Paris: Gallimard, 1992), 568. Translations throughout this article are mine except where otherwise noted.

Academy he founded was French and in 1784 the Academy sponsored an essay competition on the question of why French had become and would continue to be the universal language of Europe. The top prizes went to two essays, one by a Frenchman, the other by a German, "that praised the French language for its superior clarity, a quality that was given, they argued, by the direct order of the French sentence."[3] The Frenchman was Rivarol, the German, Johann Christoph Schwab. It is common practice today to mock Rivarol's grandiose claims for the French language—shared, of course, by Schwab—but they live on in the recent construction of a Francophone commonwealth, built on the ruins of the French colonial empire.[4] French government institutions continue to adhere to a discredited linguistic universalism and to wage an increasingly ineffective campaign to ward off the encroachment of

3. Harold Mah, "The Epistemology of the Sentence: Language, Civility, and Identity in France and Germany, Diderot to Nietzsche," *Representations*, Special Issue: *National Cultures Before Nationalism* 47 (Summer 1994): 66.

4. In December 1995, I received in my mailbox an unusual fax addressed to "Mesdames et Meissieurs les professeurs de français." It contained the text of a speech delivered by President Jacques Chirac on 2 December 1995 at Cotonou (Benin) on the occasion of the sixth summit of *la francophonie*. It provides one of the most exhaustive and astonishing statements about *la francophonie* and its grounding in linguistic universalism that has been formulated in recent years, hence the mass mailing by the French Cultural Services of Boston to all those engaged in the teaching of French in the New England area. Taking great care to avoid any appearance of repeating past errors and mindful of the necessity to encourage the development of native languages, Chirac puts the case for the promotion of French precisely in terms of its capacity to spearhead the defense of "linguistic pluralism" and "cultural diversity" in a world threatened by globalization, the stamping out of differences, and the rise of the linguistic imperialism of English. To defend French is not merely to serve the national self-interest, but to serve a far greater human right to vernacular languages: "To call oneself Francophone is ultimately to combat a major risk for humanity: linguistic and therefore cultural uniformity. . . . To defend the extension [*rayonnement*] of French is in reality to defend the right to think, to exchange, to feel and pray otherwise. It is to defend an opening to the Other and thus tolerance." "Hispanophones and Arabophones, all those who express themselves in Hindi or Russian, Chinese or Japanese, are faced with the same threat as we are." The question is: why should French of all languages lead the campaign against linguistic globalization, when the Francophone community is numerically so small in comparison to those of Chinese or Hindi speakers, for example? To make his case, Chirac reverts to the claims that have always been made for the French language. First, French is essentially suited to express a full range of human attributes; it is "A language reputed for its capacities to synthesize reality, reflect ideas, feelings, emotions." Second, and inevitably, French is the language of the universal: "Every language has its genius. The one we [Francophones] share predisposes to a certain vision of the relationships between men and communities. A vision that inspires the values of solidarity, fraternity: a sense of the universal." Thus in a brilliant twist, Chirac harnesses France's role as leader among the nations threatened by uniformization to the hoariest claims for French linguistic universalism.

the new universal linguistic idiom: English. Thus postcolonialism is directly descended from French colonialism, which associated the spread of the ideals of 1789 with the dissemination of the French language through such institutions as the Alliance Française; indeed the conflation of universalism and colonialism has done much to discredit universalism both ideological and linguistic.

Universalism, and never more so than in its Enlightenment incarnation, was grounded in the belief that human nature, that is rational human nature, was a universal impervious to cultural and historical differences. Transcultural, transhistorical human nature was posited as identical, beyond particularisms, just as the universal French language promoted by Rivarol was a language cleansed of its impure forms: patois and regional dialects. Thus Rivarol describes with great enthusiasm the mechanical "talking heads" he sees on display in the Marais, which insure the perpetuation of an idealized, sanitized standard French:

> And we shall not hear without shuddering the coarse utterings of our ancestors. Only the talking heads, I daresay, can preserve this honorable universality due the French language, and insure it against the instability of all things human. These heads, if they are multiplied in Europe, will become the terror of the multitude of language-masters, Swiss and Gascon, with which all nations are infected and which denature our language among the peoples who love it.[5]

What the French Revolution crucially instituted was the association of universalism and human rights; what was missing from pre-Revolutionary accounts of universalism was the modern humanistic doctrine of universal human rights. Modern French universalism represents the convergence of three separate streams of universalism: the religious, the linguistic, and the ethical, for as Étienne Balibar remarks, where ethics is, there is universalism. *The Declaration of the Rights of Man and the Citizen*, which was in the twentieth century reappropriated by the United Nations and extended well beyond national boundaries in *The Declaration of the Universal Rights of Man*, articulated Frenchness onto universalism. To this day French national identity remains bound up—at least in official discourse, but also in ongoing intellectual debates—with universal human rights, of which France con-

---

5. Marquis de Rivarol, Letter of 20 September 1783, in *Oeuvres complètes*, vol. 2 (Paris: 1808), 207. For more on the talking "iron heads," see Rivarol, *L'universalité de la langue française* (Paris: Arléa, 1998), 121–25.

siders itself the inalienable trustee. French, accordingly, is the idiom of universality.

Throughout the nineteenth century, despite the emergence of the countervailing forces of nationalism, republican revolutionary ideology became more firmly implanted, reaching its apogee under the regime of the Third Republic, which, not coincidentally, marked the apex of French colonialism. The Third Republic was, so to speak, the golden age of French universalism, coinciding with what Pierre Nora, borrowing from the British Marxist historian Eric Hobsbawm, has called the "invention" of France.[6] The classrooms of the republic became the prime loci of the dissemination and transmission of an ideology of France as an elect nation and guardian of civilization. So thoroughly penetrated with universalism was that era, that while universalism underlies politics, aesthetics, and science, the word itself is strangely absent from the major texts of the period. As an -ism, universalism can be said to be like other -isms, such as Realism, largely an artifact of the twentieth century.

It would, however, be quite inaccurate to assume that the path of French universalism was unencumbered and that from the outset: for it immediately became evident that *The Declaration of the Rights of Man and the Citizen* excluded or at any rate did not explicitly include several important segments of the population, notably, women and slaves. The origins of modern French feminism lie in Olympe de Gouges's astonishing response to *The Declaration of the Rights of Man and the Citizen*, her *Declaration of the Rights of Woman and the Citizen*. And yet it is one of the foundational paradoxes of post-Revolutionary France that those left out of the universalist compact readily enlisted the very principles of the Declaration to press their own claims: for example, feminists (from Olympe de Gouges to Simone de Beauvoir) and the "Black Jacobins" of Haiti, about whom C. L. R. James writes:

> And meanwhile, what of the slaves? They had heard of the revolution and had construed it in their own image: the white slaves in France had risen, and killed their masters, and were now enjoying the fruits of the earth. It was gravely inaccurate in fact, but they had caught the spirit of the thing. Liberty, Equality, Fraternity. Before the end of 1789 there were risings in Guadeloupe and Martinique.[7]

6. Pierre Nora, *Les lieux de mémoire*, vol. 3. *Les France 2. Traditions*, 15. It is of this fictional, constructed France that *Les lieux de mémoire* is the "inventory." See also Hervé Le Bras and Emmanuel Todd, *L'invention de la France. Atlas anthopologique et politique* (Paris: Livre de Poche, 1981).

7. C. L. R. James, *The Black Jacobins* (New York: Vintage, 1989), 81.

In a broader sense the emergence of French nationalism produced a potent tension in nineteenth-century France between the Republican universalists and the Nationalist particularists (Barrès and Maurras).

THE CRISIS OF UNIVERSALISM

A consensus has emerged in recent years among historians, sociologists, and political and critical theorists that the French universalism set in place by the Revolution of 1789 and consolidated throughout the nineteenth century is in crisis, discredited, and that the Republican model will not hold. One of the most representative and symptomatic works of this troubled *fin de siècle* is Pierre Nora's monumental compendium, *Les lieux de mémoire.* Indeed, the work is, as Nora self-mockingly observes, a funerary monument, a mausoleum, "a Grave for France."[8] And a dead France is a France divested of its enlivening universalism: "What remains of the Republic when one takes from it centralizing jacobinism, 'Liberty or death,' the 'no liberty for the enemies of liberty'? What remains of the Nation when one takes from it nationalism, imperialism, and the omnipotence of the State? What remains of France when one takes from it universalism?" (Nora, 32).

Access to the universal, which at least since the French Revolution has defined France's singularity, its "exception," stubbornly remains a key phrase in France's discourse of national self-representation and identity. Whether one reads *Le monde* or *Le figaro, Le débat* or *Esprit,* one is constantly reminded of France's identification with universalism. Though France as the capital of universalism is a notion in deep peril, threatened by the emergence of the United States as a rival universalist power on the one hand, and the formation of a new Europe on the other, universalism remains the object of an intense struggle in what we might call the French culture wars: wars that oppose the upholders of the Republic and the advocates of a French multiculturalism and democracy. We might speak here of a "spectral Universalism," the shadow of a formerly vigorous and dynamic ideology that once functioned as a powerful force that ensured social cohesion, now reduced to an empty rhetoric in whose cozy and familiar terms present-day ideological battles are fought. What is coded as the Republican position is argued most polemically by Alain Finkielkraut in his *The Defeat of the*

---

8. Nora, "Comment écrire l'histoire de France?," in Nora, ed. *Les lieux de mémoire,* vol. 3, *Les France 1. Conflits et partage,* 19.

Mind[9]—a book that was quickly and revealingly singled out for praise by Roger Kimball of *The New Criterion*. But Finkielkraut, about whom more later, is not the only self-appointed guardian of the universal; there are of course others: notably Tzvetan Todorov, who, in *Of Human Diversity*,[10] enlists French universalism in the battle between universalism and its current binary opposite, relativism, all the while prophylactically demonstrating the dangers of perverted universalism: ethnocentrism and genocide. Multiculturalism too has its champions, although fewer, notably Michel Wieviorka, author of *A Fragmented Society? Multiculturalism under Debate*[11] and Jean-Loup Amselle, author of *Toward a French Multiculturalism.*[12]

What then are the stakes of the French culture wars? What are their foundations? What forms do they take? In what follows I propose to consider first the underlying reasons for France's difficulty in relinquishing the discourse of universalism and then to focus on a particularly instructive instance of the crisis of universalism, the recent *parité* movement in French electoral politics.

NOUS ET LES AUTRES

Meditations on the Other have in recent years occupied some of France's leading intellectuals. They have ranged from Emmanuel Levinas's ethical considerations on the intersubjective contract that binds self and other, to Todorov's survey of French political theories regarding the relationship between France and its Others. In the texts of Julia Kristeva and Jacques Derrida the Other is specified: the Other is the exile, the foreigner, the displaced person, the survivor, but most often the Other has the face of the immigrant, notably the immigrant from France's dismembered former colonial empire. Indeed the immigrant has emerged as the prototypical Other of this new French *fin de siècle*. Though the Other is a capacious category, an empty signifier, in late

9. Alain Finkielkraut, *La défaite de la pensée* (Paris: Folio, 1987); *The Defeat of the Mind*, trans. Judith Friedlander (New York: Columbia University Press, 1995).

10. Tzvetan Todorov, *Nous et les autres. La réflexion française sur la diversité humaine* (Paris: Seuil, 1989); *Of Human Diversity: Nationalism, Racism, and Exoticism in French Thought*, trans. Catherine Porter (Cambridge: Harvard University Press, 1993).

11. Michel Wieviorka, ed. *Une société fragmentée? Le multiculturalisme en débat* (Paris: La Découverte, 1997).

12. Jean-Loup Amselle, *Vers un multiculturalisme français. L'empire de la coutume* (Paris: Aubier, 1996).

twentieth-century France the immigrant has taken the place of the Jew as the paradigmatic Other.

Now immigration is nothing new in France, a land of immigrants, though that characterization is not part of the national discourse, as it is of the American. "Where tradition has cast American society as a melting pot of multiple cultures and subcultures, French immigration policies since the Third Republic have tended to assimilate difference in the name of a single nation,"[13] writes Steven Ungar. France, a land that vies with the United States in the number of immigrants it has absorbed in proportion to its general population, has historically been a welcoming land, with a liberal citizenship policy, in sharp contrast with Germany, to which it has often been compared by such eminent scholars of French specificity as Ernst Curtius and Louis Dumont. As Rogers Brubaker remarks, "The overall rate of civic incorporation for immigrants [in France] is ten times higher than in Germany."[14]

The erasure of France's constitutive diversity is concomitant with France's policy of assimilation, which makes of it, again in Brubaker's words, "a classical country, perhaps the classical country of assimilation" (184). Achieving French identity requires as the wages of assimilation the renunciation of public cultural particularism in the name of France's vaunted particularity, its "singularity," in short, its universalism. Assimilation does not signify tolerance; indeed it may be viewed as merely the most common form of intolerance of otherness, or rather of the otherness of the other. In this critical perspective it is but another form of false universalism. Thus Dominique Schnapper remarks:

> The universal is assimilated to the culture of the "I." "I" may then pursue a politics of assimilation, which seeks to eradicate the culture of the Other and to absorb it. . . . It is not a matter of excluding the Other, but of including it to the extent that one renders it like oneself.[15]

Forged in the throes of the French Revolution—the universal revolution par excellence—the identification of France and universalism was

13. Steven Ungar, "Introduction," in Steven Ungar and Tom Conley, eds. *Identity Papers: Contested Nationhood in Twentieth-Century France* (Minneapolis: University of Minnesota Press, 1996), 2.

14. Rogers Brubaker, *Citizenship and Nationhood in France and Germany* (Cambridge: Harvard University Press, 1992), 10.

15. Dominique Schnapper, *La relation à l'autre. Au coeur de la pensée sociologique* (Paris: Gallimard, 1998), 37.

initially applied in exemplary fashion to the Jews, whose emancipation was purchased at a price. In the celebrated words of the conventionalist Clermont-Tonnerre: "One must deny everything to the Jews as a nation and grant everything to the Jews as individuals."[16] Only the abstract individual could be granted the rights of man and citizen. What applies to the Jews applies equally to regional particularisms—hence the still festering marginal situations of the Bretons, the Corsicans, the Catalans, and the Basques.

The recent reflections on the Other and otherness have been provoked by what I will call, at least provisionally, the "new immigrant," that is, one who claims the privileges of French citizenship while refusing to renounce his or her cultural or religious otherness. It is not that the new immigrant is Islamic; rather, it is that Islam, if one may generalize about such a rich and complex nexus of religious beliefs, does not recognize the separation of church and state that undergirds modern democratic, secular states: hence the celebrated affair of the veil, the so-called *affaire du foulard.* In 1989, three girls of Muslim origin in the Paris suburb of Creil insisted on wearing the traditional scarf within the precincts of the republican school, thereby provoking an "affair" comparable, though hardly equal in its divisiveness, to the Dreyfus Affair, and evoking a breakdown of the divorce of church and state. According to the analyses so prevalent in the media and taken up uncritically by many scholars, new immigrants and their children present the greatest challenge to eighteenth- and nineteenth-century universalism, that is to French identity, to "Frenchness" itself, that it has ever faced. But are these new immigrants in fact so new, calling to mind as they do the arguments of such nationalists as the demographer George Mauco, according to whom certain ethnicities rank lower on the scale of assimilability than others? The new immigrant of today raises the xenophobic, when it is not the racist, specter of the absolute Other that always lurks in the most ecumenical discourses.

> . . . [A]mong the diverse foreign races in France, there are elements . . . (Asians, Africans, even Orientals) whose assimilation is not possible and, moreover, very often physically and morally undesirable. . . . These immigrants carry in their customs, in their turn of mind, tastes,

16. Stanislas de Clermont-Tonnerre, cited by Jay Berkovitz, *The Shaping of Jewish Identity in Nineteenth-Century France* (Detroit: Wayne State University Press, 1989), 71.

passions, and the weight of century-long habits that contradict the deep
orientation of our civilization.[17]

In fact, the notion that a particular category of immigrants is nonas-
similable is not new, not new at all. The unassimilability of the Jew is
the very subject of Sartre's *Anti-Semite and Jew*;[18] anti-Semitism is
precisely that ideology that renders the assimilation of the Jew impossible, trapping the French Jew in a wrenching bind: the imperative to
assimilate and the impossibility to assimilate. What is more, there are
some who would argue that contrary to the widely held opinion that
the Muslim immigrant presents a new and uniquely threatening force
to an alleged French ethnicity, empirical studies of the process of assimilation of Muslims reveal that it is not particularly problematic and
generally obeys the three generation rule derived from the study of
other immigrant populations:

> [T]he immigration of Maghrebi origin is viewed in France as very differ-
> ent culturally, when in fact it is rapidly integrated. . . . in ordinary per-
> ceptions, its social exclusion, linked with a racist dimension, is trans-
> muted into cultural, religious, and racial difference. [Wieviorka, 30]

As Gérard Noiriel demonstrates in his important book *Le creuset
français* (The French Melting-Pot),[19] every successive wave of immigrants in France has been considered inassimilable, but all have, by the
third generation, become fully acculturated and integrated. Rather
than viewing the case of the Muslim immigrants as exceptional,
unique, Noiriel suggests that eruptions of hostility against foreigners,
that is xenophobia, have occurred regularly in France since the end of
the nineteenth century. Rather than viewing the "new immigrant" as
a contributing factor to the crisis of universalism, we might view the
allegedly difficult assimilation of the "new immigrant" as a symptom
of a larger crisis of universalism.

One thing is certain: the pressure to assimilate in France is such
that identity politics cannot thrive there; there is a logical and insu-
perable incompatibility between promoting assimilation and encour-
aging identitarian micro-communities based on gender, race, and sex-

17. George Mauco, cited by Patrick Weil, *La France et ses étrangers. L'aventure d'une
politique de l'immigration de 1938 à non jours* (Paris: Points, 1991), 44.
18. Jean-Paul Sartre, *Anti-Semite and Jew*, trans. George J. Becker (New York: Grove
Press, 1960); *Réflexions sur la question juive* (Paris: Gallimard, 1954).
19. Gérard Noiriel, *Le creuset français. Histoire de l'immigration XIXe–XXe siècle*
(Paris: Seuil, 1988).

ual orientation, what we in the United States have taken to lumping under the term *multiculturalism*. Viewed from the French perspective, multiculturalism is nothing short of a cultural disaster, threatening the polity with fragmentation, and the nation with dissolution.

Remarkably there have been to my knowledge no significant debates in France regarding the incorporation of other cultures into the French educational system, so long one of the prime disseminators of republican ideology and values. The debate, such as it has been, has rather been cast as a debate with American multiculturalism, or, to be more precise, a one-sided attack on American *multiculturalism*, which has, of course, been the object of a lively and massively ideological debate in the United States. The question then arises: why do most French intellectuals reject *multiculturalism*?

WHO IS AFRAID OF MULTICULTURALISM?

The answer is, as I have argued above, France's well-honed traditional policy of integration through civic and cultural assimilation. The predominance of the integrative model of nationhood has made the welcoming of the differentialist new immigrant exceedingly difficult, confronting the host country as it does with a veritable Derridean aporia, an impossible double moral imperative:

> The *same duty* also dictates welcoming foreigners in order not only to integrate them but to recognize and accept their alterity: two concepts of hospitality that today divide our European and national consciousness.[20]

The host nation's dilemma is precisely the mirror image of the immigrant's; thus Françoise Gaspard and Farhad Khosrokhavar characterize the young Muslim women's gesture as a means of negotiating the gap between their parents' traditional culture and the modern French society in which they live:

> Finally the scarves of the young women who claim a "veiled identity" cannot be interpreted as a rejection of French citizenship, but as a desire for integration *without* assimilation, an aspiration to be French *and* Muslim.[21]

20. Jacques Derrida, *The Other Heading*, trans. Pascale-Anne Brault and Michael B. Nass (Bloomington: Indiana University Press, 1992), 77.

21. François Gaspard and Farhad Khosrokhavar, *Le foulard et la république* (Paris: La Découverte, 1995), 204.

Assimilation, as it functions in France, cannot accommodate the copula, the alliance of a universal and a particular identity.

The following offers a precious view of multiculturalism as seen through French eyes, indeed those of one of the leading French intellectuals concerned with these issues, the above-mentioned Alain Finkielkraut. In an article that appeared in the *New York Times*, Finkielkraut begins by recalling a story by Milan Kundera in which Edward, a teacher in Communist Czechoslovakia, feigns to believe in God in order to seduce a pious young woman. When caught in the act of crossing himself, Edward is called into the directress's office and is offered a course of re-education.

> Whenever I am confronted, at some American campus bookstore, with the section on gay and lesbian studies, or Native American Studies, women's studies, Afro-American studies, etc., I recall that story. A real paradigm shift has occurred with the decision to designate intellectual disciplines not by their methods but by their subject. Henceforth what we have is learning not to understand but to heal: heal white heterosexual males of their superiority complex and give other people back their pride. Bring down the offenders, raise up the offended: such is the mission of the humanities in the era of multiculturalism.[22]

Finkielkraut casts his scathing critique of multiculturalism as therapy and redress in the very same terms as earlier French critics couched their attacks on political correctness; it is in fact the same critique in a new key, as becomes apparent in the following paragraph:

> . . . the entire tradition of European art and literature stands convicted of ethnocentrism. Whereas "culture" in the singular was a kind of conversation, multiculturalism is an inquisition: the D.W.E.M. (dead white European males) and their current accomplices have been summoned before a tribunal thoroughly determined to liberate us from their hateful grip. [Finkielkraut, 49]

It would be all too easy to mock this outdated and uninformed critique, but my concern here is not to adjudicate between two conflicting points of view—there is merit on both sides, multiculturalism has produced some dubious effects and universalism is in many ways a glorious ideal. My concern is rather to bring out the differing political foundations on which they rest, for ultimately, what is at stake in the

---

22. Alain Finkielkraut, "A Second Issue: How the World Sees Us," *New York Times*, trans. Linda Asher, 8 June 1997, 49.

American promotion of multiculturalism is the belief that culture can have political efficacy, that it can heal neither victims nor victimizers, but democracy itself. In a France rent by the new split between republicanism and democracy, democracy has become the exclusive responsibility of the left.

THE CRISES OF FRENCH UNIVERSALISM

I began this essay by speaking of a singular crisis of universalism, one bound up with recent events: the massive immigration of new immigrants, the Bicentenary of the French Revolution and the reflections it inspired, the formation of the New European Community. To do so is to suggest that this crisis is a singular, unprecedented event, whereas in fact universalism has been in crisis in France ever since the early twentieth century, if not before.

The history of French thought in the twentieth century has been marked by a series of increasingly intense crises of universalism: I will name three. The first was that denounced by Julien Benda in his epoch-making *The Betrayal of The Intellectuals* (1927). In this work—reprised by Finkielkraut in his *The Defeat of the Mind* (1987)—Benda denounces particularism as a German import (Herder) and views the rejection of abstract universalism as leading to the exacerbation of local and in turn national, indeed racial differences. What the *clercs*—writers, intellectuals, spiritual leaders—are accused of betraying is universalism itself. If Benda's polemical text, written during *l'entre-deux-guerres*, proved chillingly prescient of the extremes toward which German anti-universalism led—for Nazism was nothing if not an anti-universalism—, in the immediate aftermath of the Second World War and the Shoah, universalism was once more on the defensive, this time under the joint impetus of decolonization and the birth of second-wave feminism. Under the aegis of Sartre and those writing in the orbit of *Les temps modernes*, notably Frantz Fanon and Simone de Beauvoir, abstract universalism was repudiated as a bourgeois, Enlightenment ideology inimical to those principally excluded from *The Declaration of the Rights of Man and the Citizen*, notably women and slaves, or those included at the cost of relinquishing their otherness, notably the Jews. At mid-century, what comes sharply into focus is the central paradox of French universalism: the very universalism that is enlisted to press forward claims to human rights is reviled as legitimating oppression and masking inequity. As the falseness of universalism is uncovered, the claim for specificity is recast as a call for differences, although on this score Fanon's position cannot be assimilated to Beauvoir's, nor for that matter Beauvoir's to Sartre's. Whereas Beauvoir views access to the universal as the royal way to greatness for women writers and any cult of a female specificity as a regression to the discourse of misogyny, in *Black Skin, White Masks* Fanon wishes to linger for a moment in a rediscovered Black specificity; for him the universal is a swamp of uniformity that blurs—to mix metaphors—the difference between those who have barely emerged into the light of universalism and those, principally white males, who have always basked in its glow.

> I've barely opened the eyes which had been muzzled, and already one wants to drown me in the universal? And the others? Those who "have no mouth," those who have "no voice" . . . I need to lose myself in my negritude.[23]

The third crisis brings us right up to the present day. Throughout the 1990s the most violent, not to say vicious, debates swirled around the *parité* movement, which brought gender to bear on French universalism, completing the unfinished business of the Revolution.

The *parité* movement, spearheaded by Françoise Gaspard, Anne Le Gall, and Claude Servan-Schreiber, authors of *Au pouvoir, citoyennes. Liberté, égalité, parité*,[24] *parité* came into being in 1992 and, in the words of Gaspard, "certainly testifies to a turning point in French feminism."[25] Its main plank calls for an equal representation of men and women in various elected bodies and institutions. Whereas the second wave of French feminism drew on linguistics, psychoanalysis, and Marxism, the newest French feminism is in the most literal sense political, concerned with questions of political theory as well as with the strategic practice of electoral politics.

Like the earliest crisis of universalism, this third crisis begins by a severe attack on particularism as a germ that attacks the French body politic from without: in the instance of Benda's diatribe, the infectious external agent is Germany; in the instance of the *parité* debates—as

---

23. Frantz Fanon, *Peau noire, masques blancs* (Paris: Seuil, 1952), 151.
24. François Gaspard, Anne Le Gall, Claude Servan-Schreiber, *Au pouvoir, citoyennes. Liberté, égalité, parité* (Paris: Seuil, 1992).
25. Françoise Gaspard, "Parity: Why Not?," trans. Jennifer Curtiss Gage, *differences* 10 (1998): 3.

recorded in the significantly titled volume, *Le piège de la parité* (The Parity Trap)—the new hereditary enemy is the United States and its identity politics, just as for Finkielkraut, multiculturalism is a foreign plague visited on the French social body. Multiculturalism—of which women's studies is a key component—threatens France like a spreading epidemic, a fatal virus, a form of intellectual AIDS. Thus Finkielkraut's conclusion to his article is ominous:

> Would Edward be happier in the Old World? I'm not so sure. In France, too, you have to watch your step these days. The Gay Pride movement is powerful, and the expression of any skepticism about its mandate renders you a homophobe. And if you have the temerity to criticize contemporary art, you're immediately denounced as a reactionary.
>
> The "healing disease" is particularly virulent on American campuses, but conformism can establish its reign anywhere by brandishing the flag of subversion. [Finkielkraut, 49]

The threat to universalism always comes from without; and the fear of the threat is rooted in French xenophobia; to embrace *parité* is thus to betray the founding principles of French democracy, with the emphasis on "French." America, with its fragmentation into separate but equal identitarian communities and special interest groups each clamoring for its rights represents for most French thinkers the very image of a society in disarray. "An American import, equity is the bearer of the best and the worst,"[26] writes Evelyne Pisier; Élisabeth Badinter accuses the *paritaires* of seeking to impose "the communitarian democracy of quotas imported from the United States" (*Le piège*, 18); "Has the time come here to imitate belatedly the United States?" (*Le piège*, 23), asks Danièle Sallenave; and finally Mona Ozouf accuses the *paritaires* of borrowing from "the conceptual arsenal of American feminism" (*Le piège*, 152).[27] The American arsenal is viewed as particularly threatening because it

26. Evelyne Pisier, "Universalité contre parité" in Micheline Amar, ed., *Le piège de la parité. Arguments pour un débat* (Paris: Pluriel, 1999), 17.

27. In 1995, Mona Ozouf, a leading French historian of the Revolution, published a work that generated a major polemic among French and American feminists, *Women's Words: Essay on French Singularity*, trans. Jane Marie Todd (Chicago: University of Chicago Press, 1997). For Ozouf, France's singularity refers oddly and provocatively to women's privileged role in French society. For, according to Ozouf, male-female relationships in France, rooted in a tradition of civility fashioned in the salons of the eighteenth century and strengthened by modern-day republicanism, are unusually harmonious. Ozouf's characterization of American feminism—which bears all the marks of the anti-political-correctness campaign—is as a differentialist one, one that would be impossible in France, given French feminism's participation in the ideology of univer-

leads to quotas, the French translation of what we describe, eu-
phemistically, as affirmative action, and quotas bring with them a
nightmarish vision of a society unraveling, riven by an endless proliferation of identitarian communities of minorities; first women, then
blacks, then, as Françoise Duroux would have it, the "obese" and the
"nonsmokers" (*Le piège*, 170), and who knows where it will end?

The denunciation of *parité* as complicitous with America is not,
however, limited to the denunciation of American "communitarianism"; it takes another, more insidious and more revealing form: the association of *parité* with that other French bugaboo, deconstruction; the
paritaires are equated with the deconstructionists (*Le piège*, 33). Luc
Ferry's remarks typify what the French would describe—the expression is untranslatable—, as this *amalgame*. He begins on an ironic but
conciliatory note:

> In the 1980s, the period during which the French discover with irony
> the American fashion of the "politically correct," the questions posed
> by the feminist movements across the Atlantic aroused in us only con-
> tempt. Little by little the attitude changed, as though the humiliating
> realization that the United States always sketches out our destiny fif-
> teen years in advance was once again confirmed: with the claim for par-
> ity, a large majority of our fellow citizens accustomed itself to the idea
> of "affirmative action," which seemed to them ridiculous or contrary
> to the Republican idea some years before.[28]

He goes on to distinguish two great currents within feminism, the
French republican (i.e. universalist) model and the differentialist
model, which predominates in the United States, "where it has been
subjected to the influence no longer of existentialism, but of the ideologies of 'Deconstruction'" (130). QED.

---

salism: "American feminism can claim without trouble that the universalism of hu-
mankind has been appropriated by men, French feminism cannot because it is itself universalist" (*Les mots des femmes* [Paris: Fayard, 1995], 391).

As the author of an article entitled "French Feminism is a Universalism" (*differences*
7:1 [Spring 1995], 15–47), I can only agree with Ozouf's statement, but I cannot endorse
the general thrust of her argument, the consequences she draws from her assertion of
French feminism's universalism, its Frenchness. And I am not alone. Whatever their
points of view, whether French or American, all of Ozouf's respondents in a recent dossier
in *le débat* denounce her representation of American feminism for its lack of nuance, its
reductiveness—caricature is a recurrent term. See the interventions of Elizabeth Badinter, Michelle Perrot, Lynn Hunt, and Joan Scott in *le débat* 87 (November-December
1995).

28. Luc Ferry, "La parité et les 'valeurs féminines,'" *Le piège de la parité*, 113.

Though the case for their association is never made—what exactly does deconstruction have in common with *parité*?—it participates in the general rejection of all movements tainted by their association with the United States. Because the *parité* debates became the occasion for a gigantic settling of accounts, it is not surprising to find Derrida, the most controversial and brilliant unsettler of the Enlightenment foundations of French universalism, cited by several participants in the debates. There is, in fact, a clear connection between Derrida and the *paritaires*, but it remains as the great unsaid. Sylviane Agacinski, by far the most visible and powerful ally of the *paritaires*, is, as is well known, one of the earliest feminists to work in the orbit of Derrida and to enlist, along with Hélène Cixous and Sarah Kofman, the strategies of deconstruction in the critique of phallogocentrism and the metaphysics of presence—a critique that is, it might be argued, as beholden to feminism as feminism is to it. Agacinski readily acknowledges her debt to Derrida when she writes:

> Thinking sexual duality requires remaining within difference, that is in the in-between, thinking otherness without wanting that it come down to the same, nor to a simple identity. In short: renouncing the logic of the center and the metaphysics of presence to dare to confront this irreducible difference suggested to us by mixedness.[29]

The misunderstanding that separates French and American feminists, which is, of course, grafted onto a broader cultural misunderstanding—universalism as a positivity is, as I have tried to show elsewhere, a difficult notion for American feminists who tend to conflate universalism with imperialism, pluralism, and other despised -isms, and who think in a cultural context where universalism has no ethical purchase[30]—operates to mask what is perhaps the real situation, namely, that *parité* is a growing pain of the forging of Europe. As Evelyne Pisier points out: "Born of the proceedings of the Council of Europe and of the French delegate, Françoise Gaspard, the idea of *parité* is also inscribed as a decisive stage in the transformation of feminist themes" (*Le piège*, 192). And she goes on to say: "the proportion of women elected in the assemblies make of France the 'red lantern' of Eu-

29. Sylviane Agacinski, *Politique des sexes* (Paris: Seuil, 1998), 56. I have translated *mixité* by "mixedness," which conveys the literal meaning of the French term, but not the pun on "co-education."

30. Naomi Schor, "French Feminism is a Universalism," *differences* 7/1 (Spring 1995): 15–47.

rope, and the permanence, since 1945, of this 'non-eligibility' is indeed the index of a discrimination" (*Le piège*, 193). It is France's anomalous situation in Europe, and notably when compared to the situation in certain Scandinavian countries, and not the existence of affirmative action in the United States that presided over the birth of the *parité* movement.

> This feminization of the political world is already very broadly advanced in the Northern countries, notably Sweden where the government is strictly [*paritaire*] and where women hold the Ministries of Foreign Affairs, Justice, Labor, Agriculture, Transportation, and the Interior. [*Le piège*, 234]

It is time now to look more closely at the terms of this debate over universalism. Early on, the powerful couple Élisabeth and Robert Badinter framed the debate as one opposing the *paritaires* to the "universal republic"; to call for a special article of the constitution as a means of redressing the imbalance of men and women in positions of institutional power was, from their self-proclaimed position as the guardians of the republic, tantamount to calling for a revolution, or a counter-revolution. Thus one participant in the debate opines: "There is no doubt about it: *parité* is a real counter-revolution. Furet was able to write that the French Revolution was finished; *parité*, entering into synergy with current school reforms, returns us to a period prior to the principles of 1789. . . . The Revolution fades away, the Republic is erased" (*Le piège*, 162). One could multiply such expressions of dire doomsday predictions.

However, and this is what needs be emphasized, no *paritaire* has ever called for abandoning the universal, which France takes to be its birthright, and to this extent it remains a profoundly Franco-French debate. Indeed, what is striking is that, from the first, the *paritaires* seek to convince their opponents, not to say themselves, that not only are they not anti-universalist, but that their movement is designed to strengthen, to prop up a weakened or wounded universalism. Here I can only echo Joan W. Scott when she writes: "It is important that the *paritaires* understand themselves to be operating within the terms of the universalist discourse, even though their critics decry them as its enemy."[31]

31. Joan W. Scott, "'La querelle des femmes' in the late Twentieth Century," *New Left Review* (November-December 1997): 11.

Thus Françoise Collin asks: "is *parité* supposed to be opposed to or to realize universalism? Its adversaries will no doubt opt for the first answer, its defenders for the second."[32] She goes on to say: "It is thus *parité* that would be the true universalism (no longer a monoversalist universalism, but a pluriversalist universalism)" (*Projets*, 103). Similarly, Agacinski rejects the accusations of those who equate *parité* with an abandoning of the universal: "To take sexual difference into account theoretically and practically does not thus represent any abandoning of the universal, but rather makes possible the recognition of the concrete and differentiated content of the universal" (Agacinski, 81).

Thus we find the *paritaires* seeking by all means to preserve and uphold universalism, either by attempting to separate a bad, namely abstract (when it is not false) universal that they wish to denounce, from a concrete or good or true universal that they wish to retain and nurture back to health, or in a more radical mode by displacing the very terms of the debate. This latter strategy is the one adopted by Agacinski, an intransigent opponent of abstract universalism, for whom universalism resides not in reason but rather, and paradoxically, in the biological given of sexual dimorphism, in what she terms *mixité*. What is universal is not human rights, but the conditions necessary to reproduction, sexual difference, indeed heterosexuality, which is of course a highly problematic argument on which to build one's case.

How then do the *paritaires* make their claim that *parité* and universalism are not only *not* mutually exclusive, but in fact at this juncture necessary allies? And concurrently one might ask: how is it that feminism in France, in the form of *parité*, recognizes that it cannot do without universalism, while French universalism continues to imagine that it can progress without attending to the feminist protest? Here lies the crux of the issue: to bring gender to bear on French universalism is not as one might have wished at an earlier moment to imagine a female universal, it is to revisit universalism in the light of feminist critiques, ranging from the empirical and political to the conceptual and theoretical. The *paritariste* critique of universalism is threefold. It grows from the recognition of an incontrovertible, objective, numerical fact: the number of women occupying positions in the governmental hierarchy is pitifully low in comparison with the number of men occupying such positions in France on the one hand, and the number of

32. Intervention by Françoise Collin, in "Parité et universalisme (1)," *Projets féministes* 4–5 (February 1996), "Actualité de la parité," 99.

women occupying such positions in other European nations on the other. It would appear that there is a wide gap between the utopian ideals of republican universalism and its translation into reality and that differences, including sexual difference, continue to make their presence felt under the equalizing, homogenizing discourse of universalism. Abstract universalism, let us recall, makes of the citizen of the republic a neutered subject devoid of all particularities: in order to become a rights-bearing abstract individual the citizen is unsexed, ungendered, unraced, unclassed, but the failure of universalism suggests that the neutering operation is not complete, for the neuter is a man. Historically, the rights of the universal citizen have been appropriated, not to say confiscated, by men. If there exists no female universalism, there does exist a de facto male universalism: masculinity is the default drive of universalism.

Given the impossibility of imagining a French system of laws outside of *The Declaration of the Rights of Man and the Citizen*, the *paritaires* have no choice but to rescue an imperiled, patently inadequate universalism. Surely the most reasoned, the most logical statement on this point is made by Dominique Schnapper in her contribution to the *parité* debates, "La transcendance par le politique" (Transcendence through Politics), where she essentially argues that we need not throw the baby out with the bathwater:

> But because a great principle was often poorly applied and invoked in the wrong sense, and because it constantly risks being so if we are not careful, one must not conclude that it must cease to be what it is. One must ceaselessly struggle for it to be effectively applied.[33]

Conceding the bogus neutrality of universalism, she goes on to say in terms that are both suggestive and problematic: "Universalism does not coincide with any particular historical reality. The universal is not a content, it is a reference and an aspiration. . . . It is in the name of the true universal that women must continue to wage their battle" (*Le piège*, 115).

Parité is then anything but a threat to universalism; it is rather a wake-up call. It is a reminder that the Revolution is not over because for some it has not yet begun. But what then is "veritable universalism"? What is the true universalism always implied by the naming of

---

33. Dominique Schnapper, "La transcendance par le politique," in *Le piège de la parité*, 113. Cf. Schnapper, *La relation à l'autre* (Paris: Seuil, 1998), for a broader but similarly tempered and wise view of universalism.

a false universalism? Can there be meaningful falseness without a countervailing truthfulness? Or, to get straight to the point: is there any such thing as a utopian universalism? Here I want to home in on a series of remarks made almost in passing by some of the most perceptive participants in the debates, often historians, and the consequences of which they refuse to draw. Thus Michèle Riot-Sarcey remarks: "The entire representational system was built on the shifting base of exclusion, particularly of women. This apparatus is today in crisis" (Le piège, 102). Similarly, in a jointly-authored article, "Parité ou mixité," Helena Hirata, Danièle Kergoat, Michèle Riot-Sarcey, and Eleni Varakas note by the by:

> We in France are the heirs and the heiresses of the institutions implemented since 1789. The exclusion of women, constitutive of representational democracy, served to legitimate the monopolizing of representation by a minority of men belonging to the "economic, political, and intellectual elite" which seized, for its own benefit, the universal republican principles. [Le piège, 12]

It is this constitutive role of the exclusion of women to which Joan Scott also alludes in her critique of male universalism:

> We cannot write women into history, for example, unless we are willing to entertain the notion that history as a unified story was a fiction about *a universal subject whose universality was achieved through the implicit processes of differentiation, marginalization, and exclusion.* Man was never, in other words, a truly universal figure. It is the processes of exclusion achieved through differentiation that established man's universal plausibility that must, to begin with, constitute the focus for a different, more critical history.[34]

It is difficult to read the documents that make up the *parité* dossier without wishing to push it to its extreme logic, a point that is made incidentally here and there but whose implications for universalism are never fully worked out. Not a single participant in the debates would contest that women have been shortchanged in the wake of *The Declaration of the Rights of Man and the Citizen.* The statistics speak for themselves and they are damning. All would agree that change is called for; what is contested is the form that this change must take: constitutional or political. The solution to these questions I leave to the politi-

---

34. Joan W. Scott, *Gender and the Politics of History* (New York: Columbia University Press, 1988), 197.

cians. My concern as a student of universalism, and especially in its French incarnation, lies elsewhere: is it just French universalism that excludes women? Is it just the exclusion of women that is constitutive of French universalism? These questions lead me to far more disturbing ones: to what extent can it be argued that universalism requires, or entails exclusion as though by definition? To what extent does universalism function precisely by that which it claims to eliminate—discrimination based on differences? To what extent does universalism rely on exclusion in order to function? It is surely disturbing that to this day there is no example of a universalism that is all-inclusive. *Parité* may save French universalism, but the future of universalism as anything but an illusion at worst, or at best a noble ideal with unsurpassed emancipatory potential, remains in doubt.

DANIEL GORDON

Democracy and the Deferral of Justice in France and the United States*

Today one speaks of the "cultural wars" to refer to disputes among American academics about the significance of race and ethnicity in the educational curriculum. The term may also be used, however, to describe the growing disagreement between American and French professors over whether this kind of dispute is meaningful at all. Americans approach the debate with passion and seriousness because they recognize that perennial questions about democracy are involved. For multiculturalism is not so much an external challenge to American democratic thought as a particular way of interpreting this tradition. More precisely, multiculturalism draws energy from the widespread American belief in pluralism: the conviction, expressed by the framers of the Constitution themselves, that democracies benefit from the inclusion of different groups with different interests. This is not to say that a pluralist is logically bound to be a multiculturalist. Rather, there is a historical relation between the two: pluralism, which nearly everyone accepts, is the context in which multiculturalism acquires meaning for some.

In contrast, French intellectuals often seem to consider the American debate about multiculturalism to be an insult to democratic life. Several recent French articles portray American universities as places where fractures over curricular issues are displacing the rational discourse and universal solidarity necessary to sustain a democracy.[1] This

*I wish to thank Ralph Sarkonak for organizing this forum and for his valuable comments on an earlier draft of this essay. My thanks also go to Charles Rearick, Jennifer Heuer, Jeremy King, and David Glassberg for suggestions they made when I was researching the paper.

1. Jean-François Revel, "États-Unis: Universités, la tentation minoritaire," *Le point* (20 March, 1993), 45; François Furet, "L'Amerique de Clinton II," *Le débat* 99 (March–

YFS 100, *FRANCE/USA: The Cultural Wars,* ed. Ralph Sarkonak, © 2001 by Yale University.

displeasure with the American scene is giving rise to a new kind of anti-Americanism. French hostility used to be directed against the American economy for creating excessive inequality; now it is directed against the American university for creating too much diversity. As a product of Marxism, the older form of anti-Americanism had subversive implications at home as well as abroad. But the new form of criticism is potentially more destructive of Franco-American relations precisely because it stems from no iconoclastic doctrine, but from the very core of French nationality since the eighteenth century: republicanism. Paradoxically, the French do not like what they see in the only other democracy in the world that was founded in the Enlightenment.

On the American side, too, one senses growing hostility toward the intellectual life of the other country. A skeptical and sociological, as opposed to appreciative and esthetic, image of France is becoming more common. The tendency of French departments in the United States to move away from the intensive reading of classic texts and toward interdisciplinary and Francophone studies has inevitably brought French institutions under more critical scrutiny. Instead of studying French as a series of literary achievements, one is more likely to observe that entry into the higher levels of French society is regulated by a concept of Frenchness that is remarkably indifferent to the languages and literatures of other groups.

In short, the French tend to see America as heading toward multicultural anarchy, and Americans tend to see the French as stuck in Franco-solipsism. Each views the other as having an academic ethos that is inconsistent with true democracy. For the historian, the problem is to demonstrate how subtle differences in the way each country formulates its commitment to equality yield profoundly different visions of the cultural prerequisites of democracy. To explain these differences more fully is the scholarly purpose of comparative analysis. But comparison also has an ethical purpose, which is to create an equilibrium: to replace condemnations with a more refined and balanced perspective, one that illuminates the genius and the pathos of each system. But even more, comparative reflection should help the members of a country to envision changes in their way of life that would temper those very shortcomings that comparison exposes.

April, 1997): 7–10; "L'avenir du multiculturalisme" (a forum with several contributors), *Le débat* 97 (Nov.–Dec., 1997): 131–84. See also Eric Fassin's discussion of French views of multiculturalism in his "The Purloined Gender: American Feminism in a French Mirror," *French Historical Studies* 22/1 (1999): 132–33.

MEANING IN COMPARISON

The comparison of France and America is especially well suited for these philosophical goals. It is possible to compare any two regimes, but the act of comparison does not always promote a fruitful learning process. Certain modes of comparison portray societies as antithetical organizations, as entities that cannot integrate features from each other because they have never shared any common goals. Preference ought to be given to finer comparison—in other words, to a nuanced comparison of different nations belonging to the same type of civilization, as opposed to stark comparison of entirely different civilizations. Typically, one finds the second type of comparison in anthropological thought. For the sake of reasoning against one of the most distinguished representatives of this approach, one could consider Louis Dumont, the French anthropologist whose books compare "holism" in traditional Indian society with "individualism" in Europe and America since the Enlightenment.

The magnitude of Dumont's enterprise is impressive, but the binary framework is problematic. First, since it brings a single polarity (holism/individualism) to every inquiry, it produces distortions. Dumont, for example, describes the Enlightenment as individualistic.[2] But then how to explain the rise of Dumont's own style of thinking in the Enlightenment, the new and acute consciousness of distinct social totalities in thinkers such as Montesquieu and Millar? How to explain the popularity of words designating the whole community, such as "society" and "civilization," compared to the infrequency of the word "individual" in the Enlightenment?[3] How to account for Sieyès: "France must not be a collection of small nations. . . . It is a unique whole. . . . France is and must be a single whole."[4]

Secondly, such frameworks make it difficult to explain how regimes undergo change. In India, how did democracy (a form of individualism) manage to emerge out of the caste system (an embodiment of holism)? Dumont does not address such questions.[5] In his work (as in that of

2. Louis Dumont, *Essays on Individualism* (Chicago: University of Chicago Press, 1986); *From Mandeville to Marx* (Chicago: University of Chicago Press, 1977).

3. Daniel Gordon, *Citizens Without Sovereignty: Equality and Sociability in French Thought, 1670–1789* (Princeton: Princeton University Press, 1994).

4. Abbé Sieyès, "Dire sur la question du veto royal," *Écrits politiques*, ed. Roberto Zapperi (Paris: Éditions des archives contempiraines, 1985), 234, 237; cited in Pierre Birnbaum, *La France imaginée* (Paris: Fayard, 1998), 350.

5. It is true that in his last book Dumont changes course (*German Ideology: From*

other French anthropological thinkers, such as Marcel Mauss and Roger Caillois), comparison does not include the study of change; it is based on a cross-sectional approach to the study of civilizations. The goal is to display an incongruity, to create a shock effect by revealing a foreign mentality that has nothing in common with the reader's own.[6] Indeed, the practitioners of this approach seem unable to imagine how meaning could be produced in comparative discourse other than through the juxtaposition of radically different customs. They relish the existence of absolute alterity—so much so that they are willing to invent it through their own static dichotomies.

Moreover, the members of this school have never been clear about how they expect a reader to react after the shock effect of otherness sets in. If the purpose of comparing one's own way with the way of another is not merely to engender self-distance but to make self-reform possible, this approach does not seem to promote the latter. Its foreign reference point always stands for what one's own society cannot attain. Hence, the very terms of comparison prohibit a reciprocal influence.

The purpose of comparison is to establish an exchange, and where no exchange is possible, social science can serve no constructive purpose. Besides the polarized anthropology of Dumont, there are two other influential styles of history that are problematic in this context. The first is universal history, the second is postmodernism. Universal history is a strategy of comparison that relies exclusively on temporality to establish the meaning of difference. Societies vary depending on their stage in a linear scheme of evolution. In the seventeenth and eighteenth centuries, Europeans regarded America as their lost state of nature. "Thus in the beginning, all the world was America," said Locke (*Second Treatise,* Chap. 5). To represent the other as the primitive ver-

---

France to Germany and Back [Chicago: University of Chicago Press, 1994]). The book is a series of essays on the German conception of *Bildung* and nationhood. Dumont proposes that in German humanism, from Herder to Thomas Mann, it is possible to find combinations of individualism and holism. This is a novel point, since in his earlier works, Dumont did not explore the fusion of the two structures. But instead of using this fusion to temper his ethnographic polarities, he simply makes it the basis of a new polarity by frequently referring to France as a nation whose self-conception is entirely individualistic (see 25, 146, 199–200, 208, 215–16, 218). Thus we have a Germany/France dichotomy instead of an India/Europe comparison. The contrast is no more nuanced in the first case than in the second.

6. James Clifford, in *The Predicament of Culture: Twentieth-Century Ethnography, Literature, and Art* (Cambridge: Harvard University Press, 1988), 117–151, discusses the technique "of coupling irreconcilable realities" in the history of French anthropology.

sion of the self can produce narcissistic nostalgia. It cannot produce a serious will to change, because the other, located in a time that is absolutely past, cannot be resurrected in one's own space. Conversely, to look to the other as one's future, as the intellectuals of less economically developed nations have sometimes looked to the United States and other industrialized nations, is to create a one-way street: here the past is to learn from the future, but not the future from the past. Moreover, it only creates the false hope that "progress," that is, moving forward in time, will solve all of a nation's problems at once.

As for postmodernism, its shortcoming is not that it offers questionable comparative frameworks, but that it is resistant to comparison in general. Postmodernism avoids the concept of nationhood, which is the most important tool of comparative thought. It favors a mode of analysis that is geographically unspecific, that moves lightly across national boundaries. Like universal historians, such as Adam Smith and Marx, postmodernist theorists, such as Jameson and Lyotard, use a terminology that is generically about time, not distinctively about place. "Advanced industrial societies," "the crisis of representation," "the decline of narrative," "the commercialization of knowledge" are concepts that know no borders. In this way, postmodernist theorists neglect the distinct structures of idealism and power that are present in the constitutions, laws, and political vocabularies of different nations.

This tendency to think generically is characteristic even of the more scholarly and rigorously historical postmodern authors. Thus, in *Discipline and Punish*, Foucault attempts to show the emergence of surveillance as a technique of power in the eighteenth century. Most of his examples come from France, but enough (such as Bentham's Panopticon) come from other countries to show that he considers this new technique to be a pervasive feature of modern Western civilization. It may well be, but then it would also be worth knowing how the judicial systems, police forces, and educational programs of different countries sometimes protect citizens from certain forms of surveillance and sanctify the right to privacy. In this way, one could undertake a comparison of the different modes of interaction between power and rights in different countries. In the absence of such comparison, one is left with the deceiving sense that the institutions of modernity are uniformly absorbed in the task of disciplining the population.

A more subtle case of the evasion of nationhood is Roger Chartier's

The Cultural Origins of the French Revolution.[7] Here the thing being explained is specifically French, but the "cultural origins" doing the explaining are generically transnational. Chartier sees the Revolution as an outcome of certain gradual trends, such as desacralization and the rise of a reading public. Yet, since these trends were not limited to France, they are not adequate to explain an event that occurred only in France. When reading Chartier's account of the spread of contraception in the Old Regime, one may well be convinced that this shows increasing disregard of the Church's precepts on sexuality, hence a process of desacralization. But what does this slow, uncoordinated process of desacralization have to do with the Revolutionaries' deliberate effort to thoroughly de-Christianize France as rapidly as possible? What accounts for the transformation of a social fact into a political act? What is missing is an account of the special pattern of interaction between secularization and state authority in the French nation.

Granted that nations are not primordial realities but historical products: they are not simply there to explain everything else, but must themselves be explained. Yet, for this very reason, it is remarkable that postmodern thinkers have displayed so little interest in the formation of nationally distinct conceptions of governance and liberty. Considering the interest that postmodernist authors have in colonialism, they ought to have studied the different legal cultures of colonizing countries and their different effects on the identity and history of colonized peoples. Malick Ghachem, a scholar with a special interest in French colonialism and with training in both history and law, has noted that the failure of historians of France (not just in France, but in England and America as well) to study the legal relationships between colonies and metropoles "has much to do with the influence of postmodern thought on the writing of colonial history." He continues:

> First, postmodern thought has directed attention away from the study of formal law and institutions in favor of constantly multiplying "sites" of non-governmental, "immanent" authority. The paradigmatic thinker in this respect is of course Foucault, whose famous injunction to "conceive of sex without the law, and power without the king" has become a rallying cry of the burgeoning school of "postcolonial" studies . . .

After quoting a passage from *The History of Sexuality*, in which Foucault denigrates the significance of legal history, Ghachem resumes:

7. Roger Chartier, *The Cultural Origins of the French Revolution* (Durham: Duke University Press, 1991).

The impulse to "expel" law from history resonated perfectly with the postcolonial determination to restore "agency" to the "subaltern" populations of the European empires. But despite all the focus on indigenous resistance to the imposition of metropolitan authority, it is not at all clear that recent scholars of empire have hearkened to Foucault's warning that "there is no binary and all-encompassing opposition between rulers and ruled at the root of power relations."[8]

By citing one of Foucault's own maxims, Ghachem cleverly turns the postmodern love of paradox in a distinctly unpostmodern direction. The point of his article is to show that in the eighteenth century, the spirit of independence in one of France's colonies, Saint-Domingue, evolved not against, but by means of, the images of native culture embedded in French colonial law. The rebellious colonial subject was a product of Enlightenment jurisprudence.

In the discipline of history, it has become common to reject the study of high politics and political ideas in favor of exhaustive treatment of the everyday living conditions of ordinary people. But modern history becomes incomprehensible when the political is subordinated to the quotidian. Here the work of postmodern scholars is again instructive. For on account of their reluctance to classify regimes in terms of legal, constitutional, or party ideologies, postmodern thinkers have made little contribution to the scholarly understanding of the two most original forms of power in the twentieth century: communism and fascism. More generally, those who insist that every assertion of authority, no matter how particular it may be, is as political as any other, run the risk of hyper-inflating the concept of politics. The end result is to ignore those texts and institutions in a regime that functions to guarantee that certain norms will count for the community as a whole.

One thing that methodological critique reveals is that newer methods are not necessarily better than older ones. A new method may suddenly shed light on an area of the past that had been neglected, but its blind spots may be bigger than those of the method it claims to supersede. The problem is to determine which methods allow one to pursue the largest questions in the most nuanced way. The approach recommended here—to study the distinctive features of nation-states, and to

8. Malick Ghachem, "Montesquieu in the Caribbean: The Colonial Enlightenment between Code Noir and Code Civil," in *Postmodernism and the French Enlightenment,* ed. Daniel Gordon, a special volume of *Historical Reflections* 25/2 (Summer, 1999): 185–87.

compare those that have similar political forms but vary in their historical development—is not new. It was popular in the 1950s and 1960s. Some examples are Seymour Martin Lipset's effort to produce a rigorous social science in *The First New Nation: The United States in Historical and Comparative Perspective* (1963), and Jacques Maritain's methodologically unpretentious but no less meaningful meditations in *Reflections on America* (1958). Patrice Higgonet, the author of *Sister Republics* (1988), and Donald Horowitz, the co-editor (with Gérard Noiriel) of *Immigrants in Two Democracies* (1992) are insightful practitioners of this approach in the present.

But the founder of this method was of course Tocqueville. Tocqueville worked with the Aristotelian premise that the theorist must classify on the basis of governmental regimes, of which there are only a limited number of types (rule by one, by few, by many). But with the help of Montesquieu, he added the perception that historical accidents produce different modes of the same regime; and it is the mode, not merely the regime, that shapes the *moeurs* of each country as well as its special dynamic of change. In what follows, Tocqueville is never far from view, though I have tried to present a novel "mode" of the Tocquevillian "regime" of description: a different set of claims about the separate paths between France and America today. After sketching the fundamental resemblances between the two nations in terms of their common commitment to equality, I suggest, on the basis of their constitutions, that the many in France—"the people"—is officially ethnic in character, while in America it is presocial. This difference accounts for the distinctive strengths and limitations of each country in its pursuit of equality for all its citizens. Each country sustains a magnificent tradition, but each one has also reached an impasse in its pursuit of justice: a point where the official concept of peoplehood blocks it from pursuing reforms that are necessary to complete its egalitarian mission. As a result, each nation perennially defers the pursuit of justice for certain of its members. The current attitudes toward multiculturalism in each country are signs of this deferral of justice—not solutions to that particular problem.

"THE PEOPLE" AND THE DEFERRAL OF JUSTICE

France and the United States share the same form of government—democracy—in which citizens elect leaders who are obligated to preserve freedom for all citizens. Both spell out this fundamental relationship between citizens and government in written constitutions that are binding upon the entire population. Both are countries with multi-religious and multi-ethnic populations. They share a conception of open admission to the political community and make naturalization liberally available to foreigners. In fact, the two countries have been pioneers in forging the very ideal of civic equality: the universalist commitment to provide membership in the nation regardless of a person's origin. In this way, the two nations separate citizenship from ancestry. Just as everyone is theoretically eligible for citizenship regardless of origin, so no one is automatically granted citizenship on account of origin. In contrast to Israel and Germany, France and the United States offer no right of return—no guaranteed naturalization—to "blood-carrying" members of the community who live in other countries.[9]

Another way of saying this is that citizenship in the two countries is *sui generis*—it is a distinct status that is not reducible to other aspects of one's being. But not only is citizenship distinct from other forms of affiliation, it is also the object of intense pride. Other countries, such as Germany, may possess a democratic constitution. But Germany lacks the tradition of attaching its national pride to democratic institutions. Hence the urgency with which democratic intellectuals, such as Jürgen Habermas, advocate "constitutional patriotism" (*Verfassungspatriotismus*). In France and the United States, there is a tradition of regarding democracy as the nation's greatest invention. People also perceive democracy as an unfinished project to which they can connect their own spiritual aspirations. Without necessarily studying much history, they imbibe the future-oriented philosophy of the era in which their democracies were founded. They acquire a dynamic sense of freedom and equality, of moral truth expanding through an endless series of confrontations with inequality and injustice. The two nations do celebrate their past, especially their creation myths. Yet, what they celebrate then are revolutions, so even their nostalgia makes them look forward. For this reason, France and the United States are places in which national history is not the special property of the Right. They are places in which adoration of the past is regularly accompanied by self-criticism and the announcement of new aspirations.

9. Israel promises citizenship to Jewish immigrants. German naturalization policies are in the process of becoming more liberal toward non-German immigrants, but ethnic Germans still have special status. The government, for example, grants citizenship automatically to nearly all Russian and Eastern Europeans of German descent—see Rogers Brubaker, *Citizenship and Nationhood in France and Germany* (Cambridge: Harvard University Press, 1992), 82–84.

It goes without saying that each of these generalizations does not apply in the same degree to each country, or to every group within each country. One cannot speak of equality in the United States without noting the disadvantages of being African American. One cannot speak of ethnic neutrality in France without noting that it is the only country in the European Union that refuses to honor the principle that governments ought to encourage the use of regional dialects. (President Chirac disavowed this principle because the constitution states, "The language of the Republic is French.") These features do not cancel the supposition that the two countries have profoundly democratic political cultures, but they do underscore a tragic feature of democracies, that they never function without inequities of some kind and never completely fulfill their own spirit. To call it tragic is not to suggest that injustices should be accepted as they are. It does mean, however, that certain anomalies persist in a democratic regime, not from a prejudice against democracy, but from a prejudice in its favor. This in turn means that while any problem can be ameliorated to some degree, the resources available to address certain inequities are limited by the country's constitutional commitments. The country does not openly avow its reluctance to address a certain form of injustice; it simply postpones dealing with it in the name of some higher principle. In France, that principle is indivisibility; in America it is individuality.

The current French constitution was enacted in 1958. Article 1 is a paragraph that begins with the words: "France is an indivisible republic." It then links the republic to a series of other attributes, such as secularism, democracy, and legal equality. It ends with the words, "It [the republic] respects all forms of belief." In reality, the principle of indivisibility and the principle of respect for multiple beliefs are at cross-purposes. This tension is disguised by the insertion of so many other abstractions in the middle. The effect is to suggest a gradual slope from principle 1 (indivisibility) to principle 2 (secularism) to principle 3 (democracy), and so forth, until the reader arrives at the principle of respect for difference. Yet, when one considers what the first principle really means, it becomes clear that, far from authorizing respect for all beliefs, indivisibility diminishes the range of beliefs that can be respected. In this way, the constitution establishes, without explicitly affirming, that unity is paramount and that respect for diversity will have to be deferred.

The term "indivisible" occurs in every republican constitution in France from 1791 to 1958: seven separate constitutions. But the idea of indivisibility actually predates republicanism. It entered political thought through the works of defenders of royal absolutism in the seventeenth century. The argument was that every community contains a multiplicity of private interests and beliefs. These will bring people into violent conflict with each other unless they subordinate their particular inclinations to the will of the government, which is to say that they must opt to let the public power represent them. As Hobbes wrote:

> A multitude of men, are made one person, when they are by one man, one person, represented. . . . For it is the unity of the representer, not the unity of the represented, that maketh the person one. And it is the representer that beareth the person, and but one person; and unity cannot otherwise be understood in the multitude.[10]

In France, this absolutist logic was taken seriously in the wake of many years of religious war, and it informed the official vision of government.[11] The difficulty facing those who opposed absolute monarchy was to explain how one could remove absolutism and still have unity. Republican thinkers of the Enlightenment rose to this challenge in a specific way. They did not argue, as economic liberals and theorists of human sociability did, that human beings are inherently cooperative in their social lives. Instead, they retained absolutism's pessimistic conception of society, but transferred the public responsibility of transcending social disunity from the monarch to the people themselves. Thus, the vital center of republican philosophy, the conceptual area in which its democratic passion was most concentrated, has always been the sovereign people; the people *qua* state, not the people *qua* particular individuals. The essential question was: How to forge a people who will not be divided when they govern themselves in the ways that they are divided when they are governed? How, as Rousseau put it, to produce sovereign "citizens" who will not have the same divisive commitments that they have as "subjects"? (*Social Contract*, Bk. 1, Ch. 7).

As one can see in Rousseau, these republican dilemmas, when taken seriously, produce a radical version of democratic thought—radical in the sense of a serious commitment to include ordinary individuals in the government. At the same time, republicanism is the most absolutist form of democracy: it transfers power from the king to the peo-

---

10. Thomas Hobbes, *Leviathan*, Chap. 16, anthologized in Hannah Fenichel Pitkin, *Representation* (New York: Atherton Press, 1969), 27.

11. See the discussion of indivisibility in Bossuet's *Politique tirée des propres paroles de l'Écriture sainte*, Book 2, Article 1, Proposition 8 (Geneva: Droz, 1967), 54–55.

ple, but the power it transfers undergoes no change in the process—it remains "indivisible" and "always right" (*Social Contract*, Bk. 2, Chap. 2, "That Sovereignty is Indivisible," and Chap. 3, "Whether the General Will Can Err"). Republicanism, then, inevitably involves a repressive disposition toward prepolitical culture—to all those groupings, customs, and convictions that exist separately from the social contract and that do not fit into the program of reeducating men into the ways of democratic citizenship. During the French Revolution, "regeneration" was the popular term used to express the project of admitting new groups, such as provincials and Jews, into the citizenry, while condescendingly requiring them to shed the particular traditions that made them different from other citizens. It is no accident that the abbé Gregoire, the leading champion of Jewish emancipation, insisted that Jews should stop reading the Talmud. He was also an ardent supporter of the movement to eradicate regional languages.[12]

To this day, the French envision democracy as the project of forging citizens out of raw, prepolitical human material. They believe that a collective republican ethos must be superimposed upon the given culture of individuals—must supersede this given culture when the latter appears to be divisive. "Divisive" does not necessarily mean that a group is explicitly seditious or hostile to the government. It means that the group has a will that is "general in relation to its members and particular in relation to the state," as Rousseau put it (Bk. 2, Chap. 3). The group, in other words, offers a worldview that seems complete to its members and that does not rank the republic as the highest good. The task of republican government, then, is not so much to diminish the range of group affiliations an individual can have, but to make sure that the individual never openly affirms that these affiliations are more important than being a French national.

The French constitution itself conveys the principle of nationality. That is why it is more than a constitution in the American sense of the word. It does not merely delineate the formal structure of government; it is also an instrument of cultural unification. Thus, Article 2, entitled "On Sovereignty," reads:

> The language of the Republic is French [added to the Constitution in 1992].
> The national emblem is the tricolor flag, blue, white, and red.

12. Birnbaum, *La France imaginée*, 67, 90.

The national anthem is the "Marseillaise."
The motto of the Republic is "Liberty, Equality, Fraternity."

The American constitution has no articles like these that assign specific cultural practices to the sovereign people. In fact, it is noteworthy that the very idea of "sovereignty" has no counterpart within the system of federalism established by the American constitution. The American constitution not only omits to stipulate the republic's *cultural* emblems; it does not even try to constitute a unified *political* entity. The word "sovereignty," like the word "indivisible," does not occur in the American text. This is proof that the terms are not inherent in democratic thinking. They are characteristic only of that mode of democratic thinking that has borrowed from absolutism the conviction that the public power must have a higher order of unity than the society over which it governs. Thus, in the French Constitution, Article 3, which is also part of the section "On Sovereignty," states:

> National sovereignty belongs to the people, who exercise it through its representatives and by means of referendum.
> No section of the people nor any individual can appropriate the exercise thereof.

This clearly means that the central government is supreme over local government—a French tradition that stems from the very ideal of sovereign, indivisible authority. The American constitution, in contrast, grants particular powers to the central government and stipulates that all remaining powers "belong to the states or to the people." It is thus a system without sovereignty in the technical sense of a unitary locus of authority.

It is true that Americans have developed the habit of describing their system as based on dual sovereignty—State and Federal. But this is a departure from the more rigorous language of early-modern political philosophy and remains an oxymoron from a French point of view. In Alden v. Maine, a 1999 Supreme Court ruling placing limits on the ability of Congress to make Federal law binding on the states, Justice Kennedy wrote:

> Although the Constitution grants broad powers to Congress, our federalism requires that Congress treat the states in a manner consistent with their status as residuary sovereigns and joint participants in the governance of the nation.

Elsewhere in the same decision he stated:

When Congress legislates in matters affecting the states, it may not treat these sovereign entities as mere prefectures or corporations. Congress must accord states the esteem due to them as joint participants in a Federal system.[13]

This ruling created some anger when it appeared because it seems to allow the states to circumvent minimum-wage and civil-rights legislation by the federal government. It may be true that the ruling was guided by hostility to progressive federal legislation. But the point is that the American constitution plainly makes this ruling possible because it erects no unified, all-powerful public authority. In France, where there are no "states" possessing their own governments but only "departments" that are pieces of a unified national system, such a decision could never occur.[14]

One term that does occur in both constitutions is "the people." But closer study shows that this common term is the sign of another important difference. When Article 3 of the French constitution says that no "section of the people" can appropriate its sovereignty, it presumes that "the people" as a whole is not inherently sectionalized. As a matter of sociological fact, diverse interests and opinions are inevitable in any large group. Yet, since the purpose of Article 3 is not to establish a balance among sections of the population but to assert the sovereignty of "the people" over all sections of itself, it must be presumed that the people is not many but one. This singularity of the French people is not an intended consequence of the constitution, not an ideal goal; it is an *a priori* supposition. But not only is the people preconstitutionally unified; it is also preconstitutionally French: "The French people has adopted . . ." "The French people solemnly proclaims . . ." (The first

13. The complete opinion can be found on the website of the Legal Information Institute, http://supct.law.cornell.edu/supct.

14. Although my argument here is centered on constitutional discourse, it could be deepened with a close analysis of non-constitutional documents, including even the speeches of the most nationalist thinker in American history, Abraham Lincoln. Lincoln did say, "A house divided cannot stand" (speech of 16 June 1858), and his speeches in the years prior to and during the Civil War do emphasize the need for American unity. However, even this extreme example, taken from the only serious internal crisis the United States has ever known, illustrates the point that the French idea of indivisibility is different. For Lincoln did not oppose the concept of federalism that grants vast powers to the separate states. He did not assert the absolute sovereignty of the national government in matters pertaining to slavery either. For him, indivisibility meant only that no state has the right to secede from the union established by the constitution. For him, America is *constitutionally* one, but it is *politically* plural. (See First Inaugural Address, 4 March 1861).

phrase quoted here comes from the lines leading up to the Preamble of the 1958 Constitution; the second comes from the Preamble itself.)

Now, what is striking in all of this is that the use of "the people" in no way harkens back to the state of nature. There is no evocation of a time prior to the existence of the sovereign nation. There is no reference to a moment when, either before the making of all constitutions or in between constitutions, diverse individuals decided to exert their natural rights to authorize a new government. The unified French people is always already there and stands in for the people of the state of nature when it approves of the constitution. This is a vital point, for it means that in spite of the fact that French citizenship is extensible to the members of any other ethnic group, French citizenship implies entry into a community that has the same primordialist and unified self-image that is characteristic of ethnic ideology. In other words, the Constitution is written as if "the French people" were an ethnic group that has always existed, that is unified, and that happens to subscribe to democratic principles. The constitution is thus designed to protect not only democracy, but also the specific national identity of "the people" who created it.

This is a remarkable fusion of two very different principles: ethnicity (which is exclusive) and democracy (which is inclusive). It permits only one possible synthesis: you do not have to be born ethnically French to be a citizen, but you must become ethnically French to be a citizen. In practice, this means that you must not merely know how to speak French but must actually speak it. You must be schooled in the history of the nation. You must be willing to say, "I am French," without further qualifications. Many people have observed that the French do not employ hyphenated terms to express identity, whereas Americans refer to themselves or others as Italian-American or Jewish-American, for example. The reason is now clear. It is because being French represents the ethnic and the political sides of identity simultaneously.

The language of the American constitution is different. The text often refers to individuals in the plural as "persons," "free persons," "other persons," "the citizens of each state," and so forth. Even when it is grammatically singular, "the people" represents a loose amalgam of individuals, not a unified whole. The most frequent and formulaic use of "the people" occurs in the original ten amendments; specifically in the recurrent phrase, "the right of the people" (as in "the right of the people" to assemble, "the right of the people" to be free against arbitrary searches, etc.). This term could be paraphrased as "the right of every citizen" and in no way implies the existence of a collectivity that acts or thinks in unison. Even "We the people" of the famous preamble bears no resemblance to "the French people." First, it does not say "We the American people" but "We the people of the United States," which points to the plurality of states within the union. Secondly, "the people" act to form not an "indivisible republic" but "a more perfect union." This implies that the previous union among the people was tenuous (hence there is no primordial unity among the people) and also that the people will continue to remain distinct from each other even after they create a stronger federation (hence unity is not the *telos* of the constitution either). The phrase "We the people" institutes a myth that Americans—as individuals—have unanimously opted for this new social contract. Yet, it deliberately avoids imputing to the people a national identity, so that their rights—again, as individuals—can never be subordinated to goals defined by the federal government.

CULTURAL CONSEQUENCES OF CONSTITUTIONAL DIFFERENCES

In short, French democracy is formally constituted by the French people, whereas American democracy is formally constituted by individuals. Two different ontologies are at work. The French system is set so that the whole is prior to the part. Individuals have rights, but individuals are essentially building blocks of something, the French people, whose existence makes rights possible. The American system turns each individual into a microcosm, and there is no macrocosm that subsumes the part. Constitutionally speaking, the individual is the only America that is. From this it follows that each country has a distinctive strength: in America, the ability to restrain power for the sake of rights; in France, the ability to give priority to national over private interests. Each also has a distinctive weakness: in America, an unwillingness to define great projects of national reform; in France, an unwillingness to confer dignity on nonnational cultures.

The weakness of the American system is most evident in its failure to deal with inequalities that individuals experience but for which they are not responsible as individuals. The salient case throughout the nation's history has been the situation of African Americans. Antidiscrimination laws currently help to keep the effects of racism in check. Overcoming racism, however, is only part of the problem because many of the communities in which African Americans live do not have the economic infrastructure and educational traditions that would permit them to develop fully as individuals. Since many of the social problems stem from the fact that African Americans were the only group to be enslaved on a large scale in this country, they ought to be the unique beneficiaries of a special, long-term national policy designed to elevate their opportunities and living conditions. The country has the financial resources to embark on such a program, but it lacks the necessary national spirit. Democratic individualism does not generate the kind of historical consciousness and intense sympathy that would inspire whites to approve of the preferential treatment of blacks. The recent retrenchment of affirmative action is one example of this limited sympathy. Only national sentiment is powerful enough to make a community feel moral outrage over the persistent inequality of some of its members.

Yet the problem is even deeper. A program to reconstruct the condition of African Americans in America would have to be, in part, a program of acculturation. Better educational facilities would be part of the program, but no less important would be the process of educating African Americans as to the value of attaining a higher level of instruction. But what sort of instruction? One that emphasized standard American English? One that steered African Americans away from those aspects of their own culture that appear to handicap it economically and intellectually in American society? Such efforts have already taken place on a local level, and are often led by African Americans themselves. But for the federal government to undertake a national program of acculturation would require a degree of consensus on the components of American ethno-nationality that the United States has never had—or else it would take an act of authoritative imposition that the U.S. government is not set up to exercise.[15]

Finally, there is the constitution. Would it permit resources to flow

15. Not all historians, of course, would agree that there has never been an official definition of nationality in the United States. Rogers Smith (*Civic Ideals* [New Haven: Yale University Press, 1997]) argues that citizenship through much of U.S. history was chauvinistically Anglo-Saxon. He admits, however, that no conception of citizenship is built into the Constitution (115). He also concedes that American citizenship is dedicated first and foremost to abstract individual rights (135). These points are hard to square with his general argument. As Donald L. Horowitz ("Immigration and Group Relations in France and America," *Immigrants in Two Democracies: French and American Experience*, ed. Horowitz and Gérard Noiriel [New York: New York University Press, 1992], 1002) argues, American nationality has never had a permanent ethnic core. While whites have excluded others, they have always disputed each other's claims about who among the white population are the truly indigenous Americans. The fact that the Revolution was against the

to one group and not to others? Is this not a form of discrimination? And even if it permitted the program to exist, would it not interfere with its smooth functioning? A government cannot expend vast resources on a group without requiring the group to pledge some loyalty and responsibility to it. But can a government require a minority to salute the flag when the majority is exempt from doing so? Can a government set out to integrate, that is to Americanize, a minority while it makes no effort to acculturate the majority?

In earlier periods, notably in the reconstruction years after the Civil War and in the 1960s, the federal government did try to enforce a high standard of integration for African Americans. The older efforts, however, relied largely on the individualistic tradition of the constitution: to guarantee constitutional rights, such as the right to vote, was the rallying point of reformers until the 1970s. American liberals (namely, those calling on the government to bring about more equal conditions) hoped that a federally-guaranteed extension of constitutional rights to African Americans would bring about their integration in American society. Today it is evident that rights are not enough to create either economic parity or a psychological sense of unity among the races. Any vision of reform that is more than juridical in character has to be cultural in character—it must be religious or ethical. Hostility toward governmental imposition of values on the entire population, however, is one of the few things that Americans, including liberal Americans, do have in common. An impasse has been reached.

This impasse affects everyone. For as long as it exists, it means that nothing the government does can be based on a social goal with spiritual content. The power of government to regulate is in fact expanding, but the ideals guiding its action are contracting. Thus, the American vision of the welfare state has become largely an affair of bodily health. One can limit ads for hard liquor on TV, but not the violence in children's programs. One can ban smoking in public places but not meetings of fascist groups. Governmental regulation of the market is increasingly being reduced to the control of those things that directly threaten the longevity of the individual. There is a deep constitutional logic here. For it makes sense, given the individualistic ontology of the

---

British diminished from the start the authority of those who claimed that Englishness is the core of America. I would add that a national system of education is the principal means that a state uses to impose fixed conceptions of citizenship and national consciousness on a populace—and this is precisely what the United States lacks and France has. See Michael Kammen, *The Mystic Chords of Memory* (New York: Knopf, 1991), 290.

political system, for individual rights to win out in the long run over most forms of governmental control. In this way, whole areas of society, such as the press, have been thoroughly freed from supervision. But people cannot possess rights unless they exist, are alive. The physical body is the only thing that is obviously prior to the rights-bearing individual. So it is no wonder that the reformers who are having the most success in pushing state regulation forward are those who argue in terms of the consumer's health.

The French still like to smoke in public places. The government is not indifferent to health, but it is more concerned with promoting national solidarity. The integrity of the political body, not the well-being of the individual body, is the standard of legitimacy. The myth of indivisibility, the effort to make a citizenry that is not in contradiction with itself, renders suspect all forms of ethnicity other than Frenchness. For Americans, ethnicity is a personal "lifestyle" associated mainly with food and domestic culture. The French tend to see other groups' ethnic interests as a political threat. It is only with difficulty that they can separate ethnic culture from ethnic politics. They associate ethnicity with the aspiration for statehood.

In nineteenth- and twentieth-century Europe, ethnicity has in fact often served as an argument for dividing up existing states and remaking boundaries. But minority ethnicity has rarely taken this form in France. A French expert on education thus reveals more about his own republican mentality than about French politics when he belittles the efforts of some educators to promote the study of regional languages in public schools. After suggesting that the majority of French people willingly abandoned their regional languages as "obsolete and useless," he states:

> This collective and voluntary abandonment has been denounced only recently by French-speaking regionalists, educated people, elitists mourning for a lost identity. . . . They demand that their children learn local languages, which they themselves are sometimes unable to speak or are in the process of learning, in school. In some cases, e.g., the Corsicans, they demand compulsory teaching of the regional language to every child. . . . Clearly, this claim is more than cultural, it is nationalist, and comes from separatists who are fighting the indivisible Republic. Teaching half-dead or entirely dead regional languages is a means not only of preserving a heritage, but of building new nations.[16]

16. Antoine Prost, "Immigration, Particularism, and Republican Education," *French Politics and Society* 16/1 (1998): 16.

The author finds it impossible to believe that one would study a regional language without having treasonous thoughts. There is no sign of what Michael Walzer calls "the aesthetic endorsement of difference."[17] The author also never considers the possibility that knowing a regional language might enhance one's philosophical understanding of the dominant language. By politicizing language and treating the case of the Corsicans as if it were typical, he permits himself to adopt a repressive attitude toward all forms of regionalism. He reports with satisfaction that few French pupils opt to study regional languages; that immigrant students who wish to study their mother tongue get no assistance from the French government and are taught only by teachers who are paid by their country of origin; and that overall France is still far from adopting a philosophy of multiculturalism.

What are the practical consequences of this attitude toward ethnicity, of this fear of a state within a state? First, it shapes the treatment of foreigners. They are, for example, exposed to the indignities of an important political party, the National Front, that seeks to expel them in accordance with the principle of *La France pour les Français.* Such a party would be illegal in Germany because the constitution there forbids associations based on exclusionary and racist principles reminiscent of Nazism. France is the leading incubator of extreme right-wing politics in Europe today. It must be stressed: the National Front enjoys a degree of political legitimacy it could not attain elsewhere because it is a form of French republicanism. It draws its strength from the sense that France is a unity, that Frenchness is prior even to constitutional arrangements. The key difference of course is that other republicans are optimistic about the possibility of converting foreigners into Frenchmen, whereas the National Front regards immigrants as incapable of assimilation. This difference is important enough to mark a boundary between the National Front and other parties. It is, however, a difference of secondary importance compared to the common belief that France must be French. For this reason, the National Front could not be banned without throwing republicanism itself into confusion. Here too we have an impasse. It seems that foreigners in France will always face a hostile political system.

But the question matters not only to foreigners. As republican hos-

17. Michael Walzer, "The Politics of Difference: Statehood and Toleration in a Multicultural World," in *The Morality of Nationalism,* ed. Robert McKim and Jeff McMahan (New York: Oxford University Press, 1997), 246.

tility to regional languages shows, French citizens themselves may be treated as alien enemies when they publicly express their interest in forms of culture that are not sanctified by the national system of education. Here the history of the Jews is most instructive. Not that Jews are currently the worst scapegoat of French nationalism. Rather, their centuries-long presence in France makes them the best index of the *longue durée* of a pattern of injustice. On the one hand, the French were the first to formally emancipate the Jews, to admit them into equal citizenship (this in 1792). On the other hand, as Ira Katznelson points, America never emancipated the Jews because they had never been disenfranchised. Jews had full voting rights and were eligible for office even in colonial America. They attended universities and participated in state militias.[18]

More importantly, after emancipation, Jews continued to be a symbol of cultural recalcitrance and treason in France. The Dreyfus affair is only the best known example of this anti-Semitism. As Pierre Birnbaum has eloquently shown, hostility toward Jews as a threat to the unity of France has been a common threat running through all of the regimes in France, from the officially Catholic absolute monarchy to the officially secular republic of today. His discussion of the Vichy regime is particularly important, for he shows that French collaborators with the Nazis were often ardent republicans before France's defeat. There was, in other words, an easy conversion from democracy to deportation by means of the principle of national unity.[19] Today, strains of anti-Semitism are evident in the hostile reactions of French journalists and intellectuals to Jewish pleas to schedule important examinations so that they do not take place on the Sabbath (the French hold classes on Saturdays). Birnbaum has documented this hostility, as well as the self-righteous anger against Jews who have asked that political elections not be held on Passover (*La France imaginée*, 342–43). Of course, the French would never consider holding elections on Easter. The government is secular, but it is sensitive to the presence of Christianity and avoids unnecessary provocations. It is not sensitive, however, to other religions. With such a low threshold of tolerance for diversity, it produces conflicts that do not have to exist.

18. Ira Katznelson, "Between Separation and Disappearance: Jews on the Margins of American Liberalism," in *Paths of Emancipation: Jews, States, and Citizenship*, ed. Pierre Birnbaum and Ira Katznelson (Princeton: Princeton University Press, 1995), 166.

19. Pierre Birnbaum, *The Jews of the Republic: A Political History of State Jews in France from Gambetta to Vichy*, trans. Jane Marie Todd (Stanford: Stanford University Press, 1996).

France could probably benefit from a relaxation of its republican logic. To raise the threshold of tolerance for the public expression of diversity would probably ease some tensions. At the same time, it would enhance the country's cultural achievements and prestige to modify its educational system, at the university level, so as to make it more cosmopolitan. In the social sciences and humanities, French thought is largely folded in upon itself. A few first-rate experts study foreign cultures. But if one is in search of a critical mass of excellent scholars working on contemporary East European politics, or the Italian Renaissance, or ancient Chinese philosophy, one must turn to the countries in question, or else to Germany, Britain, or North America. It is particularly striking that French specialists in American history and literature are very rare. The Germans, who have large institutes devoted to American studies, are doing much better. The French seem to expect us to take a serious academic interest in their cultural patrimony, without taking much interest in ours. This disposition harms cultural exchange.

There is, however, no reason to belabor these points. For one thing, there are signs that the republican tradition is already softening and that pluralism is making some headway in the French educational system.[20] For another, a scholar should not pose as a prophet in a foreign land. The authentic question is what should be done at home to bring the polity and its educational system closer to a golden mean that combines national consciousness with appreciation for diversity. If the French have overemphasized nationality, that is no reason to fetishize diversity in the U.S. The fundamental problem in the U.S. is the lack of a method to address inequality and moral problems on the largest possible scale—the lack of a strong state empowered by a national philosophy. Multiculturalism deepens this problem instead of counterbalancing it.

The role of critical intellectuals, after all, is not to be part of "the people." In France, "the people" is French, so the role of intellectuals ought to be to think critically about Frenchness. In the U.S., "the people" are a plurality of individuals affirming their own rights, so the role of intellectuals should be to think critically about the problems of subjectivity and disunity in such a nation. The flaw in American multi-

20. This is Birnbaum's main argument in *La France imaginée.* I believe Birnbaum exaggerates the degree to which France is becoming like the United States. But he does reveal some significant changes.

culturalism is not its enthusiasm for diversity *per se*, but its complacency with regard to the problem of commonality. Multiculturalists deride any effort to define a common American value-system or system of civic responsibilities. The historian David Hollinger refers to "the pathological fear of the common" among many educators today.

> The value of civic nation-states in protecting rights and providing basic welfare is undervalued by proponents of postnationality. Against the view that the United States is more a container of ethno-racially defined cultures than a basis for an ethos of its own, I defend the notion of a national culture as an adhesive enabling diverse Americans to see themselves as sufficiently "in it together" to act on problems that are genuinely common.[21]

In other words, social reform, even of the piecemeal, locally-rooted kind that alone is possible in the U.S., cannot take place unless people arrive at a more common understanding of their nation's values and history. Fearful of any form of hierarchy, multiculturalism will not set any order of priorities, even for the reform of social injustices.

The history of the United States plainly shows that a vision of happiness based on the free exercise of individual rights is the basis of American culture. To explore the grander expressions of this vision—in political documents, philosophy, and art—should be part of a humanistic education in the United States. The national history also shows patterns of injustice. While many groups have suffered discrimination to some degree, only two of them, African Americans and Native Americans, have been systematically mistreated and excluded from the American dream over a long period of time. Attention to the history of these groups—but not necessarily any others—must also be a part of the American humanistic program.

Finally, education should deal with societies and value-systems that are not American at all. Without foreign reference points, one cannot grasp the existential tensions and creative limits of the American way. Thus, there is room for multicultural thinking; but multiculturalism, as the French well know, defeats its own progressive purpose.

21. David Hollinger, *Postethnic America* (New York: Basic Books, 1995), 14–15.

CHRISTIE McDONALD

Changing Stakes: Pornography, Privacy, and the Perils of Democracy*

As the millennium closes and a new one opens, the question of the changing boundaries between privacy and public morality has become an arena of intense controversy. My purpose in what follows is to explore briefly the ways in which certain twentieth-century arguments about sexuality and pornography look to the French Enlightenment for explanation and support, and how the different attitudes toward these issues in France and America focus on the relationship between freedom and equality. I am interested in the ways biopolitics, as a touchstone for expressing social and political malaise, can be argued as either liberating or harmful. My hypothesis is that the focus on sexual scandal, as it is transmitted through the media, both translates and fosters the uncertainty surrounding ethics in the sociopolitical sphere; in particular, the connection between the personal and the political for women as well as for men has been caught between an increasingly invaded private realm and a contested public morality. This has led to a mythification of national differences that stymies rather than furthers discussion among public intellectuals on the question of individual and social responsibility and on the kinds of interpretation necessary to meet the demands of the future.

DEBATES AROUND PORNOGRAPHY

In an article published in *The Nation* in 1993, journalist Carlin Romano fantasizes about raping Catharine MacKinnon, author of *Only Words*, as part of his research on the topic of her book, pornography. He imagines that *The Nation* publishes his article because of its commitment to free speech. He also imagines that another reviewer decides to rape

*I would like to thank Missy Schwartz for her assistance in the research for this article and Gary Wihl for his reading of the manuscript and very helpful suggestions.

YFS 100, *FRANCE/USA: The Cultural Wars,* ed. Ralph Sarkonak, © 2001 by Yale University.

MacKinnon physically: "He acts on the idea,"[1] and publishes his review in the *New York Review of Books*. Both authors go to trial and to jail, which suggests that words and acts carry the same value in MacKinnon's legal perspective. In support of his *ad hominem* argument, Romano refers to Lynn Hunt's preface to the collection of essays she edited, *The Invention of Pornography: Obscenity and the Origins of Modernity, 1500–1800*:

> One of the most striking characteristics of early modern pornography is the preponderance of female narrators. . . . The pornographic whore . . . is most often portrayed as . . . independent, determined, financially successful and scornful of the new ideals of female virtue and domesticity. Such texts, written by men, consequently elide the very sexual difference that was increasingly coming into vogue in medical tracts and domestic manuals.[2]

Hunt's book should be required reading for all law school courses dealing with pornography, Romano contends, because it stresses what MacKinnon ignores: "pornography's historic role in weakening the authority of the state."[3] In acting out the kind of backlash against women and feminism in popular culture and the media to which Susan Faludi has referred,[4] Romano's reference to Hunt's scholarly edition suggests more than a passing connection between early modern pornography in Europe and contemporary American debates about the role of the state in such matters.

Hunt focuses on pornography as a category of conflict and change,

1. Carlin Romano, "Between the Motion and the Act," *Nation*, 15 November 1993, 563. The article reviews three books: Catharine A. MacKinnon, *Only Words* (Cambridge: Harvard University Press, 1993); Cass R. Sustein, *Democracy and the Problem of Free Speech* (New York: Free Press, 1993); Lynne Hunt, ed., *The Invention of Pornography: Obscenity and the Origins of Pornography, 1500–1800* (New York: Zone Books, 1993).

2. Hunt, 38, cited in Romano. While Romano imputes these ideas to Hunt, he collapses summaries articulated by Hunt of articles within the edited book: the first reference is to the transgression of the role played by female narrators in defining sexual difference; the second refers to the pornographic whore in Aretino.

3. The provocative and deeply insulting article drew sharp responses from the Mens' Anti-Rape Resource Center, Men Against Pornography, as well as a protest letter from Lindsay Waters at Harvard University Press, MacKinnon's publisher: "[Romano's] argument, the attempted *reductio ad absurdum* that ends up in attempted rape, is philosophically wrong. The force of the review depends on the denial that words are sometimes acts. This denial is false. Romano's words perform an act." Letter to *Nation*, 24 November 1993.

4. Susan Faludi, *Backlash: The Undeclared War against American Women* (New York: Crown Publishers, 1991).

a cultural battle zone: "pornography names an argument, not a thing" (Hunt, 31). In her book she locates a passage from *before* to *after* the French Revolution, specifically noting that, prior to 1790, the function of pornography was to channel social and political criticism, whereas after the beginning of the French Revolution, the purpose of pornography was to arouse the reader sexually (90).[5] Sade was a key figure here in that he prepared the way for the modern "apolitical genre of pornography. . . . Pornography now became identified with a general assault on morality itself, rather than a specific criticism of the irrationalities of the *ancien régime* moral system" (301, 330). Pierre Klossowski wrote that the crimes of the Revolution constituted a kind of original sin after which legitimating morality would become more and more difficult. Hunt phrases the problem of pornography in sociopolitical terms: pornography participates in a democratizing effect in the transition from a male elite readership to a more popular one:

> Democracy was established against monarchy through pornographic attacks on the feminization of both the artistocracy and monarchy. It was accelerated in and after 1789 by especially vicious attacks against the leading female figure of the ancien régime, the queen herself. At the same time, the fraternal bonds of democracy were established—in pornography, at least and perhaps more broadly—through the circulation of images of women's bodies, especially through print media and the effect of visualization through pornographic writing. . . . Women were thus essential to the development of democracy and, in the end, excluded from it. [329]

How do women contribute to the foundation of democracy and then become excluded from it? Libertine literature of the eighteenth century has been described in terms of "cultural dissent," as Robert Darnton shows.[6] The books circulated "*sous le manteau*"; the "*mauvais livres*," "*marron*," or "*livres philosophiques*" posited the relationship between liberty and libertinism and necessitated free-thinking readers who could conceive of themselves as autonomous individuals.

The term *libertin* comes from the Latin *libertinus*. It appears in the 1400s in French writing and refers to the emancipation of freed slaves.[7]

5. See Jean-Marie Goulemot, *Ces livres qu'on ne lit que d'une main. Lecture et lecteurs de livres pornographiques au XVIIIe siècle* (Aix-en-Provence: Alinéa, 1991).

6. Robert Darnton, *The Forbidden Best-Sellers of Pre-Revolutionary France* (New York: Norton, 1996).

7. The meanings and history of the terms were collected from the *Le dictionnaire de l'ancienne langue française* and from the *Encyclopédie ou dictionnaire raisonné* (1765).

Freedom from the constraints of religion evolves into freedom from social constraints in general around 1600, and the noun *libertinage* enters the language, to mean both freedom from religious belief and an attitude of independence.[8] From the Gallican Catholic perspective, the libertines' position is both morally and eschatologically unsound; in the late 1600s the *libertin*'s appetite for independence is understood as freedom to move away from strictures and rules of conduct, then reinterpreted as a transgressive and threatening desire that first associates *libertin* and *libertinage* with sexual excess and debauchery.

The 1740s and the 1790s were periods of transformation that linked the intellectual with the erotic, the spiritual with the material. During this period of ferment at all levels (philosophical, social, and political), print culture played a crucial part in catalyzing change: the narratives of *causes célèbres* and notorious people, the *libelles*, the *mémoires judiciaires*—all enabled dissemination of information to the public.[9] At the same time, desacralization of monarchy and kingship opened a space in which the pornographic imaginary—without reproductive consequence—contested the hierarchical relationships of body and spirit, sexuality and metaphysics. With regard to gender, for example,

---

In the first religious connotation, the term referred to Sarrasin slaves who had converted to Christianity. In the early 1500s, *libertin* designates a group of Jews who had been captured by the Roman army, enslaved, and later set free and allowed to practice their faith once again, according to *Le grand dictionnaire historique, ou mélange curieux . . .* (compiled by Louis Moréri). For Biblical references, see Acts of the Apostles 6:9, 7:58.

8. Some of the major players were Théophile de Viau, Cyrano de Bergerac, Pierre Gassendi, François de La Mothe Le Vayer, and Charles Sorel. Certain members of this movement, for example, T. de Viau, *were* engaged in the sorts of liberated sexual practices that would characterize *libertins* and *libertinage* in the eighteenth century; all of the *libertins* of this period challenged social norms in one way or another. And it appears that society did not really condemn them; strong negative associations around *libertin* and *libertinage* did not begin to appear until the second half of the 1600s. See the *Dictionnaire de l'Académie française* (1694 edition) and the *Dictionnaire général et curieux* (1684; compiled by Cesar de Rochefort). The *Encyclopédie ou dictionnaire raisonné* gives 1674 as a turning point in the meaning of the term *libertinage*, a transition from independence to debauchery. As the 1700s begin and progress, the change becomes more and more definitive. The *Oxford English Dictionary* (1961) notes that the term "libertine" rarely being applied to women is obsolete.

9. See Gayot de Pitaval, *Causes célèbres et intéressantes . . . avec les jugements qui les ont décidées* (Paris: 1738–43; 20 volumes); Nicolas-Toussaint Moyne, ou le Moine, des Essarts, *Causes célèbres, curieuses et intéressantes de toutes les cours souveraines du Royaume avec les jugements qui les ont décidées. Supplément à l'essai sur l'histoire générale des tribunaux des peuples tant anciens que modernes, ou dictionnaire historique et judiciaire* (Paris: 1784). See also Sara Maza, *Private Lives and Public Affairs: The Causes Célèbres of Prerevolutionary France* (Berkeley: The University of California Press, 1993), and Darnton, 81–95.

Darnton reads the novel *Thérèse philosophe* as a story about a woman who pursues her own pleasure and controls her body, while challenging the *ancien régime*. This is a contestatory voice indicative of the sweeping transformations that would come with the end of kingship at the moment of the French Revolution. "Should Thérèse's account of sex therefore be dismissed as just another literary version of men exploiting women," Darnton asks, "as many feminist critics would have it?" (Darnton, 111). And he refers to the work of Catharine MacKinnon. Darnton has here touched on the vexed heritage for progressive political thought coming out of Enlightenment narrative. In grounding the agency of the individual woman in sexual prowess, pornographic texts such as this left a problematic legacy on the issues of gender, equality, and particularly inequality between genders.

What then is the relationship between eighteenth-century pornographic literature and current debates about pornography in the United States? What are the controversies today, and why have they become important to us? In order to address these questions, it is necessary to look at the most radical position opposing pornography today.

For Catharine MacKinnon, feminism plays a dissenting role in contemporary society, one that pornography suppresses: "Free speech silences free speech of women."[10] Pornography is not an expression in need of protection by the First Amendment; it is an action. This is what Frank Michelman of the Harvard Law School has called the "consequences model," which involves a time lapse before a "shutting up, or an inability to be credibly heard" takes effect.[11] The silencing is removed "both conceptually and in real time" from its effect. MacKinnon, Michelman, and others have worked to model the causal relationship between speech and harm in the anticipation of harmful consequences. While obscenity engages morality,[12] pornography in MacKinnon's view is a "political practice" that opposes the powerful and the powerless. MacKinnon is determined to move the terms of the debate away from "governmental authority threatening to suppress genius and dissent"—obscenity issues—to the violence of the gender imbalance located in pornography.

---

10. MacKinnon, in *The First Amendment Reader*, ed. John H. Garvey and Frederick Shauer (Saint Paul: West Publishing, 1992), 73.
11. Memo from Frank Michelman to Lindsay Waters.
12. Mackinnon's point is that "protecting pornography means protecting sexual abuse as speech, at the same time that both pornography and its protection have deprived women of speech, especially *speech* against sexual abuse" (*Only Words*, 10).

MacKinnon defines pornography as:

The graphic sexually explicit subordination of women through pictures or words that also includes women dehumanized as sexual objects, things, or commodities, enjoying pain or humiliation or rape, being tied up, cut up, mutilated, bruised, or physically hurt, in postures of sexual submission or servility or display, reduced to body parts, penetrated by objects or animals, or presented in scenarios of degradation, injury, torture, shown as filthy or inferior, bleeding, bruised, or hurt in a context that makes these conditions sexual. Erotica, defined by distinction as not this, might be sexually explicit materials premised on equality. [*First Amendment Reader*, 312]

These words pack a wallop, inflicting the sting of an aggressor on an aggressed woman. It should be noted that MacKinnon and other radical feminists center their main arguments on heterosexual pornography, giving little attention to other complex issues such as child pornography or gay pornography, or the more general problem of pornography on the internet. MacKinnon's first point is that the reality she seeks to uncover is not verbal, but experiential. "Pornography does not simply express or interpret experience; it substitutes for it. Beyond bringing a message from reality, it stands in for reality; it is existentially being there" (*Only Words*, 25). MacKinnon's second point is that pornography must be curtailed to create equality within society, and referring to the United States, she suggests that First Amendment issues have derailed the debate. "The First Amendment has grown as if a commitment to speech were no part of a commitment to equality and as if a commitment to equality had no implications for the law of speech" (MacKinnon, *Only Words*, 71). MacKinnon and Andrea Dworkin argue pornography as defamation and discrimination, not as a First Amendment question: "Pornography is a civil rights issue for women because pornography *sexualizes inequality*."[13] Free speech merely offends; pornography causes harm.

MacKinnon challenged United States law and repoliticized pornography by drafting a law with Andrea Dworkin for the city of Minneapolis, Minnesota,[14] based on pornography as a human rights viola-

13. Andrea Dworkin, "Pornography is a Civil Rights Issue for Women," *Journal of Law Reform* (21/1 & 2 Fall 1987, and Winter 1988): 63.

14. Hearings were held in Minnesota, Massachusetts, Indianapolis, and Los Angeles. See Catharine A. MacKinnon and Andrea Dworkin, *In Harm's Way: The Pornography Civil Rights Hearings* (Cambridge: Harvard University Press, 1997).

tion. Testimony in these hearings broke the silence of abused women's voices. Pornography was shown through testimony to be harmful because it is a matter of power and not simply freedom. For MacKinnon, there is no going back once it is established that pornography involves issues of harm and power. She is a statist and has challenged the laws on pornography, departing from classical liberalism in a way that makes liberals uncomfortable with the role of government in regulating the circulation of offensive material.

FREEDOM VERSUS EQUALITY

Whereas Catharine MacKinnon warns of an impending "collision" between "the law of equality" and the law of freedom of speech (*Only Words*, 71), Isaiah Berlin warned that in making choices within a democratic society, it may well not be possible to "have it all": to choose one value without diminishing or excluding another. Freedom, for example, is not equality or justice. Where ultimate values are at stake, there may not be clear and distinct solutions. Berlin put forth two forms of liberty: negative liberty, the space within which an individual or group may act without interference from others, and positive liberty, the question of by whom or what and how much one is to be ruled. The ideal of freedom encompassed both: rights protect the individual against inhuman infringement of the individual (or group) by any power, and at the same time set limits, make frontiers and rules to separate what is inhuman or inadmissible from what is humanly acceptable.[15] While Berlin leaned toward negative liberty, he understood that sacrifice is often necessary, that is, if the highest goal is freedom, then equality may suffer; if the highest goal is equality, then incursion into freedom may be necessary. He believed that freedom within democracy required some combination of the two. Ronald Dworkin espouses these two forms of freedom and argues that pornography has been fought using concepts other than freedom: religion, morality, and family values, for example. And he notes how the emergence of questions about race and gender have "transformed old alliances and divisions."[16] Citing MacKinnon's argument that "negative liberty for pornographers con-

15. Isaiah Berlin, *Four Essays on Liberty* (Oxford: Oxford University Press, 1969), 121–22, 164–65.

16. Ronald Dworkin, "Pornography, Feminism, and Liberty," in *Pornography: Private Right or Public Menace*, ed. Robert M. Baird and Stuart Rosenbaum (Buffalo: Prometheus Books, 1991), 167.

flicts not just with equality but with positive liberty as well," he concurs that "pornography leads to women's political as well as economic or social subordination" (R. Dworkin, 169). But Dworkin differs from MacKinnon in making a liberal argument: "Freedom of speech, conceived and protected as a fundamental negative liberty, is the core of the choice modern democracies have made, a choice we must now honor in finding our own ways to combat the shaming inequalities women still suffer" (R. Dworkin, 171).

The right to free speech was one of the most important articles of the 1789 *Declaration of the Rights of Man and the Citizen.* Robespierre exalted the French Revolution as "the first revolution to have been based on the theory of the rights of man."[17] In the struggle to work out whose principle of authority would emerge, the *Declaration* became a major arm in the movement toward the legitimation of the fledgling French nation. But the contradictions inherited from the Revolution go back to Rousseau, who charted the tension between defining the norms for collective power and the limitation of influence on the individual. The *general will* posited an ideal balance between dependence and independence in Rousseau's work and has been the subject of debate ever since he formulated the concept in the 1760s. As Marcel Gauchet writes of discussions about the *Declaration:* "The blind reversal that occurs in the inaugural move is profoundly significant: the will to assure absolutely the natural independence of individuals leads to the containment and complete subjugation of the will to social power" (*Revolution,* 121, my translation). In two instances, at least, purity of principle won out over questions of the social application: first, the question of universality as an autonomous principle conflicted with constitutional monarchy; second, the definition of how the universal subject was to be defined: as abstract individual or man in society. To wit, a privilege may not always be considered unjust even though in principle it infringes on the liberty of certain individuals; the question is, who predominates in the balance of power—the will of all or the general will in Rousseau's terms? Gauchet chronicles how this kind of choice arises throughout the discussions concerning formulations for the articles of the *Declaration* (*Revolution,* 142). The debate resolves itself in Article 4 of the *Declaration,* defining negative liberty, then putting the individual under collective control: "freedom is de-

17. Marcel Gauchet, *La révolution des droits de l'homme* (Paris: Gallimard, 1989). My translation.

fined as that which does not harm another, anyone else; thus, exercising each person's natural rights has as its only limit that which ensures the right of all other members of society to enjoy their rights. These limits can only be determined by law" (my translation).

Now if we look take a look at Article 4 of the *Declaration* as revised and parodied by Olympe de Gouges in her publication of *La déclaration des droits de la femme et de la citoyenne*, we see that it was written in September 1791, after the Assemblée adopted the Constitution of 1791 which excluded women from political rights. "Liberty and justice are defined as giving what belongs to another; thus the exercise of the natural rights of *woman* has as its limit only the tyranny which man imposes on her: these limits must be reformed by the laws of nature and reason."[18] What has Gouges changed? Not only has she added woman to the notion of universal man as in her version of Article 1 ("Woman is born free and remains by right equal to man"); she has added the concept of justice, and she has divided men and women into the powerful and the powerless, assuring a measure of protection for the weaker. Gouges clearly judges that the abstract principle not only may exclude certain men in society, but does exclude women. She calls not for a determination by the law, but for a reform through reason and nature.

Gouges's demand for the recognition of difference and a balance between right and duties had already been anticipated theoretically in questions asked by Sièyes and Grégoire: can duty or obligation be deduced from rights by others? Rights, they agreed, involve duties. But whose and which ones? Gauchet concludes that the *Declaration* contains within it both the first revolution, based on rights, but also a terrible realization of the inability to put into practice a system that would ensure both the rights of the collectivity *and* the rights of the individual (*Revolution*, 201). The lesson of the *Declaration* is that balance between equality and freedom involves a painful negotiation, and hence the questions of principle in the discussions raised, but did not solve, the inequities that remained.

That struggle continues in the debates about pornography, as the controversies surrounding the publication and criticism of Sade's works during the twentieth century amply demonstrate. The reading

18. "Les droits de la femme," Article 4 in *Opinions de femmes. De la veille au lendemain de la Révolution française.* Preface by Geneviève Fraisse (Paris: Côté-femmes, 1989), 52. My translation.

of the Enlightenment in general, and of Sade in particular, raises the question of the present, a subject that Michel Foucault and Guy Scarpetta have addressed. Foucault wrote about a kind of "blackmail" in twentieth-century thought that forces one to take a position for or against the Enlightenment.[19] Scarpetta describes a mythologized eighteenth century, reconstituted in parts newly sewn together in the present. Repeatedly coming to the realization of his Frenchness while in America, he locates the difference in an eighteenth century to which he is attached, and which has defined who he is, concluding that the French and American peoples have widely diverging collective imaginaries.[20] In North America, the eighteenth century that strikes Scarpetta (along with others) is marked by the burden of Puritan religion and spirit. It is complicated by the connection of virtue with politics (and the relationship to commerce), whereas the French eighteenth century links Enlightenment in a singular way with libertinism (A. Dworkin, "Pornography," 169).[21] Sade, among others, is a particularly French phenomenon.

THE MARQUIS DE SADE

Simone de Beauvoir asked whether or not we should burn Sade's work on the issue of freedom: "On the verge of his adult life he made a bru-

19. Michel Foucault, "What is Enlightenment," in *Michel Foucault: Ethics, Subjectivity and Truth*, ed. Paul Rabinow, trans. Robert Hurley and others (New York: The New Press, 1994), 313.

20. Guy Scarpetta, *Pour le plaisir* (Paris: Gallimard, 1998), 169–72. I thank Pierre Saint-Amand for comments on this passage.

21. J.G.A. Pocock writes: "It has been established that a political culture took shape in the eighteenth-century colonies which possessed all the characteristics of a neo-Harringtonian civic humanism. Anglophone civilization seems . . . to present the picture of a number of variants of this culture—English, Scottish, Anglo-Irish, New England, Pennsylvanian and Virginian, to look no further—distributed around the Atlantic shores. The Whig canon and the neo-Harringtonians, Milton, Harrington and Sidney, Trenchrad, Gordon and Bolingbroke, together with the Greek, Roman, and Renaissance masters of the tradition as far as values and concepts were . . . a civic and patriot ideal in which personality was founded in property, perfected in citizenship, but perpetually threatened by corruption." *The Machiavellian Moment: Florentine Political Thought and the Atlantic Republican Tradition* (Princeton: Princeton University Press, 1975), 507. In his analysis of the "Machiavellian moment," the confrontation of "virtue" and "corruption" (or "fortune"), the "paradigmatic legacy—concepts of balanced government, dynamic *virtù*, and the role of arms and property in shaping civic personality"—Pocock shows how the eighteenth century forged the modern and secular sense of history, transforming the Machiavellian vocabulary of "fortune" into "commerce" and opposing "virtue" with either "corruption" or "commerce." The dialectical conclusion of Enlightenment in Europe finds "a utopian perception of global space in America" (Pocock, viii–xix).

tal discovery that there was no reconciliation possible between his so-cial existence and his private pleasures."[22] For Beauvoir, what was at issue was not so much the opposition between the public and the pri-vate, but that which links the individual with the universal: "Can we, without renouncing our individuality, satisfy our aspirations to uni-versality? Or is it only by the sacrifice of our individual differences that we can integrate ourselves into the community?" (12) The problem concerns every person. If, for Sade, the differences are carried to the limit of outrage, Beauvoir claims that "it is the immensity of his liter-ary effort that demonstrates how passionately he wished to be accepted by the human community. . . . It is the paradox and, in a sense, the tri-umph of Sade that his persistent singularity helps to define the human drama in its general aspect" (12). Singularity is taken to mean both that which is idiomatic in Sade, but also that which defines him in the re-lation of the human to universality. And in Beauvoir's view, this is the ethical stance for which he took responsibility by writing literature, and what made him original.

Beauvoir answers the question: what is the relationship between the singularity of an individual and universality? by stating: "the part of him that is free." In other words, Sade is important because his ex-cesses give access to that part of each of us that is common to all. While Beauvoir examines how class interests translate into universal princi-ples for Sade, the hierarchical relationship and any potential harm be-tween sexual partners remain outside her interest. One can even say that they remain unanalyzed and virtually unrecognized as a problem within the argument. While she accepts that "the original intuition which lies at the basis of Sade's entire sexuality, and hence his ethic, is the fundamental identity of coition and cruelty" (31), the issue of gen-der or equality does not figure into her argument; the question of free-dom is primary here.

Jean-Jacques Pauvert fought to publish Sade's works on similar grounds: as an act of freedom, freedom of expression.[23] Censorship,

---

22. Simone de Beauvoir, *Faut-il brûler Sade?*, trans. Paul Dinnage (New York: Grove Press, 1954), 15.

23. At the appeal, Georges Bataille, André Breton, Jean Cocteau, and Jean Paulhan, with support from Heine, Gilbert Lely, and Pierre Klossowski, were witnesses. Pauvert won on appeal and the fine imposed during the initial trial was rescinded, but the re-mainder of the seized books by Sade were sent to the Bibliothèque Nationale. See Jean-Jacques Pauvert, "L'affaire Sade," in *Nouveaux (et moins nouveaux) visages de la cen-sure. Suivi de L'affaire Sade* (Paris: Les belles lettres, 1994).

which had been abolished in France in 1881, was reinstated in 1958, and Pauvert was taken to court for having published the works of Sade from 1947 on.[24] Writing in 1994, Pauvert declared that freedom of expression is for everyone, or no one—and he referred to *The Declaration of the Rights of Man and Citizen* (Pauvert, 32). Seemingly oblivious to the American legal debates about pornography, he proclaimed that "we all know that pornography is a danger to no one," (36–37, my translation). Pauvert brushes strangely close to Romano's written attack on MacKinnon asserting: "In 1971, one knows the difference between acts and their literary description." (Pauvert, 37, my translation).[25]

When Andrea Dworkin denounces Sade the author, by contrast, it is in the name of a violence, transmitted by literature, whose effect can be measured: "Sade's advocacy and celebration of rape and battery have been history's sustaining themes. Sade's spectacular persistence as a cultural force has been because of, not despite, the virulence of the sexual violence toward women in his work and his life."[26] And she, too, generalizes, although very differently from either Beauvoir or Pauvert: "Sade's work embodies the common values and desires of men" (A. Dworkin, 99). It is the *man* in Sade that exhibits violence, according to this argument, and pornography cannot be dissociated from it. Dworkin separates Sade from the erotic literature of the mid-eighteenth century that linked the autonomy of the individual with the mores of the libertine.

> Sade's importance . . . is not as dissident or deviant: it is as Everyman, a designation the power-crazed aristocrat would have found repugnant but one that women, on examination, will find true. In Sade, the authentic equation is revealed: *the power of the pornographer is the power of the rapist/batterer is the power of the man.* [A. Dworkin, 100]

24. See Pierre Klossowski, *Sade mon prochain* (Paris: Seuil, 1947); Maurice Blanchot, *Lautréamont et Sade* (Paris: Minuit, 1949); Georges Bataille, *L'érotisme* (Paris: Minuit, 1957), 183–218, and *La littérature et le mal* (Paris: Gallimard, 1957), 113–40; Phillipe Sollers, "Sade dans le texte," in *L'écriture et l'expérience des limites* (Paris: Seuil, 1968), 48–66; Roland Barthes, *Sade, Fourier, Loyola* (Paris: Seuil, 1971). See also Francis Ferguson, "Sade and the Pornographic Legacy," *Representations* 36 (Fall 1991): 1–22; Jane Gallop, *Intersections: A Reading of Sade with Bataille, Blanchot and Klossowski* (Lincoln: University of Nebraska Press, 1981); and Laurence L. Bongie, *Sade: A Biographical Essay* (Chicago: University of Chicago Press, 1998).

25. The same year, Pauvert published another pornographic text, *L'enfer du sexe*, not because of the value, literary or other, of the book, but on principle.

26. Andrea Dworkin, *Pornography: Men Possessing Women* (New York: G. P. Putnam's Sons, 1979), 99.

For some like Andrea Dworkin, pornography stands in as the authoritatively emblematic "legal text" of patriarchy. But Robin West makes the case that "women's experience of pornography is contradictory" and contradictions form a part of patriarchy, "since patriarchy is the political rule [that] women inhabit by virtue of their sex."[27] Again, we see a totalizing move on West's part: all legal texts engender conflicted reactions about oppression and liberation. Yet, she ascribes the split among feminists on pornography to the *indeterminacy* of its status. That is, American feminists have divided on the nature and the extent of the causal relationship between pornography and male sexual violence; they have differed about the importance of pornography to patriarchy and the way in which it may inhibit progress for women; they have split on the meaning of pornographic texts and images in the portrayal of violence and rape, as opposed to scenes of consensual sex. Even the significance of the "experience of contradiction" for feminists is subject to debate, particularly in the action-oriented forum of legal modification. Although both sides claim to be feminist, the point is that these arguments are less about feminism than about legalism. Here we see the way in which, within the American context, legal change becomes a way of channeling philosophical, political, and social discourse by attempting to limit behavior through the law.

When Drucilla Cornell makes the case against MacKinnon's view (and implicitly Andrea Dworkin's as well) of pornography on legal and philosophical grounds, she invokes an underlying psychoanalytic model of the subject: pornography communicates an unconscious scene of fantasy.[28] Sade's belief that knowledge could provide mastery over a feared woman was part of a fantasy, itself the condition of the pornographic scene. Cornell's argument is that without the fear (of castration, for example), there would be no reason for pornography. And while pornography is about sexual difference (a binary in need of rather strong revision), Cornell maintains that *the law can only do so much*; it is important to find more ways to symbolize the feminine. Thus Cornell takes MacKinnon to task for behaviorist assumptions and a belief that there is a *truth of what men want*. "I argue that pornography signifies fantasy. Fantasies themselves are not separate from reality."[29]

27. Robin West, "Pornography as Legal Text," in *For Adult Users Only*, ed. Susan Gubard and Joan Hoff (Bloomington: University of Indiana Press, 1989), 111.

28. Drucilla Cornell, *The Imaginary Domain* (New York: Routledge, 1995); see also Cornell, *Abortion, Pornography and Sexual Harassment* (New York: Routledge, 1995).

29. Cornell's argument is that "one brand of linguistic philosophy . . . does not ade-

The problem is one of the gender hierarchy and how it *furthers* or *limits* thinking about *equality* and *freedom*. Is the figure of the victim the only figure of feminine difference? Are there affirmative metaphors for the feminine, as the irreducible other?[30] Cornell calls for a recognition of femininity through the opening of a different psychic space other than the one that has been imposed by the dominant culture.

The link between sex and violence in all of these arguments is also about the violence of hierarchy during times of transition and change. What is at stake in the debates around pornography is the negotiation between legal theory based on a universal notion of what is moral and a sense of the ethical that is nonfoundational. Reworking the engagement of feminism with deconstruction to offer a sense of "groundless solidarity," Diane Elam writes of an ethical commitment without belief in the authority of an absolute moral standard:

> The ethics resulting from the engagement of feminism and deconstruction do not set a moral standard or ideal, nor do they propose shared moral perspectives for women. In this respect, ethics would not have its foundation in sexual difference. It would be more accurate to think of the work of deconstruction and feminism as *creating* an ethics that has responsibility to issues of sexual difference.[31]

Creation is not opposed to authority, but, rather, is construed as a kind of side-stepping operation whereby authoritative pronouncements (about truth, morality, and the essence of woman) require "justice in singular cases," a social justice consonant with an unfinished project that must be unceasingly renewed.[32]

---

quately address the way in which social fantasies, particularly those about how one is gendered or sexed, are at the basis of our symbolic order and therefore our form of life . . . I believe that imagination is itself a crucial aspect of what constitutes reality. Women must have this imaginary domain protected" (Cornell, *The Imaginary Domain*, 157).

30. Cornell, *Transformations: Recollective Imagination and Sexual Difference* (New York: Routledge, 1993). Cornell points out that "because of the legal interpretation of sex to be gender, the differential treatment [of gay men and lesbians] is an inequality not reached by the current form of discrimination law" (*At the Heart of Freedom* [Princeton: Princeton University Press, 1998], 4).

31. Diane Elam, *Feminism and Deconstruction: Ms. en abyme* (New York: Routledge, 1994), 117.

32. Elam refers to the distinction proposed by Jacques Derrida between law and justice: "law (*droit*) is not justice. Law is the element of calculation and it is just that there be law, but justice is incalculable, it requires us to calculate with the incalculable; and aporetic experiences are the experiences, as improbable as they are necessary, of justice, that is to say of moments in which the decision between just and unjust is never insured by a rule" (Jacques Derrida, *Cardozo Law Review* II/506 [July/August 1990]: 947).

The problem of how to bridge feminist theory and practice brings us back to issues raised earlier with the *Declaration of the Rights of Man and Citizen* concerning the relationship of the abstract principles of egalitarianism to concrete inequalities. The image of the strong women of the libertine tradition in pre-Revolutionary France finds few counterparts in contemporary French public life. The lag in participation of women in French politics—ranking in representation within the National Assembly far behind other European and non-European countries—has been a source of concern on many levels.[33] Perhaps it is in the very radicalism of French thought that one can find the explanation. Mona Ozouf writes that "For the French, the only alternative to exclusion seems to be complete assimilation and absolute equality. Since that equality on principle was contradicted by experience, women were slow to capitalize on it and make it a reality" (271). And she sees the force of this belief in equality as positive in the long run: "The force of that equality also lies in its radicalism, so that the apparent disadvantage can in the end turn into an advantage" (271). The focus on universalism rather than on particularism locates the most striking difference between French and American arguments about political representation as well as feminism, and it has polarized many intellectuals. Ozouf argues the case for French feminism which, in resisting communitarianism, evokes both the "memory of the aristocratic world, which initiated happy exchanges between the sexes, and the reality of an 'extreme democracy,' which places no limit on the idea of egalitarianism" (281). It is in the deliberate subordination of differences that a new tack in French feminism has emerged, avoiding the perceived pitfalls of certain American strategies in the search for equality.[34] The *parité* movement has reinvigorated feminism within political life to overcome the failures of universalism through a differential argument that nevertheless avoids particularism: the universal difference of the sexes. By refusing the concept and tactics of American affirmative action (translated as "positive discrimination"), in favor of a concrete concept of universality in line with the rights of mankind (an equal number of candidates from each sex for elections), the Parity movement hopes to promulgate equality in political representation

33. Mona Ozouf, *Women's Words: Essays on French Singularity*, trans. Jane Marie Todd (Chicago: University of Chicago Press, 1997), 267.
34. "The result is a paricular society, where the demand for equality among individuals remains fundamental, but can be combined with an emphasis on differences, which are always held to be subordinate" (Ozouf, 81–82).

and counter the *de jure* androcentrism of abstract universalism (found in Beauvoir's work) and its *de facto* effects within political life.[35] This is an activist and pragmatic move from within the Left in France, different from the problems of the American Left fraught with postimpeachment fatigue syndrome.

LEFT, RIGHT, DEMOCRACY

The ability to discern Left from Right on issues such as abortion, welfare, and crime, during the year 1999, has, as the *New York Times* pointed out, citing Francis Fukuyama, "collapsed."[36] The lines have been crossed, making political assessments often more difficult both to understand and to formulate. Fukuyama attributes the "end of history" to the emergence of the market-driven economy within democracy. Some assume an antirelativist position with respect to the legacy of the 1960s.[37] For others, such as Katha Pollitt, a columnist for *The Nation*, the dimming of the Left as a consequence of the fall of communism leaves nevertheless a "commitment to equality."[38]

The dividing and crossing of paths between Left and Right found one of its more quixotic moments when Catharine MacKinnon was accused of "getting into bed" with the Right on the issue of pornography. MacKinnon responded by showing how the pole-bending between Right and Left finds common cause. When Rush Limbaugh accused her of equating sex with rape, MacKinnon countered that such a false statement was "political libel," designed to discredit her in "a community in which sex is the secular religion."[39] What gives common cause in this argument is "the real threat to male dominance posed by this law" (MacKinnon, "Left and Right," 145). Astonishment at the convergence of Right and Left comes out of an expectation that they should diverge. Indeed, the terms go back as far the Constituant Assembly of September 1789 where sitting to the left or right carried not only hierarchical position (the nobles, the third estate), but political implications as well.

35. See Sylviane Agacinski, *Politique des sexes* (Paris: Seuil, 1998). This is an important, positive argument on philosophical grounds for the political movement called parity.

36. Cited in *New York Times*, 13 July 1999, Sunday Week in Review, sect. 4.

37. Gertrude Himmelfarb, *One Nation, Two Cultures: A Moral Divide* (New York: Knopf, 1999).

38. Cited in *New York Times*, 11 July 1999, Sunday Week in Review, sect. 4.

39. MacKinnon, "Pornography Left and Right," *Harvard Civil Rights-Civil Liberties Law Review* 30/1 (Winter 1995): 144.

If what began as ceremony became political,[40] then apprehension at the end of the twentieth century about the collapsing of the Left/Right distinction may reveal the extent to which privacy issues have taken precedence over issues of state.

The Clinton scandal involving Monica Lewinsky brought into sharp relief controversies that took a dramatic form in a human story. It occupied the press during much of 1998, ending with an impeachment trial, and ushered in the last year of the twentieth century with acquittal by the Congress. The problem was that the relationship between the president of the United States and a young intern was both *consensual and unequal;* it was a combination that put people of many persuasions ill at ease. Whatever the *quid pro quo,* it came from the wrong side; the young intern was demanding a job. The muddiness of the situation made difficult any clear-cut position for many liberal feminists, and this left them open to attack from a newly constituted feminist Right that accused liberal feminists of faltering on principles. This was a change in position from the charge that feminists do not distinguish between consensual sex and coerced sex. The Right suddenly began to sound, on the question of sexual harassment, like those they had for so long opposed.[41]

To blame the Clinton scandal on feminists for having opened the area of the personal to public scrutiny was a way of blaming an effect of change for the problem it unearthed; some saw this as progress, while others situated the root of the problem in a shift they labeled tragic during the 1960s. It was not *because of feminists, but because feminists inaugurated an examination of accepted mores and revealed the silences that surrounded private relationships, that changes within society began.* The goal of second generation feminists had been to expose the invisible inequalities within society and make them visible. Media hounding of public figures (beginning with the exposure of Gary Hart's private life when he was running for political office) was a different issue. It raised the question of how much knowledge of sexual behavior tells about *character,* and what the relationship is between character and position.

---

40. MacKinnon refers to Thomas Carlyle, *The French Revolution: A History* (New York: The Modern Library, 1934), 174, and takes the definition of "center" from the *Oxford English Dictionary.*

41. Linda Chavez called the Clinton-Lewinsky scandal "the most important sexual harassment case in U.S. history" (Chavez, quoted in Pete Beinart, "Hypocrites: The Right's Newfound Feminism," *The New Republic* [30 March 1998]: 9).

Gloria Steinem countered that feminists are indeed able to distinguish consensual from nonconsensual sex in a measured fashion: "welcome sexual behavior is about as relevant to sexual harassment as borrowing a car is to stealing one."[42] And she pointed to the real harassers of Monica Lewinsky: first the F.B.I. agents who detained her at the Ritz in January 1998, without a lawyer present; then, Kenneth Starr, who used brutal tactics in pursuing the president through the former intern. On both sides of the Atlantic, the Starr report was likened to a pornographic novel,[43] destined to "inflame" public opinion;[44] some compared it to "vaudeville"[45] and Starr himself to a "religious fundamentalist," a "pornocratic ayatollah" dangerously out of control.[46] In what seemed to some like a reversal of the feminist position that "the personal is political," Steinem argued for keeping sexual behavior private. Opinion polls showed that not only was that what "the American people" wanted, but that lying in such circumstances could be condoned, at least politically, since the President was by all accounts doing his job well. American public opinion was thus consonant with what opponents came to call the "French solution."[47] Coded positively, this solution indicated a way of being discreet about private sexual matters; coded negatively private character was excluded from the judgment of leadership.

One columnist queried: "Will this spectacle teach us to seek and elect leaders of personal rectitude for our country, or will 1998 be remembered as a year-long course in how to be French?"[48] Such comments conjure up ways in which odd or deviant sexual behavior, or its effects, have long been attributed to foreign cultures, for example to the French for the Anglo-American tradition. Dictionaries of slang docu-

42. Gloria Steinem, "Feminists and the Clinton Question," *New York Times,* 22 March 1998, Op-Ed page.

43. Patrick Sabatier, *Libération,* 14 September 1998.

44. See William Bennett, *The Death of Outrage: Bill Clinton and the Assault on American Ideals* (New York: The Free Press, 1998).

45. Daniel Soulez-Larivière, "Clinton mais aussi Juppé, Fabius," *Le nouvel observateur,* 31 August 1998.

46. Pascal Bruckner, "Les deux Amérique," *Le monde,* 30 September 1998. See Eric Fassin, "Le roi médiatique américain est nu," *Le monde,* 21 September 1998. Fassin remarked on the power of the media, relayed by the justice system, in the name of morality and truth. The danger is that one might take the truth of the media to be *the* truth.

47. David Broder, "The French Solution," *Denver Post,* 28 January 1998, second edition.

48. Christopher Matthews, "Clinton v. America?" Review of *The Death of Outrage,* by William J. Bennett, *Weekly Standard,* 7 September 1998.

ment the terms relegating sexual practices in general and fellatio in particular to the French: "French cap" or "safe" (condom); "French kiss"; "French," "French language expert," "French way," "French tricks" (fellatio); "French by injection" (gay fellatio); "French love."[49] Also associated with this kind of negative stereotyping is venereal disease (mostly syphillis): "French disease" (late sixteenth through late eighteenth century), "French marbles" (late sixteenth century), "French pox" (early sixteenth through late eighteenth century), "being Frenchified" (late seventeenth through the nineteenth century). Many of these have their counterparts in French, with terms such as *capote anglaise* (condom). Expressing it in positive terms, with an emerging historical sense from the libertine tradition of Enlightenment France, one might say that the acceptance of sexuality concurs with a secular view that the private world of the individual is off-limits to public scrutiny (Agacinsky, 159). It is the question of privacy and its relation to the public world that was at the heart of the polarized controversy around Clinton.

William Bennett best expressed the outraged view of those on the Right for whom character was the issue.[50] Distinguishing American politics, in which "morality is central," from European attitudes, Bennett excoriates the "culture of permissiveness" (quoting John Silber) in the name of American ideals. "Europeans may have some things to teach us about, say, wine or haute couture. But on matters of morality in politics, America has much to teach Europe" (Bennett, 9). The threats that Americans now face in this view are not so much those from the outside; they are the problems that have been interiorized: "the threats are from within. They are . . . difficult to detect, . . . insidious: decadence, cynicism, and boredom" (Bennett, 130). If one had difficulty distinguishing the Right from the Left on other issues, attitudes about Clinton were split in such a way as to prohibit consensus. Richard Posner goes so far as to call the Clinton controversy America's Dreyfus Affair. With this difference: he says that Clinton was "as guilty as Dreyfus was innocent."[51] In this view, the emotional charge, a hold-

---

49. Jonathon Green, *The Cassell Dictionary of Slang* (London: Cassell, 1998).

50. "It is said that private character has virtually no impact on governing character; that what matters is a healthy economy; that moral authority is defined solely by how well a president deals with public policy matters; that America needs to become more European (read: more 'sophisticated in its attitude about sex')." (William Bennett, *Outrage*, 8).

51. Richard Posner, *An Affair of State* (Cambridge: Harvard University Press, 1999), 10.

over from Puritanism, rendered the country dysfunctional for the duration of the investigation and the impeachment trial.

At issue in the question of character is the president as role model. Whereas in other countries, the head of state and principal executive are delegated to different people, in the United States they are wrapped up in one person. The defendant, William Jefferson Clinton, needed another scheme of reference to make his defense. That it was not based on "consensual truth" is what outraged Republicans and many Democrats, who felt that a president's political survival had risen not only above issues of individual ethical principles but above democratic social and political goals as well. Clinton lied to his family, his close associates, and the nation. Clinton lied in a deposition to the Grand Jury in the Paula Jones case.[52] But neither strict legalist arguing, nor partisan politics between Republicans and Democrats, nor fixed moral positioning could deal with the new situation that had been created by the independent counsel, Kenneth Starr. Starr himself became a sparring partner equal to Clinton. In a column titled "Abroad at Home: Pattern Of Deception," Anthony Lewis commented on Starr's testimony to Congress: "It was a pattern of evasion, stonewalling, falsification." Starr was not just Clinton's equal. He was more dangerous by far: "Some of Mr. Starr's defenders argue that it does not matter what he did—only his conclusions count. That way lies the rot of liberty for all of us. To say that a prosecutor may abuse witnesses and violate the law in pursuit of his quarry is to forget bitter lessons of history."[53]

Clinton himself indicated the differing levels at which one might understand what was occurring. In resisting what he labelled the truth of partisan attack on the part of Starr and the Republicans, he gave himself over to semiotics, in which he showed himself to be a rather deft practioner, dancing around the legalistic definition of what constitutes sexual relations as it had been defined in the Paula Jones trial.[54] According to the definition, Clinton had not "engaged" in sex with Monica Lewinsky since sexual intercourse never occurred. In one of the key

52. Judge Susan Webber Wright fined President Clinton for lying to the Grand Jury.
53. *New York Times*, 24 November 1998.
54. "For the purposes of his deposition, a person engages in 'sexual relations' when the person knowingly engages in or causes . . . contact with the genitalia, anus, groin, breast, inner thigh, or buttocks of any person with an intent to arouse or gratify the sexual desire of any person. . . . 'Contact' means intentional touching, either directly or through clothing." (Clinton 1/17/98 Depo. At 22–23; 849-DE00000586 [Clinton Dep. Ex. 1, cited in Starr Report, 202]).

moments of Clinton's grand jury testimony in the investigation by independent counsel Starr, the following, now famous dialogue took place:

> Q: Mr. President, I want to . . . briefly go over something you were talking about with Mr. Bittman. The statement of your attorney, Mr. Bennett, at the Paula Jones deposition. . . . Counsel is fully aware that Ms. Lewinsky has filed, has an affidavit which they are in possession of saying that there is absolutely no sex of any kind in any manner, shape or form, with President Clinton. That statement is made by your attorney in front of Judge Susan Webber Wright correct?
>
> A: That's correct.
>
> Q: That statement is a completely false statement. Whether or not Mr. Bennett knew of your relationship with Ms. Lewinsky, the statement that there was no sex of any kind in any manner, shape or form, with President Clinton, was an utterly false statement. Is that correct?
>
> A: *It depends on what the meaning of the word is is.* If the—if he—if is means is and never has been, that is not—that is one thing. If it means there is none, that was a completely true statement.[55] [My emphasis]

The distinction made by Clinton had to do not with representation, but with time and the kind of truth the present tense accords. William Safire exalted (as one commited to "language dodge") in the celebration of grammar becoming "newsworthy" for Americans who had little sense of their language. He invoked the history of philosophy: "The present third-person singular of the verb 'to be' comes from the Latin *esse*, as in Bishop George Berkeley's *esse est percipi*, 'to be is to be.' It's a short jump from *esse* to is. Mr. Clinton's formulation of 'what is is' lends itself to metaphysical discussions about being and essence, and will surely be the title of tracts about virtual reality in the age of image."[56] Virtual reality in its broad sense for the age of the image—such is the reality of the media spinning out global narratives from grief (Princess Diana, John F. Kennedy Jr.), to crisis and tragedy (Kosovo, Rwanda), to political campaigns. Turning a deaf ear, however, to any such speculation about the media context in which truth is constructed from images, the questioner returned to the temporal dimension, asking

55. Cited from *New York Times*, 22 September 1998, 1; transcription for the House Judiciary Committee by Deposition Services, a private transcription firm.
56. William Safire, "On Language: Alone with 'Alone,' or What 'Is' Is," *New York Times Sunday Magazine*, 11 October 1998.

whether the president's attorney, Mr. Bennett, was "aware of this tense-based distinction." In a formulation that is quoted less frequently, the questioner shot back caustically, querying the line between the literal and the figurative: "Do you mean today that because you were not engaging in sexual activity with Ms. Lewinsky during the deposition that the statement of Mr. Bennett might be literally true?"

> A: No, sir. I mean that at the time of the deposition, it had been . . . well beyond any point of improper contact between me and Ms. Lewinsky. So that anyone generally speaking in the present tense, saying there is not an improper relationship, would be telling the truth if that person said there was not, in the present tense; the present tense encompassing many months. That's what I meant by that. Not that I was—I wasn't trying to give you a cute answer, that I was obviously not involved in anything improper during a deposition.[57]

The questioner queries Clinton's understanding of the oath: "You've told us that you understand your obligation then, as it is now, to tell the whole truth, sir. Do you recall that?" And Clinton replies: "I took the oath here." And interrupting, "You even read me a definition of the oath."

On both sides, legally, the question of definition was then determining for the meaning of sexuality as well as for truth. In a democracy not beholden to divine truth, this kind of consensual definition is meant to be binding. This is not only a question of the relative moral value of certain actions, but of their importance within the polity.

The question of words and their relative meanings is about the power to create and control reality—it is presumably the reason some people write fiction to reach truth. One commentator framed his question about Clinton's language and the question of social truth thus: "Has the President read too much French literary theory? Is he our first postmodernist, poststructuralist, deconstructionist leader, averring that objectivity is impossible, meaning self-contradictory, and reality socially constructed through language?"[58] His answer was "no." Clinton has understood that "language does have a systematic though complex relation to reality. His semantic arguments, if ultimately unsuccessful, have shown an acute understanding of the logic and psychology of language" (Pinker). That is, interpretation of meaning in

57. *New York Times*, 22 September 1998, 3; transcription for the House Judiciary Committee by Deposition Services, a private transcription firm.
58. Steven Pinker, *New York Times*, 3 October 1998.

language depends upon temporal sequences understood by both speakers, as well as a common context to which they refer. The question framed Clinton's arguments about truth in terms of theoretical controversies in philosophy, literature, religion, and even cultural studies. Clinton's aporetical style, isolating the present as separate and separable from past and future, was well known to confessors of sin like Saint Augustine. And Paul Ricoeur has analyzed the ways in which temporal speculation finds resolution in poetry and prayer, but not in theory, or in politics for that matter.[59] Marking out the present, determining one space for the private and another for what was public, Clinton attempted a weak argument in the context of social and political life. He was banking on the necessity for "consensual" speaking to allow him to retreat within the context of legal sparring. In so doing, the President walked a line between some kind of truth and the resistance to a scenario that would spell the death of his presidency: conviction through impeachment. The presupposition on the president's side was that the independent counsel's investigation was politically motivated. So the question for Congress and the American public became: in that circumstance, what kind of truth can there be? And what kind of harm does such lying bring upon the nation? The Republicans took the view that the nation had been harmed. The Democrats argued that there was a near coup under way to unseat an elected president through an investigation into sexual behavior that was largely politically motivated.

In his testimony, Clinton refused to engage in detailed discussion of his sexual encounters with Monica Lewinsky. By contrast, Lewinsky spelled out in excruciating detail the nature of the sexual relationship in order to fulfill her immunity agreement. Congress released the material on the web, and the Starr Report gave an exceptionally detailed account of the sexual relationship. Some considered it a pornographic document. Reactions to the release of the Starr Report in *Libération* and *Le nouvel observateur* invoked past collective hysterias, from the Spanish Inquisition to Stalin,[60] to McCarthyism[61]—the

59. Paul Ricoeur, *Temps et récit. L'intrigue et le récit historique* (Paris: Seuil, 1983), vol. 1, 24.

60. See Bernard Svetta, *Le nouvel observateur,* 17–23 September 1998; Chantal de Rudder, *Le nouvel observateur,* 17–23 September 1998; *Libération,* 17–23 September 1998, 28.

61. See Alan Dershowitz, *Sexual McCarthyism: Clinton, Starr, and the Emerging Constitutional Crisis* (New York: Basic Books, 1988).

reference being no longer to religion or communism, but to sex.[62] Alarmed by the sight of the most powerful nation in the world going off the tracks, one commentator analyzed the crossing of Left and Right in terms of cultural conflict: "The real battleground has become 'cultured,' that is, in fact very political."[63] As a product of the 1960s, Clinton, favoring abortion rights, the rights of homosexuals, and the rights of minorities, came under attack from a moral Right that viewed his own "hedonism" in line with "moral cynicism, arrogance and manipulation."[64]

The often caustically mocking columnist Maureen Dowd was particularly brilliant about the Lewinsky and Clinton scandal, situating the ongoing drama smack in the French libertine tradition:

> In the Washington version of *Les Liaisons Dangereuses*, two cynical middle-aged women, Linda Tripp and Lucianne Goldberg, manipulated and betrayed Monica Lewinsky. The Republicans tried to paint Monica as an innocent child, turned into damaged goods by President Valmont, but she was miscast.[65]

Dowd's titles touched on the nerve that the independent counsel had hoped to excite: "Liberties: Legacy of Lust," "Liberties: Sex and Self-Pity," "Liberties: F.O.B.'s: Femmes of Bill," "Liberties: Soft-Porn Nation," and the last, "Liberties: Choking on Lust." In these analyses, few were spared. But according to Dowd, the real pornographer, the one whose imagination was "enflamed" by Lewinsky's thong underwear, whose obsession with the young woman led to the ruin of her private life (as well as her family's) and threatened the presidency, was not Clinton, but Starr.[66] Lewinsky is playfully portrayed as a libertine not only because of her open and aggressive sexual proclivities, but because she is "something of a philosopher," akin to certain pre-Sadian heroines of erotic literature in the middle of the French eighteenth century. This was also the impression she projected in an interview with Barbara Wal-

62. *Le monde,* 14 September 1998.

63. Patrick Sabatier, *Libération,* 14 September 1998.

64. Americans along with Europeans were sensitive to abusive monarchical analogies and other historical models. And during the impeachment hearings in the House of Representatives, Congressmen spoke of a coup d'état. See Michael Lind, "The Court Inquisitor," *Mother Jones,* 10 August 1999, 1–7.

65. Maureen Dowd, "Liberties: Choking on Lust," *New York Times,* 28 February 1999.

66. Maureen Dowd, "Liberties: Legacy of Lust," *New York Times,* 23 September 1998.

ters on *20/20* after the crisis was over. Dowd presents Lewinsky the "relativist," reflecting on the question of truth in the context of hamburgers and ketchup:

> "But think about the truth—O.K.? Think about truth. Truth is synonymous with good. Truth is supposed to be good. . . . O.K.?" . . . "If truth is synonymous with good, then truth is good and good is God, O.K.? If all those things are synonymous, then the right thing to do is not hurt someone." "That's true. . . . So the truth, well, what is truth? I mean, I'm not trying to have an existential conversation with you."[67]

Lewinsky expresses this belief in a world where good and truth are equated to the very person (the President) who is unable to stop the political firestorm that followed his ensnarement. "The truth is—the truth is—what it should be," opines Lewinsky (cited in Dowd, "Liberties: Truth and Ketchup"). In the best of all possible worlds, perhaps private scenarios would only exist in the present and women in love would find that truth "is" what it should be. But the American drama of the year of scandal and impeachment showed how difficult it was to make sense of such unprecedented events.[68]

Many invoked literary precedent. Philippe Sollers bantered about the magically unrepresentable organ of the President of the United States, imagining the whole scenario as a kind of musical comedy, in an attack on political correctness and Puritanism. At the same time, he seriously defended American intellectuals capable of thought (read: influenced by French thought) who had been attacked as impostors.[69] Others likened the national melodrama to an English eighteenth-century novel: "There is a whole literature devoted to the question of adultery, transgression, and the law, and that literature is called 'literature.'"[70] But the shift from fiction to constitutional crisis stopped the laughter: "What began as a sort of restoration comedy, the impeachment of the president, on a frivolous, irrelevant matter, is suddenly turning very black indeed, and all our political arrangements are at risk as superstitious Christian fundamentalists and their corporate manip-

---

67. From the taped conversations between Monica Lewinsky and Linda Tripp, cited in Maureen Dowd, "Liberties: Truth and Ketchup," *New York Times*, 4 October 1998.

68. See Elizabeth Hardwick, "Head Over Heels," review of *Monica's Story*, by Andrew Morton, *New York Review of Books* 46/7 (22 April 1999): 6–8. See also Andrew Morton, *Monica's Story* (New York: St. Martin's Press, 1999).

69. Philippe Sollers, "Le corps américain," *Le monde*, 14 March 1998.

70. Adam Gopnik, "American Studies," *New Yorker* (28 September 1998): 39–42.

ulators seem intent on overthrowing the presidential elections in a Senate trial. This is no longer a comedy," writes Gore Vidal. "This is usurpation."[71] If it wasn't comedy, then, given the high stakes for American political life, it risked becoming tragedy and the undoing of democracy as we know it.

The shock and outrage of the Clinton scandal gave way to an impeachment process that seemed to bend the constitution and that, in the end, did not deal with pornography or even libertinism. For all the salacious gossip perpetrated by the media, the sexual titillation about oral sex and trysts, the battle over Clinton was not a battle about pornography. It was about public virtue and political power. While the dynamic between Clinton and Lewinsky involved a power relationship, it was not the same thing as the horrific rape fantasy aimed against MacKinnon by Carlin Romano.

What then is going on in the itinerary I have traced? I believe that we see a transformation, as well as a cultural divide within the matrix of power and freedom that continues to manifest itself in the arena of sexuality, but *without* the revolutionary impetus that drove it during the Enlightenment. In the end, the strangely unreal aspect of the Clinton affair was how "constitutional" and orderly, irrevocably procedural, patient, and deliberative the battle over political power proved to be; no revolutionary moment could be discerned. In some ways, this could be shown to be a real transformation of revolutionary energy into a stable system, one that could not be turned back on itself through pornography as sexualized political provocation.

When, after 17 August 1998, Clinton finally confessed to "inappropriate" behavior, he demanded to be returned to his private life with his family, showing little contrition by lashing out at the independent counsel. In contrast to concerns that Clinton had not confessed enough, the French press underscored the disparity between Starr's pursuit of (an oft quoted puritan) morality and a French or European view of politics. The case never would have happened in France because of a history that often mixed sex and politics from at least Louis XIV to François Mitterand.[72] But the larger issue had nothing to do with the

71. Gore Vidal, "Birds & Bees & Clinton," *The Nation* (28 December 1998): 5–6.

72. See Bruno Franceschi, "Une 'affaire Lewinsky,' fort peu probable en France," *Agence France Press*, 18 August 1998; Sylvie Kaufman on public opinion, *Le monde*, 18 August 1998; Alain Navarre, "Sexe, mensonge et 'exception française' présumée," *Agence France Press*, 29 January 1998.

differences between the United States and Europe; and attacks like
William Bennett's, equating the liberal point of view with Europe, seem
to come more out of a lack of precedent than a conviction of the wrong-
ness of European political life. Rather, in the cross-referencing between
French and American political mores, a transition from news item to
myth occurs. If there is any similarity between the Clinton scandal and
the Dreyfus affair it is probably not only in the reversal suggested by
Richard Posner: Dreyfus was innocent, Clinton guilty. More important
is the way in which the lack of consensus allowed people to examine
and even change their own positions over time. In *Jean Santeuil*, Marcel Proust tracks in exquisite detail the follow-up to his hero's belief,
at the moment of the Dreyfus trial, that Truth "was really something
that existed in itself and had nothing to do with opinion."[73] Without
assuming a moral position of judgment, he goes on to examine in *A la
recherche du temps perdu* the ways in which individuals deal with the
great events of their time through their own background, the truths
they hold to be true, and their ability—or lack thereof—to formulate
judgments; in so doing, they may find their own way.

I am not suggesting that literature can render solutions to the ethical problems raised either by pornography or by the pornographic aspect of the Clinton scandal. What I am suggesting is that the passage
through the impasse that the polarization of opinion suggests may
come less through legalism—although legal changes may be absolutely
necessary—or through political partisanship, however much they are
a part of political life. Finding the passage may necessitate riding out
the storm, assessing how buoys of history provide heuristic markers for
the creation of new mores and new myths to guide individuals in a
rapidly changing society. It is not so much the lack of public intellectuals in our time that indicates failure, as Richard Posner suggests
when he writes that the left intelligentsia "lacks a moral core, while
the right intelligentsia has a morbidly exaggerated fear of moral laxity."
Nor is it the opposition of a "hard" field (where "agreement on methods for resolving disagreement enables consensus to be forged despite
the differing political agendas of the practitioners") versus a "soft" field
("permeable to political disagreement") (Posner, 240). It is rather that
one might hope that the dynamics of change would take us away from
analogies such as war for social conflict (Posner's comparison) to a
crossing of Right and Left, of American and European ways, among oth-

73. Marcel Proust, *Jean Santeuil* (Paris: Gallimard, 1971), 659. My translation.

ers, that might give rise to a different kind of social and political sphere, one in which privacy would be both free and respected in the equality of individuals who are free to form the selves they want within the social and political world, unharmed by the acts or fantasies of others— as much for women as for men.

III. Crossing over
Cultures/Knowledge

FRANCESCA CANADÉ SAUTMAN

Hip-Hop/scotch: "Sounding Francophone" in French and United States Cultures

> So far from your family, on the foreign shore,
> Death swung its scythe over your brow,
> And I, in my bitter sorrow, I have come
> To ask of these crosses, these willows, these tombs:
>   Where does my brother lie?
>   —Armand Lanusse, "Un frère. Au tombeau de son frère,"
>   in *Les Cénelles* (1845).

> Look at the States where black people agonize. Calculated genocide that the state supervises. Bodies lying in a heap, a blank check for death.
>   The forces of evil are afoot. 80% of youth growing up behind bars. In the ghetto, it's a free range . . .
>   . . . Is that what you want in France, a formula made in USA? Death legalized who said crime does not pay. That's the way it is in Uncle Sam's land. Maybe soon right in front of your house . . .
>   —Faouzi Tarkhani, "Les Lascars se lassent,"
>   *Guerrier pour la paix* (1999)

BECOMING "FRANCOPHONE"

The first truly Francophone author was probably Guillaume de Salluste du Bartas (1544–90): in his trilingual dialogue of muses—Latin, French, and Gascon—written on the occasion of Catherine of Medicis's and Marguerite de Navarre's visit to Gascony, his native Gascon tongue was a legitimate competitor with French and Latin and even surpassed the other two in poetic excellence.[1] But in du Bartas's day, because French was still an uneven cultural contender with Latin and Greek,

---

1. Guillaume de Salluste, seigneur du Bartas, "Accueil de la Reine de Navarre," in *The Works of Guillaume de Salluste, sieur du Bartas: A Critical Edition with Introduction, Commentary and Variants,* ed. Urban Tigner Holmes, Jr., John Coriden Lyons, and Robert White Linker (Chapel Hill: University of North Carolina Press, 1935–40), vol. 3, 477–81.

YFS 100, *FRANCE/USA: The Cultural Wars,* ed. Ralph Sarkonak, © 2001 by Yale University.

there was no political need for a *Francophonie,* so the term had no reason to be, and would have held no currency. Du Bartas's embracing
of the Gascon muse belonged to another history, the protracted,
centuries-long cultural and political interpellation[2] by regional and
smaller national languages in relation to French. "Thinking Francophone" only became possible after French colonial interests had con-
verged in a vision of empire bolstered by the rhetoric of the *mission
civilisatrice.* Hegemonic colonial strategies were enacted through language as well as through military conquest and, later, economic control.[3] Francophone writing outside of Europe and Quebec had first to
result, even indirectly, from that colonial enterprise to then work
within and against the empire.[4] Yet, the way all of this was articulated
varied tremendously throughout the "Francophone"[5] world: on the
African continent, the focus of this essay, regional and local histories
of invasion, colonial organization, dominance, and resistance. Cultural
institutions in the United States have also received literature and ideas
conveyed in French by people who are neither French nor European, or
by French citizens who are of non-European origin and not "white" in
a variety of ways.

   This essay addresses the relationship between "being/speaking
Francophone" and forms of ethnic-cultural dissent in France and the
U.S. In both countries, terms such as *Francophone* and *Francophonie*
are often captured by specific political agendas and practices.[6] The in-

   2. Following the use in Judith Butler's *Bodies That Matter: On the Discursive Limits of "Sex"* (New York: Routledge, 1993), 7–8 and 121–24.
   3. See Anne Judge, "La francophonie. Mythes, masques et réalités," *La francophonie,
mythes, masques et réalités. Enjeux politiques et culturels,* ed. Bridget Jones, Arnauld
Mignet, and Patrick Corcoran (Paris: Publisud, 1996), 19–43; Alice Sindzingré, "À quoi
sert l'Afrique? Une question française," *Afrique, la fin du Bas Empire, LiMes. Revue
française de géopolitique* 3 (1997), 15–26. This volume will be referenced as *LiMes.*
   4. On the intricacies of this particular relationship, see Christopher L. Miller,
Nationalists and Nomads: Essays on Francophone African Literature and Culture
(Chicago: University of Chicago Press, 1998).
   5. Throughout this essay I have tried to indicate the problematic nature of terms such
as "Francophone." I use *Francophonie* in italics as a foreign word, and capitalize it as a
political institution; Francophone by itself, without quotation marks, when it is accu-
rate within a limited use, such as "Francophone literature," or a "Francophone writer";
Francophone when I refer to a term or to its usage by others; and "Francophone" in quotations marks when the term is being discussed or contested, whether by others or by
myself.
   6. See Stephen Smith, "Paris vs. Washington," *LiMes,* 53–65, and Guy Rossatanga-
Rignault, "Vieilles lunes et nouveaux empires. Un regard africain sur la France et les États-
Unis," *LiMes,* 67–79; André Bourgeot, "USA. Main basse sur l'Afrique," *LiMes,* 81–88.

herent flaws of "Francophone" as a conceptual frame have been noted increasingly in both cultures, and *Francophonie* is now redefining itself according to specific race and class parameters not only in France but also in the USA with the advent of large immigration movements from the "Francophone" world. What it means to be "Francophone" involves complex interfacings between various languages, including English and French, between competing discursive claims made on the basis of linguistic home and the particular forms of cultural and linguistic hybridity, such as French hip-hop culture and world music.

The term *Francophone* was first coined at the end of the nineteenth century, by the French geographer Onésime Reclus, to designate people who spoke French in regional or national territories where French was not the main or only language; it appeared in dictionaries in 1930, but was not really used until after World War II.[7] Different dates have been proposed for the first African Francophone literary text, based on Western cultural parameters. Lylian Kesteloot's famous 1961 thesis made *Négritude* the watershed of *Francophone* African and Caribbean literature, while all writers before the movement were "precursors." As Christopher Miller remarks, describing an author as a "precursor of Negritude," as Senghor did with respect to Maran, is tantamount to "honoring him and subordinating him at the same time" (11). In Kesteloot's title, the term "black," encompassing Caribbean and African as harbingers of Négritude, did not denote Africa in any other way, a sign, perhaps, of pre-independence Africa's "transparency" in Western eyes, as a "Black continent" (*continent noir*) that erased the historical and cultural narratives of Africa.[8] Such parameters raise once more the vexed question of whether "the subaltern can speak."[9] Subaltern by definition, pre-independence African literatures in French

7. Jean-Marc Moura, *Littératures francophones et théorie postcoloniale* (Paris: PUF, 1999), 1, note 2.

8. Lylian Kesteloot, *Les écrivains noirs de langue française. Naissance d'une littérature,* (Brussels: Université libre de Bruxelles, 1963); English translation: *Black Writers in French: A Literary History of Negritude,* trans. Ellen Conroy Kennedy (Philadelphia: Temple University Press, 1974). Kesteloot's 1967 anthology of African literature in French was widely used for decades in US universities, a real force in defining the canon outside of Africa (*Anthologie négro-africaine: panorama critique des prosateurs, poètes et dramaturges noirs du XXe siècle* [Verviers: Gérard & Co., 1967]). It also bolstered the distinction between North and ("Black") Sub-Saharan Africa. See Abdennour Benantar, "Les Arabes et l'Afrique. Nous n'avons pas besoin d'intermédiaire!" *LiMes,* 269–86.

9. This refers to Gayatri Chakarvorty Spivak's now axiomatic essay "Can the Subaltern Speak?" in *Marxism and the Interpretations of Culture,* ed. Cary Nelson and Lawrence Grossberg (Urbana: University of Illinois Press, 1987), 271–313.

were presumed to be knowable through Western eyes and Western pronouncements, hegemonic in their selection criteria and aesthetic plat-
forms regardless of their occasional anticolonial stance. For Kesteloot,
for instance, several texts were to be excluded from this early canon as
mere panegyrics of colonialism (Miller, 10). However, beginning with
Guy Ossito Midiohouan and followed by Miller (11–13), others have
identified as a first text Ahmadou Mapaté Diagne's *Les trois volontés
de Malic* (1920),[10] while an argument can be made that the first narrative Senegalese texts in French were written as early as 1850.[11] The six
years of difference with another work often mentioned as a first "literary" Francophone African work (Rouch and Clavreuil, 392), Bakary Diallo's *Force-Bonté* (1926), might seem quite minor. The discrepancy is
nonetheless symptomatic of the assumptions of Western critics about
"writing in" the Francophone literary voice, establishing a canon, and
imposing their own views of literature. Subaltern status is confirmed
by the difficulty encountered in simply reformulating the questions,
part of which is identifying a "first text." The history of Francophone
literature in the Maghreb might have been a similarly contested ter-
rain, but at the very least there is consensus that the first Algerian work
in French appeared in 1920, and other works—often of a fairly clear
colonial obedience—were being produced in French by the 1930s.[12]
Needless to say, a brief look at the Caribbean would yield much earlier
dates, well back into the nineteenth century.

Yet, during the early fifties, other voices were already formulating
a corpus of *Francophone* African literature with a history and a genealogy. *Présence africaine* was publishing interviews with and comments on African authors along with texts, for example its 1955 publication of Abdou Anta Kâ's first short story. A biographical note explained

10. Guy Ossito Midiohouan, *L'idéologie dans la littérature négro-africaine d'expression française* (Paris: L'Harmattan, 1986).

11. In 1850 a Senegalese métis, Léopold Panet (1820–1859), published a travel text
"La relation d'un voyage du Sénégal à Soueira" in the *Revue coloniale;* another Sene-
galese of mixed parentage, the catholic priest David Boilat (1814–1901), published his *Es-
quisses sénégalaises* in 1863 (Paris). Between 1912 and 1913 a third Senegalese writer,
Ahmadou Dugué-Clédor, wrote two historical essays. Alain Rouch and Gérard Clavreuil,
Littératures nationales d'écriture française. Afrique noire, Caraïbes, Océan Indien
(Paris: Bordas, 1987), 392–93.

12. Charles Bonn and Naget Khadda, "Introduction," *Littérature maghrébine d'expression française*, ed. Charles Bonn, Naget Khadda, and Abdalah Mdarhi-Alacin (Vanves:
Edicef, 1986), 5–21. The first such work was Mohamed Benchérif's partially autobiographical *Ahmed ben Mustapha, goumier*. Benchérif was a colonial administrator, *caïd*,
and captain in the French army, who espoused the virtues of French colonial power.

that he had no employment or home, came from a culturally and religiously mixed family, and had already written plays performed in Senegal, in particular on the radio (Radio-Dakar), as was often the case with African theater in the twentieth century.[13]

The term *Francophone* did not catch on right away; it began to appear in titles of works around 1963[14] coinciding with the rise of independence movements in Africa south of the Sahara. Interestingly, early texts were already heralding both the triumphant and the alarmist trends in *Francophonie*.[15] In the 1960s the term made inroads in doctoral dissertation topics in the USA, first in relation to education and economic development, and then in titles addressing literature, more frequently by the 1970s. Scholarship and commentary on Francophone literature nonetheless appear to be a phenomenon of the last decades: a cursory look at the MLA's database shows that between 1900 and 1987, 745 entries concerned *Francophone* topics; there are 881 for the 1987–2000 period alone. Nor did the term hold purchase with all: several critical works written in France in the late 1970s and 1980s consistently avoided *Francophone*, and used *French-language* or *of French expression* instead.[16]

The study of Francophone literature shifted and corrected the Eurocentric view of French literature (narrowly conceived as literature written in Europe), but could also hide the term's links to France's colonial past. The subaltern was thus ushered into the French academy, but only nominally empowered to speak since the condition of that speech remained the willingness to address, even at the onset of the twenty-first century, the relationship of the postcolonial writing subject to the French language as fount, model, and mirror. In *Francophone* subjects the French academy discovered a rich academic field, but it was rapidly lost to a unique form of discursive control. The use of French at a variety of levels—native language, lingua franca, administrative tool, academic instrument—became more than a simple classification tool. The will to classify evident in discussions of what constitutes *Fran-*

13. Abdou Anta Kâ, "L'envers du Masque," *Présence africaine* 13 (Aug.–Sept. 1955). In the interview, Kâ remarked that he had no degrees, for "degrees would separate me from the people."

14. Alfred de Soras, *Relations de l'Église et de l'État dans les pays d'Afrique francophone: Vues prospectives*. [Paris:] Mame [1963].

15. Hyacinthe de Montera, *La francophonie en marche* (Paris: Sedimo, 1966); Gérard Tougas, *La francophonie en péril* (Montréal: Cercle du livre de France, 1967).

16. Robert Cornevin's classic *Littératures d'Afrique noire de langue française* (Paris: PUF, 1976), or Rouch and Clavreuil's 1987 work. The Bibliothèque Nationale de France currently uses *littérature africaine d'expression française* as a classification category.

cophonie, geographically and linguistically, is an almost parodic version of Foucault's famous exegesis of classification norms in Western systems of knowledge.[17] The "factic" nature of the language connection established the purported link of former colonies to French culture; but other "facts" were dismissed, such as opposition to colonialism and racial strife. In Togo, a country usually classified as *Francophone*, resistance to French presence, colonial policies, and the imposition of the French language was so strong when France and Great Britain seized the territory from the Germans in 1914 that there was actually an active pro-German movement, an embarrassing detail of colonial history not mentioned in official versions. The opposition continued for decades, as student movements in 1991 issued statements rejecting "imperialist and neocolonialist" relations with France and *Francophonie*, and calling on people to "divest [themselves] of French paternalism, for Togo never has been a French colony."[18]

NEOCOLONIALISM AND EMERGING DISCOURSES OF FRANCOPHONE STUDIES

Muddled neocolonial discourses abound in texts using such linguistic classification systems. For instance, the authors of a pamphlet on the "Francophone challenge" organize the *Francophone* countries of the world according to a grid based on the connection of other languages to French. The Caribbean countries are described as close to French, most of Africa as speaking languages "more distant" from French, and Arab cultures as "very distant."[19] This peculiar set of linguistic criteria obliterates the radical differences of these linguistic families, puts all African languages, however diverse, into one category defined in relation to French, and maintains the French language as center and standard. Even more objectionable is a work entitled *1989. Vers une révolution Francophone?* in which the various speakers of *Francophonie* are classified as the "Francofaune," and are divided into "Francophones, francophonoïdes, and franco-aphones."[20] It would be hard to find

17. In Michel Foucault's foundational *The Order of Things: An Archeaology of the Human Sciences*, (New York: Vintage, 1994) [1971], see chapters 5 and 10.

18. Comi M. Toulabor, "Problèmes de frontières, francophobie et nationalisme au Togo," *LiMes*, 169–76.

19. P.-F. Chatton and Jeanne Mazuryk Bapst, *Le défi francophone* (Brussels: Beuylant/ Paris: LGDJ, 1991), 8–9.

20. Robert Chaudenson, *1989. Vers une révolution francophone?* (Paris: L'Harmattan, 1989), 41–66.

a more convincing illustration of postcolonial theory's charge that the "other" (even, in this case, the purportedly culturally close and allied Other) is silenced through zoological, entomological, and/or botanical classification grids and implicitly removed from full membership in humanity.[21]

Thus the term *Francophone* is used in this essay with a great deal of discomfort, as a term fraught with ambiguities and complicities. It conceals the sinister underside of a French-speaking world no less innocent of imperialism than its English-speaking counterpart (how did parts of Africa "get French" and can they remain so?), and, as well, it is a problematic scripting of postcolonial realities, such as the role of France as a world power in countries like Chad[22] and Rwanda. Behind the term lurk elements of the "Francophone" idiom that contribute to generate and maintain geopolitical renamings and remappings of territories conquered and controled (Indochina, French Equatorial Africa, Central Africa, etc). They have also veiled the excess of meaning that now has been heaped on apparently simple French words, such as *civilisation, progrès*, or *citoyen*. In view of all these ambiguities, Jean-Marc Moura's reminder of a distinction to be made between *Francophonie* as a state of linguistic fact and *francophonisme* as a discourse about cultural hegemony and a will to power is particularly useful (2).

These questions do obtain in the U.S. context, but both their importance and their solutions shift a bit. Before the 1970s, when the academy largely gave no place to Francophone literature in its French curriculum, or reluctantly admitted only such figures as Césaire or Senghor, the term implicitly evoked things non-Western and hence threatening to canonical French literature. This announced conflicts about territory and resources that remain with us today. Proponents of Francophone literature may not always recognize that at stake was a sort of "unbearable whiteness of being." The whiteness of the canon screamed for interrogation and resistance, paving the way for its current deconstructions as a category by scholars and critics, primarily African-American, and the elaboration of a new "race theory."[23] French

---

21. See V.-Y. Mudimbé, "Symbols and the Interpretation of the African Past," *The Idea of Africa* (Bloomington: Indiana University Press, 1994), 1–37.

22. [collective: Agir ici et Survie] Dossiers noirs de la politique africaine de la France no. 8, *Tchad, Niger. Escroqueries à la démocratie* (Paris: L'Harmattan, 1996).

23. See for instance Kimberlé Crenshaw et al., ed., *Critical Race Theory: The Key Writings that Formed the Movement* (New York: New Press, 1995), and Wahneema Lubiano, ed., *The House that Race Built* (New York: Random-Vintage, 1998).

hexagonal (and European) literature was also perceived as conservative, cut-off from contemporary strife and issues, and in need of a kind of "regeneration" that Francophone literature provided. Such a perspective, however, teetered dangerously at the edge of less noble responses to the literature and culture of the perceived "Other." "Regenerating" smacks of the Western colonial view of Africa's cultural role as providing a return to unspoiled original sources, to landscapes and sensations lost by the industrialized world.[24] Such a desire for an "eternal Africa" has been roundly condemned by African intellectuals and policy-makers who have adamantly rejected atavistic policies that amount to neglecting or refusing the economic and technological development of Africa for its own people.[25]

Interest in the literatures of the *Francophone* world has indeed shot up considerably in the last decade, and the reasons are varied. As Christopher Miller remarks, "within French departments in U.S. colleges and universities, it has become an indispensable, if not wholly understood, component of the curriculum" (1). But Orientalism is still afoot in the Academy: the wide attraction of Tahar Ben Jelloun's novels—while his politically engaged poetry[26] remains almost unstudied—and their ulterior treatment in film, may be one indication of that. The contemporary academic publishing world has also been "discovering" the emergent voices of the colonized, marginalized, and ostracized—former colonial people, people of color, lesbians, and gays—in ways that mix commercial and professional benefits with genuine intellectual interest. Francophone studies, as they still struggle for full recognition—in particular for financial parity—are at times the site of opportunistic career strategies from which the specters of colonialism have not been dispelled. Today we witness a contradiction between continued resistance to the term and the field on the one hand and empty endorsements of *Francophonie* by the academic establishment that confer to

24. On this subject see a collection of acerbic essays by François de Negroni, *Afrique fantasmes* (Paris: Plon, 1992), and his pamphlet on French *coopérants* entitled *Les colonies de vacances.*

25. See Callisto Madavo and Jean-Louis Sarbib, "L'Afrique en marche. Attirer le capital privé vers un continent en évolution," *LiMes,* 33–46; on women, technology, and survival, *African Feminisn: The Politics of Survival in Sub-Saharan Africa,* Gwendlolyn Mikell, ed. (Philadelphia: University of Pennsylvania Press, 1997); on the questions of African museums, technology, and African agency, see Peter R. Schmidt and Roderick J. McIntosh, ed., *Plundering Africa's Past,* (Bloomington: Indiana University Press, 1996).

26. Tahar Ben Jelloun, *Les amandiers sont morts de leurs blessures* followed by *Cicatrices du soleil et Le discours du Chameau* (Paris: Maspéro, 1976).

both banal currency on the other. And when faculty or graduate students not trained in any of its areas anoint themselves specialists, such attitudes betray the old topos of "uncharted territory." Considered unclaimed and uninhabited, such territory is thus open for occupation and appropriation, a form of neocolonization through discourse. Yet, such a simple characterization of the situation of Francophone studies in U.S. universities and colleges would be unfair: the *Francophone* wave has also allowed French departments to diversify to a tiny extent, with the result that an ethnic and racial pluralism has begun to make its mark, though barely. Maintenance of the field as separate can be a form of exclusion but also a protection of sorts, a guarantee that non-Western and non-hexagonal works in French will not be shortchanged, absorbed, or made to disappear in mysterious ways.

Until very recently, the important theories of Foucault, Derrida, and Deleuze, which in turn inform thinkers such as Homi Bhabha, Judith Butler, and Gayatri Spivak, had become marginalized and suspect in their country of origin. In the U.S., postcolonial theory, postmodernism, gender theory,[27] as well as the frequent ideological debates about political morality and the catch-all accusation of so-called "political correctness" create a kind of intellectual turmoil unknown in France. Eve Kosofksy Sedgwick's "rich stew"[28] seems far removed from the more ponderous, detached, and authoritative discourse of the French academy, grounded in linguistics, sociology, and political economy. But such a facile contrast would be, again, quite superficial: writers and scholars have moved from France and "Francophone" countries to the precincts of U.S. academe with ease, transposing one set of discourses to another environment[29] and blending both in an original type

27. For instance, Françoise Lionnet, *Postcolonial Representations: Women, Literature, Identity* (Ithaca: Cornell University Press, 1995); Rosalyn Terborg-Penn and Andrea Benton Rushing, ed., *Women in Africa and the African Diaspora: A Reader* (Washington, DC: Howard University Press, 1996); Aiah K. Ndomaina, "Repetition, Resistance and Renewal: Postmodern and Postcolonial Narrative Strategies in Selected Francophone African Novels" (Ph.D. diss., Ohio State University, 1998); Keith L. Walker, *Countermodernism and Francophone Literary Culture: The Game of Slipknot* (Durham: Duke University Press, 1999); Jarrod Hayes, *Queer Nations: Marginal Sexualities in the Maghreb* (Chicago: University of Chicago Press, 2000).

28. Eve Kosofsky Sedgwick, *Epistemology of the Closet* (Berkeley: University of California Press, 1990), "a rich stew of male algolagnia, child-love, and autoeroticism" (8).

29. See Franco/phone-American efforts in Claude Bouygues, ed., *Texte africain et voies-voix critiques. Essais sur les littératures africaines et antillaises de graphie française: Maghreb, Afrique noire, Antilles, immigration = African Text and Critical Voices-Approaches: Essays on African and West Indian Literatures of French Expres-*

of thought. Such has been the role, to mention only some scholars and thinkers who are also world-renowned writers, of Maryse Condé at Columbia, Assia Djebar at LSU, Edouard Glissant at CUNY, and Vumbi Yoka Mudimbé at Stanford, among others.

FRENCH, ENGLISH, AND LINGUISTIC "CROSSING ZONES"

French outcry against the ever-encroaching culture of the United States and the English language is another zone of difference between the construction of *Francophone* studies in the two countries. Indeed, in 1986, the Paris Francophone Summit marked a new turn in the field: organized political resistance to Anglophone hegemony, a will to turn the tide of the inexorable rise of English worldwide, and the desire to launch a "Francophone challenge" on the stage of world politics and economics. Yet the term now reflects the internal tensions that complicate and split it. For instance, in 1987 a small volume entitled *La deriva delle francofonie*[30] broached this very topic in its preface and declared itself the first publication to reformulate definitions by using the word in the plural. Though unitary and centralizing at its beginnings, it stated, the concept of *Francophonie* was moving to greater recognition of the "various socio-cultural and literary individualities it might apply to." In fact, the word *francophonies* had appeared by 1985, but in a limited sense.[31]

The rivalry between French and English creates a binary opposition that is deceiving, since many languages can be inscribed in the same cultural space as the one occupied by French in a given work. Lise Gauvin speaks of writers who have chosen to write in French, but nevertheless labor in a sort of crossing zone between languages ("oeuvrent à la *croisée des langues* . . . "). Their works reflect a linguistic "hyperconsciousness" born of the many contacts with other languages.[32] And

---

sion: *Maghreb, Black Africa, West Indies, Immigration,* (Paris: L'Harmattan, 1992); Laïla Ibnlfassi and Nicki Hitchcott, ed., *African Francophone Writing: A Critical Introduction* (Oxford: Berg, 1996); P. Little and Roger Little, ed., *Black Accents: Writing in French from Africa, Mauritius and the Caribbean* (London: Grant & Cutler, 1997).

30. Franca Marcato Falzoni, ed., *La deriva delle francofonie 3. Animisme et technologie dans la littérature francophone* (Bologna: Editrice *CLUEB,* 1989).

31. Doukoure Abdoul Dukule, "Afrique-Québec. Deux francophonies," *Présence francophone* 26 (1985): 45–56. Between 1987 and 2000, its most frequent occurrences were still in the title of a journal, *Francophonies d'Amérique.*

32. Lise Gauvin, "L'imaginaire des langues. Tracées d'une poétique," in Jacques

in poignant pages Assia Djebar has given voice to the various competing and coexisting languages that live in her, as in other women of her
world, who "possess" four languages: that of the rocks, the original
Berber; the language of the Book, Arabic with its dialectal sister; the
language of the former masters, French; and finally, the language of
the body.[33] The professional use of French may displace mastery of the
original language, as was the case until recently in parts of the Arab
world, creating for many a tragic absence in the daily experience of Arab
identity. The term "Francophone" is mired in complex experiences of
linguistic and societal practice in which national and individual contexts play major roles. In this interlocking network, geographical and
cultural proximity to the French language contributes to the linguistic
conundrum. In the U.S. those who are either expatriates or exiled but
continue to write in French face a new possibility, that of "inhabiting"
yet another "foreign" language, English.

Until recently, the most widely-read Francophone author in the
United States, apart from Aimé Césaire, was probably Camara Laye
whose book *L'enfant noir* was translated into English in the United
States in the early 1950s.[34] Since then it has been assigned even in high
schools in the United States. It is ironic that a fellow Guinean, Amadou
Diallo, became the figure from a country labeled *Francophone* to be
known to the general public in the United States in 2000, a position he
owed to the configuration of race and power in the United States rather
than to any "Francophonie."[35] As with the case of a Haitian immigrant,

Chevrier, ed., *Poétiques d'Édouard Glissant,* Actes du colloque international "Poétiques
d'Édouard Glissant," Paris-Sorbonne, 11–13 March 1998 (Paris: Presses de l'Université
de Paris-Sorbonne, 1993), 275–84; 276. See also Lise Gauvin, *L'écrivain francophone à la
croisée des langues* (Paris: Karthala, 1997).

33. Assia Djebar, *Ces voix qui m'assiègent. En marge de ma francophonie* (Paris: Albin Michel, 1999), 13–14. See also her March 1996 text "Les yeux de la langue," in *Poétiques d'Édouard Glissant,* 363–65.

34. Camara Laye, *The Dark Child;* with an introduction by Philippe Thoby-Mar-
cellin; trans. James Kirkup and Ernest Jones (New York: Noonday Press, 1954); and *The
Dark Child,* trans. James Kirkup, with an introduction by William Plomer (London:
Collins, 1955). On those translations and their problems, see Eloise Brière, "In Search of
Cultural Equivalencies: Translations of Camara Laye's *L'enfant noir,*" *Translation Review* 27 (1988): 34–39; Fredric Michelman, "From l'Enfant noir to the Dark Child: The
Drumbeat of Words Silenced," in Samuel A. Johnson, Bernadette Cailler et al., ed., *To-
ward Defining the African Aesthetic* (Washington, DC: Three Continents, 1982), 105–
11.

35. Amadou Diallo was an immigrant from Guinea living in New York City who was
gunned down by members of a special plain-clothes police squad because he looked like
a suspect they were seeking.

Abner Louima, held and tortured by New York City police officers, citizens of countries from the "Francophone" world are entering the vortex of police violence in the United States. The attacks on Amadou Diallo and Abner Louima, members of communities living as separate immigrant groups, quasi invisible to the mainstream, associated them with a wider community contoured by color and the exclusions pinned on it by structures of racial discrimination in the United States. Thus, both reflect the new place of immigrants from the Francophone world in U.S. life, not through the rich content of Francophone cultures triumphantly riding in with the surf, but by virtue of being black in a country where police culture is experienced daily as hostile to blacks. In their new "home," the matter-of-factness of being black in their land of origin has become the racial "fact" of blackness that intersects in sudden, brutal ways with their status as immigrants and people from poor neighborhoods. Both the exoneration of Amadou Diallo's executioners and the condemnation of Abner Louima's torturers—guilty in particular of sexual assault—dramatically engulf immigrants from different cultural horizons in United States views of race and sexuality. As the East Coast of the United States becomes a second Francophone population hub, it is increasingly problematic to study the Francophone literatures of Africa and the Caribbean in the United States without reflecting on this changing cultural horizon. The latter comprises a Haitian community rising in numbers but curtailed by hostile immigration and political asylum policies, fleeing the daily political violence and economic hardship of their country, and bringing with them memories of murder, terror, and political strife. The impact of migrations on cultural environments leaves such traces of memory that literature harbors and transmits. The great urban centers of the West have been put in direct contact with those of the developing world following new cultural axes linking Paris, New York, Montreal, Dakar, and Port-au-Prince.[36] And ironically again, it is the very subaltern status of racial minorities in the United States that has made the study of Francophone literature more desirable in local academic contexts. All in all, in the United States cultural and political context, Francophone literatures and cultures can simply no longer have outsider status.

36. Collective reflection and conversation with my colleagues at the City University of New York Graduate Center, Édouard Glissant, Lucienne Serrano, and Thomas Spear have been most helpful in inspiring this essay.

"Francophone," both as a term and a concept, has further challenges to meet. The etymology of the word should refer more properly to language spoken and heard, not written, although what we study is precisely the written word. Further, French is spoken by a minority in each purportedly "Francophone" country and written by fewer still. So the question remains of how to recognize the *sounds* that echo behind the written words of the Francophone text. And these sounds are not merely the *words* in the particular linguistic crossings and stews at work but the cultural sounds in their rich, ethnically and socially diverse, conflictual, muted, and insistent forms.

"SOUNDING" AND FRANCOPHONE TEXTS

That hidden part of the Francophone text can be accessed through an illuminating critical concept coined by a leading scholar of African American literature and culture, Houston Baker Jr., in his discussion of the Harlem Renaissance and modernity. He proposes that a variety of texts and performances by African Americans, regardless of their sometimes apparent acceptance of hegemonic views of race and of being black, encode another dimension that is authentically black and protected through internal references that do not voice African American culture but *sound* it.[37] This important theoretical tool is very relevant to the subject preoccupying us here. Francophone African writers also "sounded" Africa in texts that seemed otherwise complacent toward colonialism. Later, Francophone voices inscribed themselves in a more or less welcoming, at times hostile, hegemonic cultural environment on both sides of the Atlantic; gradually they have made themselves known and desirable but not yet at home.

In its relationship to English, Francophone literature cannot be reduced to a wall of last defense against linguistic encroachment. The primacy of French does not mean that it turns its back on other linguistic expressions. Further, the *sounds* of Francophone writing were heard in North American culture, particularly literary culture, quite early. Of special significance to the Franco/American dimensions of *Francophonie* is a literary work written in the United States, one of the earlier black Francophone texts of the Americas. This is an anthology of eighty-four poems in French, for the most part love poems, by seven-

37. Houston A. Baker, Jr., *Modernism and the Harlem Renaissance* (Chicago: University of Chicago Press, 1987), 25–69.

teen New Orleans poets, well-to-do free people of color (*gens de couleur libres*), known under the collective name *Les Cenelles*, and published in New Orleans in 1845 by poet and educator Armand Lanusse (1812–1867). This group had "a unique cultural life distinct from that of whites on the one hand and slaves on the other," and included merchants, writers, a journalist like Joanni Questy who wrote for the militant *La tribune de la Nouvelle Orléans*, or the successful playwright Victor Séjour, who had a career in Paris. The work, modeled on French romanticism, has seemed conventional to some; however, closer readings of its themes of disillusionment and death have elicited more serious echoes, reflecting "imposed limitations and twarthed ambitions" as well as a "deep cultural orientation towards France."[38]

During the Harlem Renaissance, the work of one writer in particular embodied the complex ties between North America and French socio-cultural environments thereby relativizing linguistic identity. Claude McKay, an important albeit marginalized Harlem Renaissance author who left his native Jamaica to become a major African American voice, "sounded" in such famous poems as "If We Must Die," a militant and dignified call to resistance embraced by a black community under siege by racist rioters. McKay wrote his novel *Banjo* in English about the very subject of *Francophonie*, and the work was translated immediately into French.[39] The novel concerns the lives and drifting futures of a large group of black men—and a woman of mixed South Asian parentage—from all over the Francophone world and several English-speaking countries as well. Their use of French as an idiom of cultural communication is contrasted to a desired pandiasporic idiom of black identity. French words, references to French press articles and to French song, as well as debates over Lamine Senghor's platform, all provide a rich texture to this work and create a new category of text, one that might be termed not *Francophone* but "francophonic." "Francophonic" might incorporate Houston Baker's concept of *sounding* to

38. Philip Barnard, "Les Cenelles," in *Oxford Companion to African American Literature*, ed. William L. Andrews, Frances Smith Foster, and Trudier Harris (New York: Oxford University Press, 1997), 121–22. See also: Alfred J. Guillaume, Jr., "Love, Death, and Faith in the New Orleans Poets of Color," *The Southern Quarterly*, 20/2 (Winter 1982): 126–44; Floyd D. Cheung, "Les Cenelles and Quadroon Balls: Hidden Transcripts of Resistance and Domination in New Orleans, 1803–1845," *Southern Literary Journal*, 29/2 (1997): 5–16.

39. Claude McKay, *Banjo: A Story without a Plot* (New York: Harper, 1929); *Banjo*, traduit de l'américain par Ida Treat et Paul Vaillant-Couturier, avec une préface de Georges Friedmann. (Paris: Éditions Rieder, 1931).

designate a text in which the linguistic vector itself is less important than the presence of sound, music, and song, of hearing and speaking French in displaced, disjuncted cultural contexts as experienced here by the various protagonists of McKay's novel.[40]

Francophone African writers have also incorporated references to the United States and used English as participants in a cross-Atlantic conversation with agency and control on their side, echoing on another plane another trans-Atlantic passage, this one mired in violence and abduction. In Zegoua Gbessi Nokan's hybrid text, *Le soleil point noir,* a letter written by a young woman to her lover repeatedly uses the English "my darkness" as a form of affective and erotic endearment as well as political interpellation, marking the discursive limits of French which has no equivalent term.[41] Allusions to writing in English bring out conflicts in the construction of identity around nation and gender, as in Abdourahman Waberi's "Une affair à vivre." In this soliloquy, a woman ponders her own history of exclusion, control, discrimination, and resistance; impugned for having read Betty Friedan, Angela Davis, and Angela Carter, along with Beauvoir and "the Algerian Assia Djebar" and responded to these "foreign names," she stakes her right to read texts about women her own way.[42]

The United States and the city of New York have figured in works of African literature in French as emblematic of a black history of suffering. Bernard Dadié's 1963 poem "Harlem" depicts Harlem as a crucible of relentless oppression: "a new Golgotha . . . an island of shipwreck victims . . . a zoo for tourists . . . manor house of Death . . . "[43] In another poem, Dadié views Harlem as a forlorn place ("cotton field for Wall Street") but inserts a more resistant note, concluding that, with the sun, "Harlem casts off its coat of subjection and takes back its dreams."[44] David Diop denounced racial oppression in the United

40. On McKay's work, see A. L. McLeod, ed., *Claude McKay: Centennial Studies* (New Delhi: Sterling Publishers, 1992); Tyrone Tillery, *Claude McKay: A Black Poet's Struggle for Identity* (Amherst: University of Massachusetts Press, 1992); Heather Hathaway, *Caribbean Waves: Relocating Claude McKay and Paule Marshall* (Bloomington: Indiana University Press, 1999); and Miller, 21–23.

41. Zegoua Gbessi Nokan, *Le soleil point noir* (Paris: Présence africaine, 1962).

42. Abdhourahman Waberi, "Une affaire à vivre," *Cahier nomade. Nouvelles.* (Paris: Le Serpent à Plumes, 1996), 49–57.

43. Bernard Dadié, "Harlem," *Hommes de tous les continents* (Abidjan: CEDA, 1985; 1967): "un nouveau Golgotha . . . une île de naufragés . . . un zoo pour touristes . . . hôtel particulier pour la Mort."

44. Dadié, "Jour sur Harlem," also dated 1963. Also, in the same volume, "Jésus se repose à New-Orléans (sic)," which ends on a vision of segregation abolished.

States, in his poem "À un enfant noir," an elegy for the murdered Emmett Till.[45] In Jean-Baptiste Tati-Loutard's poem "Lettre à une fille de New York," ambiguous allusions to Harlem are incorporated in an evocation of Africa: "I have all your features at the tip of my pen / And your words also, truly brilliant: / 'Harlem is Night inhabited by nights'."[46] Among these traces, one work stands out as the inverted reflection of McKay's: this is a novel by Lamine Diakhaté (1928–87), *Chalys d'Harlem*, the story of a Senegalese sailor from Rufisque who moves to the United States in 1919. Chalys tells his life story to a countryman, after living forty years as a black American in Harlem. He goes back to Senegal for a visit, only to realize how deep the gulf has become between him and his original culture.[47]

African-American music has occupied other foundational textual positions in the work of Emmanuel Boundzeki Dongala and Mongo Beti. Dongala's *Jazz et vin de palme* (1982), a work with a deliberately cross-cultural title, is intertwined with U.S. black culture in an inspired homage to John Coltrane, with whom Dongala shared a distinctive aesthetic vision and whom the writer envisioned as a teacher and a leader. In the section entitled "A Love Supreme," Dongala reacts with eloquent pain to the news of Coltrane's death. The narrator speaks of seeking identity and unanswered questions in different types of black music, "the deep and sorrowful soul of Billie Holiday and Ma Rainey," or "the jaunty and lusty rhythms of Fats Waller or Willie Smith the Lion." This music is a "museum" containing "a part of our people's history," but also a dead end.[48] The complex interactions of French and English in the context of defining black identity—African and African American—are reflected by the narrator's eulogy to Coltrane written directly in English, followed by only a partial translation into French. After the narrator has removed the words "his people" from the eulogy because they have lost meaning, he steps out in the blazing sun, right into a confrontation between the community and the police: "a thirteen-year old black youth had just been killed by a white police officer who was invoking self defense to a crowd of hostile black people."[49]

45. David Diop, *Coups de pilon* (Paris: Présence africaine, 1973), 24–26.

46. Jean-Baptiste Tati-Loutard, *Les normes du temps* (Kinshasa: Mont noir, 1974).

47. Lamine Diakhaté, *Chalys d'Harlem* (Dakar: NEA, 1978).

48. Emmanuel Boundzeki Dongala, "A Love Supreme," in *Jazz et vin de palme* (Paris: Hatier/Monde noir, 1982), 175–206.

49. He writes: "When the time comes, / May he rise again in the glory / Of his luminous sound / To be the teacher of us all / And let his supreme vibrations show the way

The "luminous sound" Dongala speaks of, produced and embodied by Coltrane, is at once music and much more, a textual matrix and mediator of cultural passage. It is also a truly *resounding* answer to a history in which that culture had been made subaltern and muffled, turning silence and constraint into a thing of beauty.

The "sounding" of African-American culture was starkly rendered as well in Mongo Beti's 2000 novel, *Branle-bas en blanc et noir.*[50] This is a parodic detective story starring a cast of characters with ambiguous professional and political identities, including the main protagonist, Eddie, a lawyer or private eye with ambiguous political contacts, and his friend George the "toubab," the "only Frenchman he can stand," adventurer, seducer of young girls, and unpredictable ally. The novel is really about the impact of economic globalization on contemporary West Africa, conveyed through an unnamed but recognizable Cameroon, and the breaking down of artificially constructed national identities, which are meaningless in the kind of multilingual, multicultural, and multiethnic societies that nations purport to encapsulate. While French is the vernacular of the novel, it is subverted by an "African French" with its own linguistic contours, and it must coexist with African languages, as well as with English. The latter is presented through an Anglophone character (264), standing in for an actual Anglophone minority in Cameroon, multiple allusions to neocolonialism and imperialism, through the IMF (205), or the consumption of foreign alcohol. But it is music, the distinctly African-American sound of jazz (Eddie has played in a jazz club, 201) and the blues (he repeatedly listens to a particular record, a duo by Billie Holiday and Lester Young [290, 351]), that give the novel a distinctive voice of black identity, transcending the farcical and parodic modes. The "musical tracks" in the novel provide a particularly effective form of sounding, because it is the resistant quality of a song like Billie Holiday's "Strange Fruit" that is encoded in a passage presenting a disconcerting caricatural fantasy on the inception of the blues in the American South (335). The song refers to a lynching, but the singer associated it with the death of her own father, who died of illness under the Jim Crow system, after being turned away from several hospitals.[51] In Mongo Beti's novel, it is through the

---

/ To us, / The living. / And may his people for whom he sang / Rise up with him." It is the last two verses that are erased (Dongala, 205–206).

50. Mongo Beti, *Branle-bas en blanc et noir* (Paris: Albin Michel, 2000).

51. See James Baldwin, "Where the Grapes of Wrath Are Stored" (*The Devil Finds*

blues, or the jazz-blues duo, that meaning is recovered and that resistant discourse reinscribes itself in a neocolonial society marred by corruption from top to bottom. Paradoxically, it is through the sounding of black American culture and its oppositional voice that a new authentic position of identity can be reclaimed by this beleagured African society. These examples of the concept of sounding are potentially rich, but should not obscure the fact that literature is not the only cultural space that allows this particular form of voicing to take place.

LINGUISTIC CROSSINGS AND THE "OTHER" FRANCOPHONIE: HIP-HOP (INTER)NATION

Contemporary France is no longer a cultural hegemony but a series of competing cultural sites that render questionable a vocabulary of mere addition with terms such as *France plurielle* or *Francophonie*. Translations of foreign literature, theatrical experiments with cultural fusion, countless international film festivals from all over the world, and the many venues for traditional musical expression, are all reflections of a new "world culture" marketed in France. But nowhere are these relations and contradictions more obvious than in the world of music crafted by a multi-ethnic youth culture that is a messenger for and witness to community healing and community strife. This music is principally French rap, which entertains special relations with world music in France, both new forms of an unrecognized "Francophone" expression. In defining the contours of Francophone studies, French rap is an important element for it is first and foremost textual, even if musical arrangements are often quite innovative. France is now the second hip-hop nation of the world, with close to a thousand different rap groups, some of whom have not yet recorded.[52] It produces a vast musical culture that nets millions of dollars in profits and mixes world, rap, reggae, and r/b with rai, chaabi, and still other forms such as flamenco. It uses the French language as a medium, mixed with Arabic, Berber, various African languages, Spanish, Marseilles dialect, English,

---

Work [1976; New York: Dell, 1990], 120–37), on the passages in Billie Holliday's memoirs in which she describes her father—an army veteran with ruined lungs—and his ordeal as he was turned away from hospital after hospital in Dallas, Texas. She added "A song was born which became my personal protest—'Strange Fruit'— . . . " (Baldwin 132).

52. See the website multimania.com/hiphopbombattack/Le_Repertoire. The entry claims that there are several thousand rap groups operating in France, many of them known only to their friends and family, and many of them underground.

and soon, probably, South Asian rhythms already imbedded in the culture of the Caribbean.[53]

Far from being a mere Western commercial invention, world music originated with African artists, whose contributions have been and still too often are overshadowed by larger commercial interests. In their work, multilinguism, polyglossia, interweavings of different linguistic traditions and practices were distinctive features. In 1970s Paris, the world-renowned artist Toure Kunda performed at the beginning of his career, concocting a type of afro-jazz-rock. Ray Lema, a towering figure in African music, used Douala, Swahili, Lingala, Kikongo, and Mango, combining the influences of his native Zaire with jazz, Jimi Hendrix, the Beatles, Mozart, and Bach. The tradition is kept up by contemporaries such as Toups Bebey, a Cameroonian born in Paris, whose group Paris Africans mixes instruments, styles, and nationalities. As well, Sita Lantaa, led by the Centrafrican Maixent Landou, which began in 1992, mixes French, Lingala, Kikongo, Dioula, and Wolof, performing a Congo-Zairian rumba with Western influences. Rai constantly produces new artists who also blend their musical genres with chaabi, gnawa, reggae, and rap.[54] Based in Grenoble, the Franco-Algerian fusion group Gnawa Diffusion is led by the son of Kateb Yacine, Amazigh, an iconoclast and virulent political satirist who lambastes political adversaries in France and his native Algeria. Playfulness and transgression are present in the name of the group ONB, "Orchestre National de Barbès," which mixes rai and Chaabi in front of packed audiences. Multiple criss-crossings of language and culture are effectuated as well by rap artists who mix a discordant chorus of voices speaking in their own languages as well as French with a variety of accents, and provide entire sets of such "speech performances," or in the economy of a particular album, performative speech acts.[55] Examples are the piece called "Jackpotes" by the group 113,[56] or several songs from the older group, Massilia Sound System.[57]

53. "Guadeloupe Kali Ceremony," East Indian Music in the West Indies, The Alan Lomax Collection, Caribbean Voyage: the 1962 Field Recordings (Cambridge, MA: Rounder Records, 1999).

54. See Joan Gross, David McMurray, and Ted Swedenburg, "Arab Noise and Ramadan Nights: Rai, Rap and Franco-Maghreb Identity," Diaspora 3/1 (Spring 1994): 3–39.

55. I use the term in an analogy with Sedgwick's analysis of the closet, that is "initiated by the speech act of a silence," a silence "that accrues . . . in relation to the discourse that surrounds and differentially constitutes it" (Sedgwick, 3).

56. 113, Les princes de la ville (np: Alariana, 1999).

57. Massilia Sound System, Commando Fada ([Marseilles]: Ròker Promocion, Shaman, 1995).

Manu Dibango and his Wakafrica plunged into their own roots through an exploration of black American music and its political discourses of resistance to racism in the 1960s. This revelation took place when he arrived in Los Angeles in 1969, discovering the political movement of the Black Panthers. He brought back this awareness and a newfound genealogy of resistance to a France in which resistant discourses about blackness, Fanon notwithstanding, were still barely known. And in another significant genealogy, the reverse journey had been made by James Baldwin, who first moved to France to get away from racism in the United States. Then, tired of sitting in Paris discussing the Algerian War, he returned home when the first Civil Rights Movement and the torches of the Black Liberation Movement lit up the streets: in 1963, Baldwin was in Selma, participating in the voting drive among black Americans. Today, young people in working-class neighborhoods of France, whether black, Beur, or white have reinterpreted and retooled a musical culture of African-American origin to make it their own, inflecting it in decisively French and "Francophone" ways. They have gradually but firmly moved away from borrowings of English phrases and sentences to a more distinctly French vernacular.[58]

For many people in France, U.S. imperialism is manifest in the constant flow of music, cinema, food habits, and language emanating from the "barbarian" United States. The efforts of Chirac's government to stymie the *mainmise* of English on French culture, by demanding that a minimum of 30% of songs played on air waves be in French, have paradoxically favored singers who incorporate their own musical heritage with forms from the United States and the use of French. Thus the young public of French working-class suburbs militantly endorses a certain type of American culture, through the rediscovery of black roots and black American music, reinterpreted in the crucible of

58. On the one hand, moving away from English to French represents a closer tie to urban youth communities. On the other, being able to take advantage of French laws on 30% French content on airwaves generates a proliferation of groups, not all of them thought to be authentic by urban youth, especially project audiences. French communities of rap listeners resist academic conclusions on the subject as often based on incomplete and inauthentic information, but accept a magazine like *L'Affiche. Le Magazine des autres musiques* (Clichy). How much *respect* researchers show for the performers and communities they write about is a strong issue. For these insights, as well as musical documents, and information unavailable in printed sources, I want to thank a graduate student from Paris on exchange at the CUNY Graduate Center in 1999–2000, Maboula Soumahoro. For other comments, I also thank my graduate students in my Spring 2000 "Constructions d'Afriques" course, especially Sophie Saint-Just, Anna Lerus, and Rosa Attali.

French urban, marginalized life.[59] This music is sometimes rerouted to the African continent, as is the case with groups like the Ghetto Blasters, Senegalese rap artists,[60] and now the growing movement of Algerian rappers singing in Arabic such as the women rappers of Hyphen and the better known Intik or Le Micro Brise le Silence. As well, many of the leading French rap artists were in fact either born in Africa or are sons and daughters of African immigrants: MC Solaar was born in Senegal; the Bamileke woman rapper Bams comes from Cameroon; Khery, lead singer for the militant group Ideal J., is from the Ivory Coast; Stomy Bugsy of Ministère Amer is Cape Verdian. French rap has also woven into its lyrics some of the barely visible strands of French multiethnic culture. The Italo-French rap artist Akhetanon (Philippe Fragione) sings about the history of Southern Italy, and intersperses fragments of Sicilian and Neapolitan on his tracks, as well as the songs of an Arab/Beur-inflected group like Fonky Family. Marseilles groups anchored in local hybrid culture also provide similar cross-cultural soundings, such as IAM, Massilia Sound System or Fonky Family. The latter's lyrics refer freely to the Koran, combining religious allusions with violent exhortations against capitalism and a racialized society. Other groups and solo artists of Maghrebi descent also sing on specifically religious Muslim themes, like K-Rhyme le Roi ("La Qibla," on the *Comme un Aimant* musical track, see below) or the group Umma.

Rap music's arrival on French shores can actually be dated precisely: in 1982 the massive impact of U.S. rap music identified with the Bronx and the legendary Afrika Bambaata group was transmitted to young black people from the most recent immigration wave.[61] The rapper

59. See V. Milliot, "Le Rap. Une parole rendue inaudible par le bavardage des stéréotypes: Expressions culturelles dans les quartiers," *Migrants Formation* 111 (1997): 61–73; Christian Béthune, "Made in France," *Autrement* 189 (1999): 179–206.

60. In Dakar alone, there are now hundreds of rap groups, working in very limited conditions, without recording materials, and singing in linguistic polyphonies of English, French, and Wolof. The successful ones have an almost heroic status, such as Positive Black Soul and Daara J (Lord Aladji Man, Faada-Freddy, Ndongo D). The latter sings on themes such as slavery, including talks by the director of the Gorée House of Slaves put to music. "Daara J: Xalima," *Webdo-L'hebdo* 9, 4 March 1999, Disques, Xalima (www.webdo.ch/hebdo/hebdo_1999).

61. See André Prevos, "Une nouvelle forme d'expression populaire en France. Le cas de la musique Rap dans les années 1980," *Francographies* (1993): 201–16; "Création, transformation, américanisation. Le Rap français des années 90," *Francographies* 2 (1995): 179–209; "The Evolution of French Rap Music: Hip Hop Culture in the 1980s and 1990s," *French Review,* 69/5 (1996): 713–25; "Rap Music and Hip-Hop Culture in France during the 1980s and 1990s: Developments and Reactions," *European Studies Journal*

Solo, from the group Assassins, commented: "It was the devil's music, the sound that heated up my shoulders and my feet."[62] In the United States, decades earlier, this devil's music was the blues at its inception. In the now thriving French hip-hop culture, alienated urban youth communities continue to identify with their place of origin, Lyons, Marseilles, Bordeaux, Grenoble, Strasbourg, Toulon, as well as the suburbs of Paris, Sarcelles, Créteil, and Vitry. They generate a rich "folk culture" of the disenfranchized in which race, unemployment, police violence, and dignity are major themes, along with friendship, love, and sex, that can only be acknowledged briefly here. Ideal J. is one of the most militant, with songs like "Hardcore" and "R.A.S. 1" in which he refuses to serve in the French army ("there is already a war in my neighborhood"). The album is packaged with a cover image of the French flag crumpled in a strong black hand on one side, and, on the other, an ambiguous image of a strong, unclad black man draped in the same flag, but devoid of white in it, like a bare-shouldered ballroom dress.[63] Faouzi Tarkhani, a blind Maghrebi solo artist, identifies himself as a pious Muslim opposed to violence, but he is also extremely political ("Le noir me met à l'abri," "Un mike est une arme," "Reste Love"), and includes a strong woman rapper like Casey Marcko on one of his tracks ("Dois-je me taire").[64] Bams, one of only a few women rappers, is one of the most forceful new voices with strong, explicit, and angry lyrics about race and gender, the status of women in relations with men, and social marginalization.[65] In the virulent lyrics of Ministère Amer, the *Francophone* concept of Négritude is derided ("Pas venu en touriste"); the group also can claim fame for its serious legal troubles when it was charged with inciting anti-police violence.[66]

15/2 (Fall 1998): 1–33; "Communication through Popular Music in the Twenty-First Century? The Example of French Rap Music and Hip Hop Culture," in Jesse Levitt, Leonard R. N. Ashley, and Wayne H. Finke, ed., *Language and Communication in the New Century* (New York: Cummings and Hathaway, 1998), 137–48.

62. "1982–1990. Le Rap débarque en France," France Culture, *L'histoire en direct*, Emmanuel Laurentin and Christine Robert, 5 July and 7 July 1999.

63. Ideal J., *Le combat continue* (n.p: Alariana, Barclay, 1998).

64. Faouzi Tarkhani, *Guerrier pour la paix* (n.p.: Polygram, Jazz Dean, 1999). He is the main Maghrebi artist played on the music program of Radio Shams (Radio Soleil), a predominantly Maghrebi station in Paris (88.6 FM).

65. Bams, *Vivre ou mourir* (n.p.: Trema, Sony: 1999).

66. Ministère Amer [Stomy Bugsy and Passi], *95200* ([Paris]: Hostile, Delabel, Sarcélite: 1994).

Akhenaton, both solo performer and organizer of collective efforts, member of the Marseilles group IAM, hails from Sicily via Naples. A working-class immigrant who became French while claiming proudly the label *métèque* (mixed breed, darker person), integrated in the multiethnic Marseilles hip-hop culture, he had dreamed since 1993 of making a movie based on these youth life stories.[67] This film came out in May 2000, entitled *Comme un aimant* [Like a Magnet] a title that alludes to the destiny of those who irresistibly come back to their old neighborhood, and cannot leave it for a better life, ending their days in a familiar place "where their dreams die."

Akhenaton directed and starred in this film in collaboration with his friend Kamel Saleh, and he produced its musical track with composer Bruno Coulais. This was not the first French film on hip-hop culture, but the film avoided both stereotypical gangster-action with rapid gunfire, and an excessively jocular tone. It tells the story of a group of friends from North Marseilles, all unemployed young men of Franco-Arab and Franco-Italian descent who hang out together, deplore the dead-end life they lead, live off hustling and small-time crook operations, half-heartedly attempt to seduce girls—as is to be expected in this type of movie, the homosocial bond proves by far to be the most important—and make an ill-fated move toward higher crime. At this point, tragic mechanisms trigger a chain of suicidal acts: Fouad's mother's death pushes him over the edge, he launches a useless hold up, and is shot down; the character played by Akhenaton and his friend Bra-Bra spontaneously beat up a mobster in retaliation for the beating of their associate Santino and are subsequently gunned down. The entire group in the end is led to death or incarceration. In a sumptuous finale, Cahuete (Kamel Saleh), alone, steals a gas truck, dumps gasoline all over the streets of Marseilles and sets them on fire, watching the city light up with ephemeral bonfires. There is an epic quality to the last scenes as he watches from afar this last desperate mark of the young men's attempt to leave their signature on an indifferent world, and the fires all suddenly go out, leaving the screen in blank darkness.

While the film itself can be judged as a contribution to visual cultures, its salient feature remains its particular performance of sounding, its sensitive and inspired interweavings of text and music, its production of music as text and of linguistic mixture. Akhenaton and Bruno Coulais composed the score by seeking *musiques témoins*, that

---

67. Olivier Cachin, "La vérité sur l'aimant, "*L'affiche* (June 2000): 60–62.

is, musical voices that acted as witnesses. They accomplished this by combining a few tracks of Akhenaton's with a complex dialogue between contemporary French and American rap artists as well as great performers of African-American soul music. Several of the French rappers use varied cultural registers to create a sound unique in that it is "French" linguistically but multicultural, and specifically Mediterranean, in its sound and poetic texture. These include Psy–4–de la Rime which signs off as "Psy-Ka-Dra," pronounced with an Arabic intonation; or K-Rhyme le Roi's "Qibla," which evokes the Prophet Mohammed's desert journey; the presence of singers of Arab, Italian, and Spanish descent working together; or, finally, Akhenaton's own class-conscious and bitter "J'Voulais dire" with its direct reference to Sicily, Naples, and a continuous Southern migration flow.

The resulting score is a powerful, wrenching polyphony, which speaks a multilingual idiom of French, English, Corsican (and through Corsican, alludes to Italianate—Sicilian-Neapolitan—cultures) and a small amount of Arabic. Musically, it is a "rich stew," in which social and political themes are expressed through a cross-cultural dialogue of musical styles. Politically, most of the songs engage the themes of poverty, unemployment, urban devastation, and international political violence. The latter is exemplifed through reference to the massacre of Palestinian villagers in Deir Yassin (Millie Jackson, "Deir Yassin"), drawing a parallel with the refugee theme narratively enacted in the film, where Sauveur (Akhenaton) is helped and fed by an adolescent Bosnian girl. The references allow in turn analogies between the Bosnian war and the "war" in which these youths see themselves as casualties. The Corsican element (perhaps the boldest because the most jarring within hip-hop musical culture from both an aesthetic and political viewpoint) brings in traditional lamento, a compelling contrapunto with the dominant elements of soul, gospel, and rap. But the most effective technique of sounding is articulated through the crossover of black American artists and French rappers. In the first track, Millie Jackson sings a duo with Shurik'N, one of the lead singers from IAM, a revised version of "Prisoners of love." This sets the tone for the multiple ways in which these African-American soul classics will be reread, a different sound created by the juxtaposition of contemporary rap, layering the original messages and their emotional "soundwaves" in a cross-cultural idiom of both resistance and despair. Thus, Isaac Hayes's "Is it really home?," Cunnie Williams's "Life Goes on," the Dells's "You Promised Me," or gospel singer Marlena Shaw's "Life" take on especially strong meanings with some of the harsher but more somber rap numbers such as Bouga's "Belsunce Breakdown," a pure Marseilles sound. Sounding is effectuated in yet another subtle way: for the soul tracks, Akhenaton did not call upon the best-known names of soul music (except Isaac Hayes); he sought out of his own musical library connections with singers who had reigned supreme at a certain point in their careers and been somewhat forgotten, such as Millie Jackson. By bringing such artists to the fore in this soundtrack, he returned these great African American performers to public space, sounding another chapter in the history of African American voice. He also used textual layerings so that they expressed pain and questioning in the African American tradition of testimony, to rearticulate the contemporary experiences and disillusioned voice of French ghetto youth and make them intelligible to a wide public. The entire enterprise "sounds" difference and resistant discourses through screenplay, musical score, and production modalities: the music is signed off by such labels as No Sell Out and La Cosca, and the producers include, along with more staid sources like Canal plus, a group called Why Not Productions.

In conclusion, it would seem that little is to be gained by a stark opposition between the place and nature of Francophone studies in France and the United States, although there are certainly differences of inflection, and most importantly, differences of context. Much might be gained, on the other hand, from a rethinking of a term with such a loaded history, one whose political import far outweighed its cultural underpinnings. On both sides of the Atlantic, this would mean engaging in an unfettered dialogue that moves beyond the now moot point of whether Francophone literature should be taught. It means not only acknowledging the inescapable role of colonialism, but also coming to terms with the Academy's enormous discomfort with matters of race, and to recognize the many shifts in thinking and discourse that they incite.

Those working in the context of the United States may acknowledge more openly the crucial need for writers of color to be taught and for scholars of color to teach, without laments about bowing to some ill-defined "political correctness." Yet the French have shown a disquieting eagerness to adopt the term "politically correct," albeit devoid of the intellectual work and harsh conflicts it reflects in the United States.[68] Such slogans merely parrot conservative U.S. politics and

68. See, for a critique of the new trend to cry "political correctness" whenever racism and anti-Semitism are being questioned, Philippe Sollers, "Les nouveaux bien-pensants," *Le monde* (17 June 2000): 1, 17.

close off all attempts to address—which is not the same thing as to "redress"—colonial and racial injustice through culture.

Yet much can be learned in the United States from the French university. In the United States, decentralized and sometimes fragmented university systems do not routinely provide access to the study of languages that the French may still call *orientales*, but at least have been teaching for a while—what high school in the United States teaches Arabic unless it has a specific Islamic orientation? Universities in the United States still need to develop the many fields that lay claim to *Francophonie* in more stable structures. These fields—distinctive cultural, geolinguistic areas within the unwieldy, globalized expanse of "Francophone" literatures and cultures—need to stand as separate areas, each with its immensely complex and exacting set of problems, bodies of primary and secondary sources, and critical tools. If we are serious about the place of Francophone study in the academy, we need to put sufficient resources into training well-rounded specialists, not opportunistic superficialists.

And on both sides of the Atlantic, "Francophone" must move beyond what is studied in books as a recognizable, formally canonic art. Cultural products need to be studied in relation to the living communities producing them, and these communities are at least partially present in Paris, New York, and Montreal. Further, we need to recognize that the children and soon the grandchildren of these communities have developed an idiom of their own, American and African in its roots, but distinctly French in its expression. This new idiom, international, resistant, and transgressive, is providing new and challenging texts, from the diaspora and the so-called "Francophone" world at once.

ANNE F. GARRÉTA

Re-enchanting the Republic: "Pacs," *Parité* and *Le Symbolique*[1]

How many times have I been asked, when in the United States, about the state and shape of gay and lesbian studies in France? My interlocutors might even be bold enough to inquire about queer studies. After all, wasn't "French theory"—whatever goes by the name—a key ingredient in the constitution of these (inter)disciplinary fields in the North American realm? My answer to such queries has been for quite a while now that there is no such thing as gay and lesbian or queer studies in France. Or rather, and in the face of my interlocutors' disappointment and disbelief, that such fields of knowledge have no autonomous, recognized, institutional presence on the French intellectual and academic landscape. And what is a field without a properly registered title and institutional demarcations? To ward off despair in my well-wishing American colleagues, I now add to my answer that, lately, one can discern a few stirrings.

Indeed, the picture is not as bleak as it used to be ten years ago. Individual researchers and academics are starting to make a difference. But the difference between scattered, individual pursuits and institutional recognition is the central conundrum of the French construing of minority communities and its resistance to acknowledging them. The uneasy emergence of a disciplinary field of study is mirrored in the uneasy articulation of gay rights evidenced in the recent enactment of the "pacs"[2] law and the controversies surrounding it. The French aca-

1. Elements of this article were first articulated in talks and conference papers presented between 1998 and 2000 at Cornell University and Duke University. I wish to thank Anne Berger, Fred Jameson, and David Bell for giving me the opportunity to test some of these ideas. I also benefited indirectly from William Eskridge Jr.'s "Gender, sexuality and the law" class at the Yale University Law School.

2. The acronym for *Pacte Civil de Solidarité* (Civil Pact of Solidarity). The acronym has spawned verbal, pronominal (*se pacser*), and adjectival (*pacsé*) uses.

YFS 100, *FRANCE/USA: The Cultural Wars,* ed. Ralph Sarkonak, © 2001 by Yale University.

demic order, its view of the proper subjects of knowledge, its criteria in legitimating disciplines might prove even more resistant to the claims of gay and lesbian scholarship than the French *polis* to the institution of a legal framework for same-sex couples.

However, the debates that arose on the occasion of this sociopolitical event might bear in paradoxical ways on the articulation of gay and lesbian studies in France (G&L studies, from hereon). The argumentation deployed around the "pacs"—whether pro or anti—relied on, exhibited, and thus betrayed many of the presuppositions of discourses borrowed from the human sciences and their conceptual apparatus. It provided at the same time the impetus for an unprecedented public questioning of the categories of gender and sexuality as these became loci of political contestation, even though in the end, in both the "pacs" and *parité* laws, gender and sexuality, in order to be *recognized*, had to wear a mask, the mask of the French universal.[3] Theoretical reflections, critical perspectives that rightfully belong in the purview of G&L studies gained a new urgency and public articulation.

A survey of what might qualify as G&L or queer studies would thus be insufficient to provide the substance of an entire article and it would miss the point of their problematicity in the French context. I therefore propose to articulate such a survey with an account of the "pacs" debates, since they both shed light on the underlying ideology preventing the institutional emergence of the new discipline and point to a paradoxical French ordering of both *polis* and knowledge.

THINKING IN TRANSLATION

But before I do so, a few reflexive considerations are in order, since this scanning of the French academic landscape for signs of a certain type of life is a rather suspicious activity. It presupposes the object it is looking for, in meaning to recognize its features—features it suspects are dispersed or concealed in it. To be able to recognize them I must have become acquainted with them somewhere else, prior to my quest: my gaze is informed by practices and knowledge alien or foreign to the landscape. How close am I then in projecting these features? Or how deluded in imagining their existence necessary or natural?

It could be argued that this procedure is characteristically "ethno-

---

3. On the *parité* debates and the universal, see in this same issue Naomi Schor's article (43–64). I wish to thank her for allowing me to read the part devoted to the analysis of the *parité* and draw it into dialogue with my own considerations of the "pacs."

centric" or "imperialist": an attempt at mapping American patterns of disciplinary construction onto a foreign land whose own structuring according to local categories and principles I risk obfuscating, imprinting in the process the patterns sought, instead of discovering them. G&L studies would in this case amount to a foreign product, species, or construct, exported and forced onto a culture inimical to it. This is more or less what many French intellectuals have denounced stridently and regularly on one occasion or another in the last ten years, demonizing in "radical American feminism," U.S.-style *"communautarisme,"* and identity politics the signs of American ideological imperialism. In this view, gender studies, gay studies, and McDonald's fast food go hand in hand. And obviously, in this view, I would be proving myself most un-French, adopting on the French landscape a point of view that has its roots in a transatlantic experience. I would be colonized and furthering the colonizer's purpose. It would be easy to point out in many recent publications or interventions on behalf of the gay or queer question in France, the influence—if not hegemony—of American sources. Emblematically, the adoption by speakers in the community of the untranslated English terms of self-designation ("queer" and "gay," as in the title of Didier Eribon's book, *Réflexions sur la question gay*),[4] even though sometimes naturalized for the French speaker (in "gai"), is interpreted by many commentators and not simply by the Académie française as a symptom, if not of corruption, at least of globalization, i.e. colonization.

An answer to this polemical charge—one of the many in the battles of these new culture wars—would take into account two crucial elements. The first points to the pattern of reciprocal misrecognition between the two discourses or forces spectacularly set one against the other in the French imagination of these cultural wars. For after all, what is taken to be the emblem and weapon of the colonizing Other—"American"—inspired gender studies or queer theory for example—betrays the heritage of what is known, and sometimes derided, on American campuses as "French theory." Many French proper names did inform these fields and theories, from Derrida to Deleuze, Foucault, Irigaray, Wittig, and others. That the product, or the thought, as it recrosses the Atlantic, should be misrecognized as pure American poison to the straight, French mind is most ironic. My second point is that we should avoid mistaking the practice of translation, however fraught

---

4. Didier Eribon, *Réflexions sur la question gay* (Paris: Fayard, 1999).

with betrayals and uneasy tension between respect for the foreignness of the other's text and the need for its assimilation into the target language and culture,[5] with that of wholesale importation and colonization. To take as queer an example as possible: translating Judith Butler into French—and in the process retranslating Foucault back into French—is not the same thing as opening a McDonald's outlet in Millau.[6] In the process of translation things are lost and gained, which are neither equivalent nor identical; meanings subtly drift; categories and demarcations are revealed and shift. Joe Doe from Ohio on a trip in the south of France will immediately recognize the same old, self-same, ubiquitous McDonald's without even the possibility of an ambiguity, a mistake, or a misreading, since everything has been *designed* to exclude such a mishap. But Dupont and Dupond encountering queer theory in an American bookstore may not recognize its Foucaldian inflections.

Thus, thinking both inside and outside of the enclosed, delimited territory, bringing home the insights gained abroad is of the essence. The desperate attempts at preserving the integrity of disciplinary and national demarcations ensures not the purity of the fields but their sterility. Subjects travel and in so doing remodel the landscape. This is the core of my justification for what I attempt in this article, and the reason I read French institutional erasures of gender and sexuality behind the mask of the Universal or of Objectivity as phenomena of resistance and denial rather than *a priori* conditions of possibility of the Political or of Knowledge.

QUESTIONS WITHOUT A FIELD OR A HOME

G&L and queer studies have neither legitimacy nor identity in the French ordering of disciplines. The North American Modern Language Association job list attests to a different transatlantic state of affairs: such descriptions of requirements for appointment in an institution of higher education are not rare. They might not be central or prevalent, but they exist and are recognized in hiring strategies, program building, and curriculum diversification. No French institution of research or

5. On this tension, see Jacques Derrida, "What Is a 'Relevant' Translation?" *Critical Inquiry* 27/2 (Winter 2001): 174–201.
6. Millau is the site of the *Confédération paysanne*'s—a farmers' league—famed assault and trashing, under the leadership of anti-globalization's iconic hero José Bové, of a McDonald's fast food in July of 1999.

higher education that I know of has to date ever advertised for a position involving such disciplinary interests or qualifications. No department, institute, or program is either nominally or explicitly devoted to either queer or G&L studies. And this shouldn't come as a surprise, in light of the related fact constituted by the *very* meager population of programs and positions in gender studies within French universities. Other European countries fare better with regard to both gender and G&L studies. I easily found references to programs of the latter sort at the universities of Amsterdam, Utrecht, and Nijmeguen in the Netherlands, at the universities of Bern, Zurich, and Basel in Switzerland, at the Universities of Köln in Germany and Bologna in Italy, and the enumeration does not pretend to be exhaustive. However small or fragile these programs may be—involving few permanent, dedicated positions—their institutional anchoring and visibility contrast sharply with a French situation marked by both atomization and quasi-invisibility.

Individual researchers and professors within recognized academic environments do however pursue lines of inquiry and teaching we might recognize as partaking of G&L studies. To gauge the vitality of this inexistent field I researched the seminars offered around its issues under various disciplinary umbrellas. For the years 1999–2001 I located six such research seminars (offered at or around the doctorate level). One at the École Normale Supérieure-Ulm,[7] offered since 1994 by Éric Fassin bears on "gender and sexuality: anthropology of reproduction in France and the USA"; one at the École des Hautes Études en Sciences Sociales, offered by Rommel Mendes-Leite deals with "socio-anthropological approaches to sexualities"; one at the Université Paris X,[8] offered by Daniel Borillo in law examines "sexualities, liberties, and discriminations"; another at the same institution offered by Françoise Gaillard and Didier Eribon on "sociology of homosexualities"; one at the Université de Reims' School of Law and Political Sciences, offered by Gérard Ignasse on "genders and sexualities"; another at the Université Toulouse II and housed by the research laboratory SIMONE dedicated to gender studies is offered on "genders and sexualities."[9] The strong representation in this sample—whose exhaustiveness I cannot guarantee, due to the difficulty in finding information on such mat-

7. http://www.sciences-sociales.ens.fr/sociologie.html
8. http://semgai.free.fr/cours/DEA_Nanterre/DEA_Nanterre.html
9. http://www.univ-tlse2.fr/rech/dea/sociologie.html

ters—of sociology and anthropology is remarkable, and some of the names appearing in their programs would be familiar to anyone who followed the episodes of the recent "pacs" wars. Queer studies appeared only on the margins, in the form of a seminar held in 1998–99, partly under the roof of the Sorbonne but without any institutional affiliation, organized by an association called the ZOO. As described on the home page of the association,[10] the seminar seemed transplanted from across the Atlantic, its theoretical references and rhetorical moves queerly mimicking the American construction of the field.

Doctoral thesis topics and problematics might provide another vantage point on the presence or absence, the possible future, and the disciplinary distribution of questions forming the core of an emerging field. A search of the computerized *fichier central des thèses*[11] returned—unsurprisingly—no result to a query for "queer" in all thesis abstracts. "Homosex*" however provided the references for 121 doctoral theses from 1972 to the present. All the disciplines of the sciences—human or not—, and of the arts and humanities are represented in the database. Among the 121 results, 26 were medical theses, 13 seemed to hail from the field of psychoanalysis/psychology, 7 from history, 5 from law or political science, 3 from religion studies, 18 from the other social sciences (mainly sociology and anthropology), 2 from film studies and 42 from literature. With a few notable exceptions, all the theses defended before 1986 were medical or "hard" science theses and were concerned mostly with AIDS. To provide grounds for quantitative comparisons, I queried the database for other notions or topics. "Narratology" (the province mostly of the humanities and literary theory) returned 141 thesis abstracts, "Balzac" 158, "Lacan" 177, "Proust" 218 (the queer theorist will no doubt remark that, in light of the discrepancy with the data for "Homosex*," French doctoral theses indulge in a wholesale degaying of the author), "Rousseau" 244, and "feminism" 267. So, all in all, the yield of the only term unmistakably indexing the topic relevant to G&L studies is rather modest. A puzzle remains: with 42 references in the field of literary studies revolving around considerations of homosexuality, why hasn't the problematic yet coalesced or gathered steam in literature departments to the point of visibility and demarcation?

Gay and lesbian disciplinary concerns are sporadically present on

10. http://perso.club-internet.fr/domarco/SQIndex.htm
11. http://thesenet.abes.fr/

the academic landscape, but the field has not even come close to establishing an autonomous identity around recognized communities of scholars. Another indication of this can be found in the fact that a journal like the *Journal des anthropologues* might devote a whole issue to the "anthropology of sexualities,"[12] but that there exists no scholarly publication analogous for example to *GLQ* in France today. By the same token, major publishers in the human sciences do publish works related to the (nonestablished) field, but propose no collection dedicated to it. The paradox is thus that there is no such entity as G&L studies in France, although such studies do happen there, as a result of individual pursuits, of informal, unacknowledged coalitions of researchers. Colloquia happen, their acts get published. French academic and intellectual institutions will allow individual pursuits but resist legitimating intellectual and scholarly minority communities, whether at the level of disciplines of knowledge or at the political and legal level.

Instituting homosexuality as more than an object choice—object of research or desire—i.e., as a critical position of articulation—conceptual and social—would run against far more than the bureaucracy, habits, and entrenched demarcations of establishments of higher education. It runs against the proclaimed ethos of the French politico-social order, as the "pacs" controversies revealed. More disturbingly, these controversies exposed a critical entanglement of power and knowledge, politics, and disciplines in the claims of concepts evolved from the human sciences to regulate and limit political deliberation. Starting with a comparison between the French and U.S. approaches to the institution of same-sex unions, and highlighting their differences, I will try to bring into focus the specificity of the discourses and strategies deployed in the French field. The *ordre symbolique* so liberally invoked by both the proponents of women's access to equal political representation—the *parité* law—and the opponents of a legal recognition of homosexual couples, has been at the center of a rearticulation of the discourses of politics, gender, and sexuality in France. How did psychoanalysis and anthropology come to work at re-enchanting the Republic? My analysis calls for an examination of the genealogy, purchase, and hegemonic nature of this concept, brought into play at a moment of crisis to provide a quasi-religious foundation to the political and social order.

12. *Journal des anthropologues* 82/83 (2000).

TRANSATLANTIC CHIASMUS

"The PACS has timidly crossed the Atlantic"[13]: thus was reported, on *Le monde*'s front page of 24 April 2000, the enactment of Vermont's civil union statute. This journalistic characterization of the Vermont event by analogy with a French law enacted the previous fall might have been no more than a pedagogical tool. The rhetoric of the article belies this interpretation. The misreading that leads *Le monde* to talk about the *"pacsés du Vermont"* reveals itself as not entirely innocent once replaced in the ideological context currently prevailing in France on issues of gender and sexuality. *Le monde*'s description of the Vermont statute, lending to the temporal priority of the French law a quasi-causal force, represents France as exporting its revolutionary achievements across the Atlantic, bestowing upon puritanical and reticent—if not retrograde—America the enlightenment of a moral *modernity.* It also manages to lay at the door of the United States an imputation of timidity, predicated on the local character of the Vermont statute as opposed to the all-encompassing national quality of the French provisions. In the process it hopes to conceal the chasm between the sweeping Vermont provisions granting full benefits to same-sex partners and the very limited rights achieved through the *Pacte Civil de Solidarité.* For two key issues are at the core of any measure destined to grant legal recognition to same-sex relationships. Should the union thus devised be structured as open to all couples or pairs, irrespective of their gender, or limited to same-sex couples? Should the union substantively follow the model of marriage and/or be equivalent to it in terms of benefits, rights, and protections? In this respect, the analogies teased out by *Le monde* article barely manage to disguise the facts of the matter: the French and the American solutions would better be articulated as a chiasmus—structural, substantive, and procedural.

The French "pacs" is open to both heterosexual and homosexual unmarried couples. Sameness or indifference would be the French road to equality. The difference in sexual orientation and sexuality itself are apparently erased: silence on the gender status of the "pacsed" individuals is legally enforced. We may know that as of May 2000, 14,000 such pacts had been signed, but we shall never know the proportion of same-sex and opposite-sex pairs thus constituted, since the *décrets d'application* of the law forbid the collection of this information. To distin-

---

13. All translations, unless otherwise indicated, are mine.

guish, it is alleged, could lead to discrimination.[14] The law is literally blind and enforces blindness. Identities seem not to matter.

In contrast, the Vermont statute strives for clarity: only same-sex couples are allowed to register for a civil union. The law thus formalizes a category of difference and inscribes homosexuality as a (minority) status.

The French went the way of what Eve Sedgwick would call the integrative approach,[15] dissolving the difference of same-sex couples into indistinction, whereas the Vermont legislature chose a formally separatist solution. Optimists might say that the French have gone the way of queer, even though they don't even know how postmodern that might make them. Pessimists might point out, however, that the layer of indifference covers up the deeper discrimination (heterosexual couples do retain the possibility of getting married).

In substantive terms, the French and Vermont legal frameworks achieve inverse effects. Vermont civil unions are endowed with the same state (but not federal, see *infra*) benefits and responsibilities accorded marriage. The law's provisions are to track those of marriage, now and in the future.[16] The logic is "separate but equal" and the difference with marriage is in name only.

The French legislature, for its part, took great pains to insure maximum differentiation of the "pacs" from civil marriage.[17] The logic

14. Thus reasoned the *Commission Nationale Informatique et Libertés* (an advisory body on liberties related to computerized information collection): "one can't take for granted the disappearance of prejudice against homosexuals, nor the abolition of all risks of discrimination on the basis of sexual orientation (*mœurs*)." The National Institute for Demographic Studies [INED] protested, in vain. See Blandine Grosjean, "Black-out sur le profil des pacsés," *Libération*, 7 March 2000. Articles and debates published in this newspaper can be found at http://www.liberation.fr/pacs/actu/.

15. Eve Sedgwick, *Epistemology of the Closet* (Berkeley: University of California Press, 1990), 78–90.

16. Parties to a civil union will have "all of the same benefits, protections and responsibilities under law . . . whether they derive from statute, administrative or court rule, policy, common law or any other source of civil law, as are granted to spouses in marriage." See the text of the law (H.847) as well as that of the Vermont Supreme Court decision, *Baker v. State*, which led up to it, at http://www.leg.state.vt.us/baker/.

17. Proponents as well as opponents of the measure concurred on the necessity of such maximum differentiation. The "pacs" was not to be a "*marriage bis.*" For a summary of the differences, see C. Fabre, "Mariage, pacs, concubinage: 3 régimes différents," *Le monde*, 17 March 1999. Records of the legislative debates are available at http://www.senat.fr/evenement/pacs.html and http://www.assemblee-nationale.fr/2/dossiers/pacs/2pacs.htm; the text of the law at http://www.legifrance.gouv.fr/citoyen/; the most complete documentation and relevant links at http://www.France.qrd.org/.

here is "indifferent but unequal." The default property regime of the "pacs" was carefully established by difference from that of marriage (at the cost, it turns out, of feeding a probable wave of litigation),[18] as were the associated tax benefits (which vest only 3 years into a "pacs" vs. immediately for marriage). Foreign partners of "pacs" are not automatically offered the benefit of residence permits and citizenship granted to married couples. Entering into a "pacs" does not affect the civil status (*état-civil*) of the partners: they remain, in the eye of the law, single. This feature is procedurally embodied in the locus of "pacs" registrations: the court instead of the town hall. The decision to dissolve a "pacs" can be made unilaterally. Finally—and this was the object of the most heated and symbolic controversies—"pacsed" couples are theoretically barred from adopting children and from access to state-sponsored artificial means of reproduction.

The French "pacs" and the Vermont civil union came about following radically different routes, and this difference highlights or puts in perspective a major contrast between French and U.S. articulations of law and politics, judicial and legislative powers, and the contrasted incidence of federal or European supranational sources of rights.

It might be deemed rather curious that the Vermont law happened in a country where many states still (or rather, anew, as a consequence of the 1986 Supreme Court's Bowers v. Hardwick decision)[19] criminalize homosexual conduct: more than half of the states of the Union have anti-sodomy statutes on their books, some recently rephrased to bring the old, blanket, polysemic crime of sodomy into a newfangled homosexual focus.[20] Also strange is the fact that it happened in a country where the first rumblings of Hawaii's possible finding of gay marriage's constitutionality[21] led to precipitous federal legislation, in the Defense of Marriage Act.[22] Finally, federal courts, particularly the

18. See Blandine Grosjean, "Pacsés largués dans la jungle de la loi," and "Trois juristes au secours des usagers," *Libération*, 22 May 2000.

19. For in-depth analyses of this decision, and the legal issues involved (privacy, equal protection, etc.), see Evan Gerstmann, *The Constitutional Underclass: Gays, Lesbians and the Failure of Class-based Equal Protection* (Chicago: University of Chicago Press, 1999), and William Eskridge, Jr, *Gay Law: Challenging the Apartheid of the Closet* (Cambridge: Harvard University Press, 1999).

20. For a survey of such statutes, see Eskridge, Appendix A1; see also Richard R. Posner and Katharine B. Silbaugh, *A Guide to America's Sex Laws* (Chicago: University of Chicago Press, 1996).

21. Baehr v. Lewin: Hawaii Supreme Court, 1993. 74 Haw.530, 852P.2d 44.

22. Known as *DOMA*, this law [Public Law No. 104–199, 110 Stat. 2419 (21 September 1996)], the constitutionality of which has not been tested, achieved two things.

U.S. Supreme Court, had seemed in the 1960s and 1970s the most promising venue in the struggle for progressive, liberal emancipation,[23] and activists thus tried for years to adduce legal reasoning and analysis that would have brought about at the federal level an extension to sexual orientation of the protection granted by the Supreme Court to suspect classes or classifications such as race and gender.[24] But it turned out in the 1990s that it is at the state level that the ground for gay rights was starting to shift.[25]

In contrast, the French legislation stemmed directly—if however discreetly—from European directives designed to enforce the antidiscriminatory provisions contained in Article 131 of the Amsterdam Treaty,[26] which France ratified on 18 January 1999. The injunction came from a supranational source and resistance to it is located at the national level, as evidenced in the highly polemical debates surround-

---

It first rephrased the definition of marriage for federal purposes as the union of a man and a woman (the language of the law had until then been oddly genderless, never explicitly stating its underlying presupposition), thus forbidding any federal recognition of same-sex marriages for purposes such as income tax or social security. Second, it relieved other states from giving full faith and credit [US Constitution art. 4, §1] to "any public act, record or judicial proceeding . . . respecting a relationship between persons of the same sex." More than 30 states have since passed their own DOMAs. See Eskridge, Appendix B3 and analysis at 139–140 and 216–217. DOMA influenced the solution devised by the Vermont legislature: opening marriage to same-sex couples would have brought any marriage contracted in that state under suspicion. By creating a separate status, Vermont circumscribed and distinguished categories of couples insofar as they might be affected by other state and federal laws.

23. For a skeptical view of the Supreme Court's progressivism, see Eskridge, Part II.

24. An example of such reasoning may be found in David A. J. Richards, *Women, Gays and the Constitution: The Grounds for Feminism and Gay Rights in Culture and Law* (Chicago: University of Chicago Press, 1998), chap. 6, 7, and 8. For a critical analysis of the legal doctrine of suspect classes and classifications, see Gerstmann, *passim*, and Eskridge, particularly Part II.

25. While a state may not afford its citizens fewer protections than recognized by the equal protection clause of the U.S. Constitution's 14th Amendment, it is not barred from extending greater protection under its state constitution or laws.

26. Article 13 undertakes to "fight discrimination on the basis of sexual orientation." The text of this treaty (as well as other legal material) can be found at http://www. europa.eu.int/eur-lex/fr/treaties/. Thus, in these matters just as in the case of *parité*, the demonizing of an American Other threatening to contaminate French political and social culture with affirmative action, quotas, minority rights, or multiculturalism hides the actual force driving the change. The (European) Other is made to wear (for obvious ideological and political reasons) an American mask. I concur in this with Naomi Schor's observation: "*parité* is a growing pain of the forging of Europe. It is France's anamolous situation in Europe . . . and not the existence of affirmative action in the United States that presided over the birth of the *parité* movement" (Schor, 60).

ing the "pacs" and in the conservative reactions of the French judiciary's upper ranks.[27]

Different European states have designed widely differing legal solutions—some predating the Amsterdam Treaty requirement—to the question of same-sex union, in both the structural and substantive aspects identified above. But a common feature of all of these laws is worth highlighting. In contrast to the American debate's framework, the key point of European, and particularly French, resistance to such unions seems centered on the question of parental rights. Most of the legal forms of union enacted in European countries in the last ten years have in some way, or at least initially, denied homosexual partners the possibility of adoption or recourse to artificial means of reproduction.[28] In paradoxical contrast, gay parenthood has been adduced in the Hawaii and Vermont cases as evidence for the legitimacy of same-sex alliances.[29]

In the course of the last twenty years, most European national codes and the European Court of Human Rights have granted homosexuals an array of individual protections on the basis of the privacy rights enshrined in Article 8 of the European Convention on Human Rights.[30] The more liberal (Nordic) countries expanded these rights well before the Amsterdam Treaty into some form of recognition of same-sex union. But *respect de la vie privée* was explicitly distinguished from *protection de la vie familiale.*[31] In the U.S. the existence of gay fami-

27. "The most liberal wing of the legal establishment unanimously considers that homosexuality must be tolerated as a manifestation of private life, but that in no case can it be recognized as a source of couples' rights. [They fear that] such recognition of same-sex unions might threaten the institution of marriage and might open the door to [homosexual] filiation," explains Daniel Borillo, in "Fantasmes des juristes vs Ratio Juris: la doxa des privatistes sur l'union entre personnes de même sexe," in *Au delà du pacs. L'expertise familiale à l'épreuve de l'homosexualité,* ed. Daniel Borrillo, Eric Fassin, and Marcella Iacub (Paris: Presses Universitaires de France, 1999), 162. This volume, which could be taken as a perfect French example of G&L studies, provides the most complete critical picture of the legal and social questions concerning same-sex unions in contemporary France.

28. For a survey of European legislation, and a history of the French measures, see Marianne Schultz "Eléments pour un débat" appended to Irène Thery, "Le contrat d'union civile en question," *Esprit* 236 (October 1997): 188–211. For updated summaries see the International Gay and Lesbian Association at http://www.ilga.org/.

29. The Vermont Supreme Court said as much, in effect reasoning along the following lines: we long ago granted homosexual couples the right to adopt, how can we logically refuse to grant the right to a formal legal union? See *Baker v. State,* at 41–44.

30. See the site of the European Court of Human rights, http://www.echr.coe.int/.

31. See the 1986 decision of the European Court of Human Rights denying homo-

lies precedes—and in the case of Hawaii and Vermont grounded—the possible right to contract a legal alliance. States that have not enacted any form of same-sex partnership laws have nevertheless allowed same-sex partners a number of family rights.[32]

In Europe, the sequence of rights' recognition thus starts from individual rights, may be extended to couples' rights, but stops at the line of family rights. Homosexuals, as individuals, might be allowed to enter into state-sanctioned unions; however, gaining recognition for the families they found turns out to be the limit. The European-U.S. chiasmus is illustrated once again in this decoupling of filiation and alliance.[33]

THE FRENCH EXCEPTION

A fine discrimination between areas of legitimate individual rights, tentative same-sex union rights, and off-limits family rights might, however, be difficult to preserve. The unresolved tensions in the French legal system between individual, civil, and family rights are now coming to the fore as never before. In February 2000, an administrative court reversed a regional agency's refusal to grant a "pacsed" woman the authorization required to adopt.[34] This reversal ran counter to the prior jurisprudence of the Conseil d'Etat which held that homosexuality is a legitimate ground for denying this administrative authorization. The welfare of the child is in such cases deemed to trump established principles of nondiscrimination. The French national policy on adoption is thus analogous to the "Don't ask, don't tell" policy enforced in the U.S. military. Single people may adopt children. No mention is made in the law of sexual orientation as a condition for adopting. However, the

sexual partners of different national origins the right to *regroupement familial*. (This is mentioned and analyzed in Shultz, 206.) This distinction between *individual, private life* and *family rights* grounds the denial of residency and citizenship acquisition for foreign partners in a legally recognized same-sex union. Kinship and citizenship are not autonomous constructs.

32. Thus, for example, New Jersey allows joint custody of adopted children for same-sex couples (R.E.M. v. S.L.V., 1998). For a detailed analysis, see Nancy G. Maxwell, Astrid A. M. Mattijssen, and Charlene Smith, "Legal Protection for All the Children: Dutch-United States Comparison of Lesbian and Gay Parent Adoptions," *Arizona Journal of International & Comparative Law 17* (Spring 2000): 309–348.

33. This point has been the focus of Éric Fassin's numerous discussions of the "pacs," and particularly of a talk he gave at Duke University on 29 March 1999.

34. Reported in *Le monde*, 26 February 2000. For an analysis of French adoption laws (article 343-1 of the *Code civil*) and practice, see J. A. Nourissat's piece in *Libération*, 11 October 1999.

grant of an authorization is a discretionary administrative decision, most obviously—if silently—discriminating against single men. The inception of the "pacs" complicated the picture. All the ambiguities of the law's language, all of its silences came to roost in the February decision. Entering into a "pacs" with a same-sex partner still leaves you, civilly, single, and as such theoretically entitled to seek to adopt. But entering into a "pacs" shows you to be engaged in a same-sex relationship; the law may be blind, but the administration may peer from under the blindfold. In the February pleadings, the state raised four objections in support of the administrative denial of the authorization. The first three are legal considerations: *Conseil d'État jurisprudence*, legislative intent (everywhere manifest in the parliamentary debates and the Minister of Justice's declaration, but nowhere inscribed in the actual law), and the analogy to medically assisted reproduction that the 1994 laws on bio-ethics explicitly reserved for couples composed of one man and one woman, whether they are married or have lived together in a stable relationship for at least two years. The fourth objection, invoking a general ethos of society, is by far the most curious to the ear of any student of French culture. In a couple composed of two women, said the *commissaire du gouvernement*, there is no man (an unimpeachable conclusion, granted), and thus no "paternal reference" (*référent paternel*); the image thus provided to the child would not even be that of an absent father, but that of a "denied father."[35] The court verdict, while defeating the government's position, was in the end no legal earthquake: the authorization to adopt—if it even survives appeal—will have been granted to one woman, even though a professed lesbian. Her "pacsed" partner will remain, legally, a stranger to the child whom they will raise together.

This tension between individual and family rights, between filiation and alliance, found its most strident and striking expression in the French context. Parliamentary debates, opinion pieces, review articles revealed again and again an obsessive focus on keeping, so to speak, the axis of filiation straight. To hear French cabinet ministers, senators, representatives, and experts in fields as diverse as law, psychoanalysis, anthropology, sociology speak, it seemed as if no society had ever con-

35. "Denied or negated father": the phrase resonates with mighty Lacanian irony. The *nom du père*, which is also (thanks to the homophonic punning in French between *name* and *no*) the *non du père*, is seen as negated, its own—quasi-metaphysical—negativity upturned.

sidered the possibility of granting same-sex couples, as couples, a legitimate interest in having and/or raising children.[36] A universal prohibition on access to homosexual parenthood was deemed to hold.[37] The conservative opposition invoked the slippery slope argument: grant a legal recognition to same-sex couples and soon enough you'll have to acknowledge "homosexual families." The socialist government steering passage of the legislation through Parliament vowed to keep such a possibility off limits, acknowledging it as fundamentally repugnant, logically inconceivable. Or, in the words of Elisabeth Guigou, the Minister of Justice: "Il ne faut pas toucher au Symbolique" (best translated as "Hands off the Symbolic"). A survey of existing legislation outside of France—and without even traveling as far as New Jersey or Vermont—would have belied this blanket assertion of universal inexistence, if not of conceptual impossibility. In March of 1999, the Netherlands had added to its 1998 laws providing for same-sex legal unions the authorization for such couples to adopt.[38] On 13 September 2000, the Dutch Parliament passed, by a vote of 109 to 33, a bill converting the country's registered partnerships into full-fledged marriages. But what is the force of *ordinary empirical evidence*, in the face of preciously-held beliefs?

36. Among others, Elizabeth Guigou, the Minister of Justice, declared: "A child needs a father and a mother," *Le monde*, 11 May 1998; Catherine Tasca, chairwoman of the *Assemblée Nationale* judiciary committee: "We chose, like the quasi-totality of European countries . . . to bar adoption and PMA, since we keep on wishing for children the filiation of a father and mother, "*Le monde*, 10 October 1998.

37. Françoise Héritier, Professor of Anthropology at the Collège de France, was the main exponent (and intellectual guarantor) of this assertion. See her contribution during the hearings held in the lower chamber of Parliament and an interview in the Catholic newspaper *La croix*, November 1998. For a more complete exposition of her views, see her book, *Masculin/Feminin. La pensée de la différence* (Paris: Odile Jacob, 1996). For a rebuttal (buttressed by Claude Lévi-Strauss's dissent) of Héritier and an examination of the abuse of scientific expertise (particularly of the discourse of anthropology) in the controversies surrounding the "pacs," see Éric Fassin "Usages de la science et sciences des usages. À propos des familles homoparentales," *L'homme* 154–55 (Summer 2000): 391–408.

38. Denmark allows same-sex registered partners to adopt their mate's children born from a preceding heterosexual union (Agence France Presse, 20 May 1999). Such liberalism is not the exclusive province of those traditionally tolerant, Nordic, Protestant nations that had a head start in the area of gay rights: the Parliament of the Navarra autonomous region, for example, passed a law (which would, however, require a revision of the Spanish national legislation to take effect) allowing same-sex couples to jointly adopt (Agence France Presse, 24 June 2000).

SPECTERS OF MODERNITY

The starkest contrast, then, with regard to gay rights is not so much between European political and legal cultures and American ones, but between the French republic and the rest of modern Western democracies. This contrast can be subsumed under one word: *le Symbolique*, a curious category that in the "pacs" as well as the *parité* controversies came to encode an order of things and of beliefs that, while purporting to be universal and foundational, appears paradigmatically French.

Whereas in the United States—or in the Netherlands—the opposition to same-sex unions is framed by those who are religiously inclined in Biblical, theological terms,[39] or at worst in terms of Western civilization's tradition,[40] in France, on the other hand, even the Catholic Church's objections and injunctions against same-sex union legislation were couched, both in official declarations and in the published admonitions of its main ideologian, in thoroughly ethico-psychoanalytical terms.[41] Granting that the French separation of church and state—far more robust in its purview than the American establishment clause—rules out both the Bible and the *Summa Theologiae* as legitimate sources of law, there remains to be investigated the intellectual genealogy of this Symbolic. The *ordre symbolique* so liberally invoked in the twin debates of the late 1990s (the *parité* and "pacs" laws) displayed in them all the troubling attributes of a lay theology: Lacan displaced Saint Thomas Aquinas, Lévi-Strauss's *Elementary Structures of Kinship* did the work of the Leviticus.

How can we account for the extraordinary rise, and current hegemony of the Symbolic from its humble Lacanian and Lévi-Straussian origins? Éric Fassin has analyzed how the anthropological work of Françoise Héritier supplemented Lévi-Strauss's original theories on

39. As the Reverend Bill Banucchi, executive director of the New York Christian Coalition, put it on 22 May 2000, in reaction to the Vermont statute's enactment: "We are fighting to keep this nation from fast-forwarding towards Gomorrah." Christine Boutin, a representative from the Right, did brandish a Bible in the French *Assemblée nationale*, but this move was widely perceived as having backfired and hurt the cause of the anti-"pacs".

40. See the tenor of the philological battle between expert witnesses on the occasion of a pivotal Colorado case, analyzed in Randall Baldwin Clark, "Platonic Love in a Colorado Courtroom: Martha Nussbaum, John Finnis, and Plato's Laws in Evans v. Romer," *Yale Journal of Law and the Humanities* 12/1 (Winter 2000): 1–38.

41. "Déclaration de la Conférence des Evêques," *Le monde*, 18 September 1998. Exactly one month later, in the same newspaper, Tony Anatrella, priest and psychoanalyst, would develop the same language under the title: "Une précipitation anxieuse."

kinship, incest prohibition, and the founding threshold between nature and culture with a second universal rule enshrining the difference between the sexes as the horizon of all cultural intelligibility (Fassin, 400). The genealogy of the psychoanalytic concept of the Symbolic is more complicated and I don't have the space in this article to retrace it.[42] One thing is clear, however: what should be examined, rather than the subtleties of Lacan's own theoretical articulations and their evolution, are the *misreadings* he occasioned, the strains that made his thought so vulnerable to its current vulgarized use, and the hidden baggage of his doctrine allowing for a return of the sacred in the French public discourse. Of the many psychoanalysts to intervene on the occasion of the "pacs" debates, at least one brought to the fore the roots of the Lacanian problematics in Catholic anthropology, and the Christian paternalist legacy encoded in his articulation of the paternal function.[43]

The "misreadings" of the Symbolic have sown extraordinary paradoxes. No wonder that the *parité* measure propounded as a radical gesture of enlightened modernity and destined to advance the cause of women's political representation manifests in its doctrinal articulation many a regressive feature, or that the logic underlying it was also the most serious ground for opposing the grant of a legal status to same-sex unions. Should it be surprising that both the "pacs" and the *parité*, rather than simply reiterating a classical Right-Left political chasm, split the left itself and its intellectual figures into warring camps?[44]

Recognizing the common features of the two debates and the ideological substrate at work in their articulation, seeing them as twin questions, may help us answer Naomi Schor's concluding questions in her analysis of the crises of French universalism: "To what extent can it be argued that universalism requires, or entails exclusion as though by definition? . . . To what extent does universalism rely on exclusion . . . to function?" The accession of women to the universal in the *parité* cannot be separated from the ambiguities of the "pacs." The theoretical re-engineering of *la différence des sexes* as *la Différence* itself,

42. This will be the object of one of my forthcoming publications.
43. Michel Tort, "Homophobies psychanalytiques," *Le monde*, 15 October 1999; and "Artifices du père," *Dialogues* 104 (1989): 46–60.
44. See E. Eliacheff, A. Garapon, F. Héritier, *et al.* "Ne laissons pas la critique du pacs à la droite," *Le monde*, 27 January 1999, claiming for the Left too a voice in opposing the "pacs." On the *parité* split, see Evelyne Pisier, "Contre l'enfermement des sexes," and Elizabeth Roudinesco "Une parité régressive," *Le monde*, 11 February 1999; Elizabeth Badinter, "La revanche des mères," *Le monde*, 22 April 1999.

the founding, primordial, symbolic difference—which can only be recognized, for it was always already there, simply hidden from view—logically entails a casting out or a dissolution of all minor or minority differences. It is no coincidence that the intellectual guarantors of the *parité* doctrine could take a position against extending legal recognition to same-sex couples.[45] It is no wonder the "pacs" proponents were at pains to underline again and again how the measure evaded instituting a minority sexuality, and how much in agreement with the spirit of the French republic was its indifference to the sexual orientation of those destined to benefit from it.[46] In setting up heterosexuality as the key to achieving gender equality, the *parité* doctrine achieved progress at the cost of a fabulous regression. *Parité*, rather than a translation of the primordial difference's recognition—for in translation who knows what may get lost or betrayed—is to be a representation of it, in the strict sense of a *mimetic representation* of the sexed bodies of the citizenry in all elected political bodies. In this "picture theory" of political representation, the mystical heterosexual body of humanity would be incarnate in all of its democratic emanations. The *ordre symbolique*, and its cortege of attendant capitalized and fetishized cognates—*la Différence, l'Autre*—thus strategically invoked, revealed in this use a quasi-transcendental quality, placing it beyond the realm of political deliberation, acquiring in the process a foundational status. And psychoanalysts of all stripes could rise in accord to the rescue of the symbolic order threatened by the specters of a a public legitimation—versus a mere toleration—of homosexuality.[47]

The logic of the Symbolic's intervention in both "pacs" and *parité* discourses was in defining a sacred realm, a realm off limits to the will and the action of the human community, but threatened by irrational transgressions such as homosexuality's claims.[48] The normative

45. In particular, Sylvie Agacinski, *Politique des sexes* (Paris: Seuil, 1998), 105–124; Héritier, in *La croix*.

46. Or, as Jean-Pierre Michel put it in his report to the Assemblée Nationale: "If it is true that the "pacs" originated with the demands of the gay community, it is, however, universal in its scope. Pursuant to our Republican tradition, founded on the *Declaration of the Rights of Man and the Citizen*, which refuses to take into account the individual through community affiliations and guarantees equality of rights as well as the right to privacy, it is excluded that we institute a status specific to homosexual couples." Report n° 1097, 23 September 1998.

47. See Anatrella; Simone Kork Sausse "Pacs et clones. La logique du même," *Libération*, 7 July 1999; D. Sibony "Pacs. Cette homo-famille qui gêne," *Libération*, 30 October 1998.

48. See, for example, Julia Kristeva, "Le sens de la parité," *Le monde*, 23 March 1999.

power of democracy is incomplete: the political and legal orders cannot sustain themselves without grounding in a realm prior to them, an order—the Symbolic itself—that transcends the institution of laws achieved through political deliberation The prepolitical conditions of the subject's construction trump, precede the determination of the citizen. The political theology underlying the *parité* doctrine and secretly informing the "pacs" ambiguity as well as the opposition to it, reactivated, under a new, apparently *modern* and *progressive*—anthropological, psychoanalytical—garb the very old conservative concept of an organic model of the primary political unit as constituted by the heterosexual couple as the basis of the political order.[49] It reintroduces at the heart of the supposedly rational, disenchanted realm of the political, the dimension of the sacred in the form of heterosexuality construed as a quasi-state universal (i.e. Catholic) religion.

L'AUSTÈRE MONARCHIE DU SEXE[50]

The doctrine of the Symbolic and its current hegemonic hold on French sociopolitical discourse accounted for the built-in limitations of the

---

In Kristeva's rhetoric, liberally alluding to Jesus and Genesis, the *parité* is a symbolic pact, a sacred refoundation, a stone in the garden of "childless virilized feminists" and an occasion for psychoanalysis to overcome "its relative current discredit."

49. An idea that can be traced back in modern French political philosophy to the counter-revolutionary philosophy of Louis de Bonald. This disturbing reactionary feature caught the attention of Irène Théry in her (uneasy) attempt at making sense of the ambiguities and paradoxes of the laws and debates she had contributed to initiate, and at (re)defining a position that would steer clear of the excesses of the Symbolic creed without, however, relinquishing the claims of both the Universal and *la différence des sexes:* "Pacs, sexualité et différence des sexes," *Esprit* 257 (October 1999): 139–181. Lacan included references to Bonald's works in the bibliography to his 1938 article "La famille" in *Encyclopédie française* (Paris: Larousse, 1938), vol. 8, 40. 3–42. 8, later republished, without the bibliography, as *Les complexes familiaux dans la formation de l'individu* (Paris: Navarin, 1984). Lacan's distrust of contractuarian theories of the social and political order arose early in his career: "[our conception of the human milieu] is opposed to the doctrines . . . of eighteenth-century individualist anthropology, and particularly to a conception such as that of Rousseau's 'social contract,' whose profoundly erroneous character stems by the way directly from the paranoid mental structure of its author," in *De la psychose paranoïque* (Paris: Seuil, 1975), 337, note 21. Bertrand Ogilvie, *Lacan. Le sujet* (Paris: Presses Universitaires de France, 1987), 57–61, traces the sources influencing Lacan's "sociological" view of the human subject to Maurras, and beyond him to Auguste Comte and the naturalism of French counter-revolutionary philosophy exemplified in Louis de Bonald.

50. "The austere monarchy of sex" is a quotation from Michel Foucault's eminently ironic last paragraph of *The History of Sexuality* [New York: Vintage Books, 1978], vol. 1, trans. Robert Hurley.

rights and recognition granted same-sex couples under the law. The "pacs," in its formulation, in the legal strategies embodied in its legislative history, and in light of the polemics that have accompanied its enactment offers uncanny analogies with what the seventeenth and eighteenth centuries have known as the idea of a civil toleration, to be granted—or withheld from—religious minorities.

In 1685, Louis XIV's Edict of Fontainebleau "revoked" the Edict of Nantes whereby his grandfather Henri IV had, almost a century earlier, put an end to the religious wars devastating the realm. Since a king could not contradict the divinely inspired will of his predecessor, the royal strategy of 1685 consisted in pretending that the circumstances that had called for granting certain privileges and tolerances to the Protestants did not hold any longer. The legitimacy of the Fontainebleau edict was grounded in the fiction that Protestants were converting in droves, that soon there would not be any left. The edict's stated purpose was therefore simply to hasten the advent of this most desirable state: the restoration of the kingdom's fundamental religious unity under one faith, one law, one king (*une foi, une loi, un roi*). The effects of this strategic legal ploy amounting to a denial of empirical evidence, a denial of the actual existence of the minority, were stark. From 1685 on, in addition to being the object of various persecutions, Protestants ceased to exist legally. Their civil death stemmed from the following institutional fact: the *état-civil* being, in the all-Catholic monarchy, in the hands of the clergy, no birth, no marriage, no death could be registered legally outside of the Church. Protestants who refused to pass, and kept relying on now outlawed and secret celebrations of baptisms and weddings (the so-called *mariages au désert*) had no civil existence. Their offspring from such marriages were automatically deemed bastards (illegitimate) and as such legally barred from inheriting.[51]

When barely two years prior to the French Revolution, which would establish both freedom of conscience and freedom of worship, Louis XVI granted an edict of toleration, he was faced with the same predicament as his great-grandfather and had to resort to similar legal devices. Louis XVI could not grant privileges, immunities, or rights to legally nonexistent entities: there was no such thing as a Protestant in *La*

---

51. It is to this situation that Voltaire is alluding in chapter 5 of his 1778 *Traité sur la tolérance* (Treatise on Toleration): "Calvinists only ask for natural law's protection: the validity of their marriages, the certainty of their children's status, the right to inherit from their fathers and their personal freedom."

France toute catholique[52] he had inherited from his forebears. And thus the title of the edict stating its purview is a masterpiece of circumlocution: "Edict of the King concerning those who do not profess the Catholic faith."[53] Toleration amounts thus to a negative recognition. The edict spells out the impossibility of spelling out a minority identity, of acknowledging and constituting it in language.

The same silence has been observed throughout the design of the law enacted two centuries later to grant a homosexual minority a measure of civil toleration: the "pacs" was designed for those "who either do not want to or cannot marry." The analogy extends further. Since the Catholic clergy, in whose hands lay the *ancien régime état-civil*, vigorously objected to officiate for Protestant subjects whose concepts of baptism and marriage were naturally repugnant to the Catholic faith, the 1787 edict instituted a specific, separate registry. In 1998, a few French mayors initiated a petition, which was signed by more than half of the mayors of the realm, by law the republic's officers of the *état-civil*, stating their objection—if not outright refusal—to deliver the certificates registering the soon-to-be enacted "pacs." Then, as now, in the all-heterosexual French republic, as in the all-Catholic French realm, the contracting parties in the minority legitimate their union in front of a local civil judge, and records of these unions are kept apart from those entered into by the then Catholic couples and the now heterosexual spouses. The civil records of modern France's unnamable minority are located exactly where the waning French monarchy finally allowed that of its unnamable minority to be held.

In this light, the French "pacs" appears as what, despite all its pretenses at enlightened modernity, it harks back to: a good old-fashioned edict of toleration. Toleration was the categorical aim of the "pacs," not plurality or equality. It offers at the same time indifference to sexual orientation and differentiation amounting to inequality in terms of the rights and duties accessible to a class of citizens. Like any edict of toleration, it can't bear to name, distinguish, or acknowledge what it tol-

52. This is the title (*All-Catholic France under the Reign of Louis the Great*) of Bayle's 1685 pamphlet, written in the Dutch Refuge, and denouncing the legal hypocrisy of the royal handling of a religious minority.

53. "Édit du roi concernant ceux qui ne font pas profession de religion catholique," reprinted in *Bulletin de la Société de l'Histoire du Protestantisme Français* 134 (Spring 1988), with the proceedings of the Paris, October 1987, colloquium on the 1787 *Édit*. See, in particular, in this issue, Anne Lefebvre-Teillard, "Les problèmes juridiques posés par l'Édit de 1787": 241–259.

erates. Now as then, the purpose of dissolving the identity or difference of those affected is to ward off the possibility for a minority "to form a distinct body within the realm." Or to put it in contemporary French terms, to ward off the specter of *communitarisme* (a loose transatlantic translation of identity politics and multiculturalism), an illness thought to characterize the un-Catholic U.S. political culture and threatening to contaminate the French body politic.

The revealing analogy is not thus between France and Vermont, but between *ancien régime* France and modern-day France, between the fate of religious minorities under universal state religion and the fate of sexual minorities under universal state heterosexuality.

It is as if the French Revolution had simply transferred to the state apparatus all the privileges, powers, and exclusivity the Catholic Church held prior to it, just as it transferred, wholesale, the sovereignty residing in the King to the citizens' body. Should one conclude that a political culture never invents anything, but only rediscovers old solutions to new problems? The recent virulence of the reaction evidenced in the *parité* and "pacs" debates should lead us however to at least question or reexamine the problematic nature in our era of this paradigm of modernity which has been dubbed disenchantment (Max Weber), secularization (Karl Lowith), or in the radical form it took in the French historical context, *laicization*.[54]

54. A good starting point for such a project would be Marcel Gauchet, *La religion dans la démocratie* (Paris: Gallimard, 1998).

Contributors

DAVID BELL teaches in the Department of Romance Studies at Duke University. He is interested in the relation between science and literature, and has recently completed a book on speed and communication in the first half of the nineteenth century in France.

ANNE F. GARRÉTA is Associate Professor of eighteenth-century French literature at the University of Rennes II (France), as well as Visiting Professor in the Literature Progam at Duke University (Spring 2001). A returning contributor to *Yale French Studies* (*Same Sex/Different Text?*, no. 90, 1996), her areas of research and publication include queer theory, literary theory, and Rousseau. She is also a novelist, and a member of the Oulipo.

DANIEL GORDON is Associate Professor of History at the University of Massachusetts at Amherst. He has written extensively on European intellectual history and is the editor, most recently, of *Postmodernism and the Enlightenment: New Aproaches to Eighteenth-Century French Intellectual History*.

CHRISTIE MCDONALD is Smith Professor of the French Language and Literature at Harvard and Chair of the Department of Romance Languages and Literatures. She is the author of *The Dialogue of Writing, Dispositions*, and *The Proustian Fabric*; editor of *The Ear of the Other*, and co-editor of *Transformations: The Languages of Culture and Personhood after Theory*.

RALPH SARKONAK is Professor of French at the University of British Columbia (Vancouver, Canada). His latest book is *Angelic Echoes: Hervé Guibert and Company*. He has previously edited or coedited two other volumes of *Yale French Studies: The Language of Difference: Writing in QUEBEC(ois)* (no. 65, 1983) and *Same Sex/Different Text? Gay and Lesbian Writing in French* (no. 90, 1996).

YFS 100, *FRANCE/USA: The Cultural Wars,* ed. Ralph Sarkonak, © 2001 by Yale University.

FRANCESCA CANADÉ SAUTMAN is presently Executive Officer of the Ph.D. program in French, and faculty member in French, Women's, Medieval and Renaissance Studies at the Graduate School and University Center of the City University of New York. Her work in the early modern field focuses on women, communities, margins, and resistant cultures, and in the modern field on race, culture, and same-sex networks between women.

NAOMI SCHOR is Benjamin F. Barge Professor of French at Yale University and author of *Zola's Crowds, Breaking the Chain, Reading in Detail, George Sand and Idealism,* and *Bad Objects.* She is founding co-editor of *differences: a journal of feminist cultural studies.*

SUSAN WEINER is Associate Professor of French at Yale University. She is the author of *Enfants Terribles: Femininity, Youth, and the Mass Media in France, 1945–1968.* Her articles have appeared in *French Cultural Studies, Contemporary European History,* and *Sites.*

The following issues are available through **Yale University Press,** Customer Service Department, P.O. Box 209040, New Haven, CT 06520-9040.

69 The Lesson of Paul de Man (1985) $17.00
73 Everyday Life (1987) $17.00
75 The Politics of Tradition: Placing Women in French Literature (1988) $17.00
Special Issue: After the Age of Suspicion: The French Novel Today (1989) $17.00
76 Autour de Racine: Studies in Intertextuality (1989) $17.00
77 Reading the Archive: On Texts and Institutions (1990) $17.00
78 On Bataille (1990) $17.00
79 Literature and the Ethical Question (1991) $17.00
Special Issue: Contexts: Style and Value in Medieval Art and Literature (1991) $17.00
80 Baroque Topographies: Literature/History/ Philosophy (1992) $17.00
81 On Leiris (1992) $17.00
82 Post/Colonial Conditions Vol. 1 (1993) $17.00
83 Post/Colonial Conditions Vol. 2 (1993) $17.00
84 Boundaries: Writing and Drawing (1993) $17.00
85 Discourses of Jewish Identity in 20th-Century France (1994) $17.00
86 Corps Mystique, Corps Sacré (1994) $17.00
87 Another Look, Another Woman (1995) $17.00
88 Depositions: Althusser, Balibar, Macherey (1995) $17.00
89 Drafts (1996) $17.00
90 Same Sex / Different Text? Gay and Lesbian Writing in French (1996) $17.00
91 Genet: In the Language of the Enemy (1997) $17.00
92 Exploring the Conversible World (1997) $17.00
93 The Place of Maurice Blanchot (1998) $17.00
94 Libertinage and Modernity (1999) $17.00
95 Rereading Allegory: Essays in Memory of Daniel Poirion (1999) $17.00
96 50 Years of *Yale French Studies*, Part I: 1948-1979 (1999) $17.00
97 50 Years of *Yale French Studies*, Part 2: 1980-1998 (2000) $17.00
98 The French Fifties (2000) $17.00
99 Jean-François Lyotard: Time and Judgment (2001) $17.00

Special subscription rates are available on a calendar-year basis (2 issues per year):
Individual subscriptions $26.00
Institutional subscriptions $30.00

ORDER FORM **Yale University Press,** P.O. Box 209040, New Haven, CT 06520-9040
I would like to purchase the following individual issues:

_____
_____

For individual issues, please add postage and handling:
Single issue, United States $2.75   Each additional issue $.50
Single issue, foreign countries $5.00   Each additional issue $1.00
Connecticut residents please add sales tax of 6%.

Payment of $_____ is enclosed (including sales tax if applicable).

MasterCard no. _____ Expiration date _____

VISA no. _____ Expiration date _____

Signature _____

SHIP TO _____
_____
_____

See the next page for ordering other back issues. Yale French Studies is also available through Xerox University Microfilms, 300 North Zeeb Road, Ann Arbor, MI 48106.

The following issues are still available through the **Yale French Studies Office**, P.O. Box 208251, New Haven, CT 06520-8251.

19/20 Contemporary Art $3.50

33 Shakespeare $3.50

35 Sade $3.50

39 Literature and Revolution $3.50

42 Zola $5.00

43 The Child's Part $5.00

45 Language as Action $5.00

46 From Stage to Street $3.50

52 Graphesis $5.00

54 Mallarmé $5.00

61 Toward a Theory of Description $6.00

Add for postage & handling

Single issue, United States $3.00 (Priority Mail)   Each additional issue $1.25
Single issue, United States $1.80 (Third Class)   Each additional issue $ .50
Single issue, foreign countries $2.50 (Book Rate)   Each additional issue $1.50

YALE FRENCH STUDIES, P.O. Box 208251, New Haven, Connecticut 06520-8251
A check made payable to YFS is enclosed. Please send me the following issue(s):

Issue no.   Title   Price

_____

_____

                                        Postage & handling _____

                                                 Total _____

Name _____

Number/Street _____

City _____ State _____ Zip _____

- -

The following issues are now available through Periodicals Service Company, 11 Main Street, Germantown, N.Y. 12526, Phone: (518) 537-4700. Fax: (518) 537-5899.

1 Critical Bibliography of Existentialism
2 Modern Poets
3 Criticism & Creation
4 Literature & Ideas
5 The Modern Theatre
6 France and World Literature
7 André Gide
8 What's Novel in the Novel
9 Symbolism
10 French-American Literature Relationships
11 Eros, Variations...
12 God & the Writer
13 Romanticism Revisited
14 Motley: Today's French Theater
15 Social & Political France
16 Foray through Existentialism
17 The Art of the Cinema
18 Passion & the Intellect, or Malraux

19/20 Contemporary Art
21 Poetry Since the Liberation
22 French Education
23 Humor
24 Midnight Novelists
25 Albert Camus
26 The Myth of Napoleon
27 Women Writers
28 Rousseau
29 The New Dramatists
30 Sartre
31 Surrealism
32 Paris in Literature
33 Shakespeare in France
34 Proust
48 French Freud
51 Approaches to Medieval Romance

36/37 Structuralism has been reprinted by Doubleday as an Anchor Book.
55/56 Literature and Psychoanalysis has been reprinted by Johns Hopkins University Press, and can be ordered through Customer Service, Johns Hopkins University Press, Baltimore, MD 21218.